AF774261

Perspectives on Crises

Jorge Emilio Núñez
Editor

Perspectives on Crises

A Multidimensional Approach to Law and Politics

Springer

Editor
Jorge Emilio Núñez
Manchester Law School
Manchester, UK

Section Editors
Danielle Mendes Thame Denny
Research Centre for Greenhouse
Gas Innovation,
Innovation, University of São
Paulo (USP), Luiz de Queiroz
College of Agriculture (Esalq)
Piracicaba, Brazil

Kay Lalor
Manchester Law School
Manchester Metropolitan University
Manchester, UK

Wei Feng
China University of Political Science
and Law Beijing, China

University of Kiel
Kiel, Germany

Natalina Stamile
Department of Law
University of Brescia
Brescia, Italy

ISBN 978-3-032-23835-1 ISBN 978-3-032-23836-8 (eBook)
https://doi.org/10.1007/978-3-032-23836-8

© The Editor(s) (if applicable) and The Author(s), under exclusive license to Springer Nature Switzerland AG 2026

This work is subject to copyright. All rights are solely and exclusively licensed by the Publisher, whether the whole or part of the material is concerned, specifically the rights of translation, reprinting, reuse of illustrations, recitation, broadcasting, reproduction on microfilms or in any other physical way, and transmission or information storage and retrieval, electronic adaptation, computer software, or by similar or dissimilar methodology now known or hereafter developed.
The use of general descriptive names, registered names, trademarks, service marks, etc. in this publication does not imply, even in the absence of a specific statement, that such names are exempt from the relevant protective laws and regulations and therefore free for general use.
The publisher, the authors and the editors are safe to assume that the advice and information in this book are believed to be true and accurate at the date of publication. Neither the publisher nor the authors or the editors give a warranty, expressed or implied, with respect to the material contained herein or for any errors or omissions that may have been made. The publisher remains neutral with regard to jurisdictional claims in published maps and institutional affiliations.

This Springer imprint is published by the registered company Springer Nature Switzerland AG
The registered company address is: Gewerbestrasse 11, 6330 Cham, Switzerland

If disposing of this product, please recycle the paper.

Editor in Chief:
Jorge Emilio Núñez

Thematic Editors:
Climate Change—Danielle Mendes Thame Denny
Gender—Kay Lalor
Gender—Natalina Stamile
Human Dignity—Wei Feng

Foreword

This book emerges at a moment of profound global disruption—from the conviction that such moments, however devastating, also offer rare opportunities for clear-sighted diagnosis of the structural pathologies that shape our collective existence. The chapters collected here were initially presented at online roundtables organized by Jorge Emilio Núñez and his group *Juris North* in collaboration with the NGO Academics Stand Against Poverty (ASAP) and Yale's Global Justice Program between April and December 2020, when the COVID-19 pandemic stopped much of the world in its tracks. As borders closed, hospitals overflowed, and familiar certainties dissolved, a diverse group of scholars and activists from nearly every continent gathered in virtual spaces to ask fundamental questions about justice, vulnerability, and responsibility. This volume is the fruit of those conversations.

The pandemic served as both subject and method for our inquiry. As a subject, it demanded urgent analysis of how legal and political systems respond—or fail to respond—to existential threats. As a method, it functioned as what several contributors call a "magnifying glass," exposing pre-existing inequalities, institutional fragilities, and governance failures that had long been glossed over by normalcy's reassuring routines. The virus itself, as Judith Butler observed during this period, does not discriminate; but social and economic inequality ensures that its effects do. What the pandemic revealed—and what this book explores—is the extent to which vulnerability is structurally produced, unevenly distributed, and systematically belittled in regard to those deemed "ungrievable" within prevailing frames of recognition.

The volume is organized around two thematic pillars that initially might appear distinct but are deeply related: human dignity and climate change. Part I examines how crisis tests and redefines the ethical and legal frameworks that sustain human dignity. José-Antonio Santos opens this section by proposing a legal ethics of vulnerability grounded in responsibility rather than compassion, arguing that the pandemic's exposure of human fragility demands a rethinking of how law engages with suffering. Wei Feng and Jingshu Wang then develop a sophisticated theoretical account of the tensions between dignity and health rights during public health emergencies, identifying four critical dilemmas—the hierarchy doubt, the naturalistic fallacy, the triage dilemma, and social determinants—that require structured normative balancing rather than absolutist assertions of rights hierarchy. Jairo Lima and Andrei Domingos Fonseca's searing chapter on Indigenous dignity in Brazil demonstrates how these abstract tensions manifest in concrete violence: underreporting of Indigenous deaths, government agents spreading the virus in isolated communities, legislative attempts to open traditional lands to mining, and the burning of prayer houses. Their account of Indigenous resistance, particularly the landmark ADPF 709 lawsuit, reveals dignity not as a static legal entitlement but as something actively claimed and defended through struggle. Natalina Stamile and Kay Lalor's response chapter synthesizes these contributions, tracing dignity's contested character—foundational yet fluid, absolute yet relational—and arguing that crisis reveals both the fragility and the indispensability of this concept.

Part II extends the lens of vulnerability to planetary scale, examining how climate governance failures intersect with and amplify existing injustices. Oswaldo Lucon's comparative analysis of greenhouse gas regulation in the United States and Brazil reveals a striking paradox: despite constitutional environmental protections and international commitments, both countries have systematically failed to regulate greenhouse gases as pollutants, creating regulatory vacuums that render climate pledges practically unenforceable. Douglas de Castro and Danielle Mendes Thame Denny's study of BRICS responses to climate governance during the pandemic shows how developmental models based on extractivism and natural resource dependence create fundamental tensions with sustainability goals—tensions that COVID-19 exacerbated rather than created. Their content analysis of BRICS declarations reveals high incidence of "cooperation" and "development" but low correlation with climate-specific concepts, suggesting that national interests continue to prevail over multilateral vision. Gabriela Cuadrado-Quesada's ethnographic study of community water governance in Costa Rica and India offers a counterpoint to these failures of formal institutions. Her concept of the "hydro-socio-logical cycle" captures the deep entanglement between water systems and social contexts, while her documentation of civic innovations—aquifer monitoring, reforestation, equitable water-sharing norms—demonstrates how communities "stay with the trouble" of climate change in the absence of adequate governmental response. Carla-Leanne Washbourne's response chapter weaves these threads together, emphasizing the need for coherent, multiscalar governance that integrates lessons from historical legislation, national policy frameworks, and local initiatives.

The volume's conclusion, authored by Natalina Stamile, Rafael González Muños, Marlène Sam, and Yarina Amoroso, returns to the philosophical question of crisis itself. Drawing on the Greek κρίσις—meaning "decision" or "turning point"—they frame crisis as simultaneously threat, revelation, and opportunity: threat to dignity's recognition, revelation of solidarity's possibility, and opportunity for ethical reconstruction. Their meditation on dignity as both mirror (reflecting injustice) and compass (guiding reconstruction) encapsulates the volume's dual commitment to critical diagnosis and normative imagination.

Several threads run through these diverse contributions. First, a shared recognition that vulnerability is not exceptional but constitutive of human existence—and that legal and political frameworks must be reimagined accordingly. Second, a commitment to pluralism that goes beyond mere tolerance of difference to what Jorge Emilio Núñez in the introduction calls a "pluralism of pluralisms": recognition that multiple legal systems, epistemologies, and value frameworks coexist globally, and that effective responses to crisis must enable coordination without erasing diversity. Third, an insistence on the interdependence of human dignity and ecological sustainability—a recognition that protecting vulnerable populations requires protecting the ecosystems on which all life depends. Fourth, a methodological openness to learning from failure as well as success, from the Global South as well as the North, from communities as well as courts.

Bringing to bear an extraordinary range of expertise—legal philosophy, international relations, political ecology, Indigenous studies, public health, environmental science—the scholars filling these pages share a refusal of disciplinary silos that fragment understanding and a common commitment to engaged scholarship that addresses urgent practical challenges. Their contributions demonstrate that rigorous analysis and ethical commitment need not be opposed; that attention to local particularity can illuminate global patterns; and that hope, properly understood, is not naive optimism but the capacity to recognize possibility within constraint.

The authors also share a deep loving respect for the many communities and individuals whose struggles for dignity and survival inform their writings: Indigenous peoples in Brazil defending their territories against mining incursions; residents of Flint, Michigan, fighting for clean water; farmers in Hivre Bazar crafting equitable water-sharing norms; ASADA members in Costa Rica protecting aquifers for future generations; medical personnel making impossible triage decisions; patients dying alone in ICUs; families separated by lockdowns. Their experiences remind us that the abstractions of legal and philosophical analysis correspond to lived realities of suffering and resistance—and that the ultimate purpose of scholarly work is not merely to understand the world but to contribute to its transformation.

The world has greatly changed since the first roundtables convened in spring 2020. New crises have emerged; old ones have deepened. The climate emergency, far from abating, has intensified, with each year bringing new records of pollution, warming, and weather extremes. Political polarizations have sharpened; multilateral institutions have been enfeebled. Yet the questions that animated our initial conversations remain urgently relevant: what do we owe to the vulnerable? How can legal frameworks protect dignity when exceptional measures become the norm? What forms of governance can address crises that respect no borders? How can communities sustain hope and agency in the face of systemic failure?

This volume offers no definitive answers. More modestly, and realistically, it seeks to provide, in the words of chief editor Jorge Emilio Núñez, a "blueprint of what is possible and realistically achievable in law and policy"; to illuminate through comparative analysis the diverse ways different societies have grappled with common challenges; to identify through failure as well as success the contours of more just and sustainable alternatives. If it promotes these aims, it will have contributed to the collective work of imagining—and building—a world in which dignity is not contingent on circumstance, vulnerability is met with responsibility rather than neglect, and human flourishing is understood as inseparable from ecological flourishing. Joined by scholars, activists, policymakers, and citizens around the world, this urgent and important work must and will continue.

28 February 2026

New Haven, CT, USA Thomas Pogge

Contents

Chapter 1
Perspectives on Crises: Introduction

Jorge Emilio Núñez

Abstract This volume compiles original research from global online roundtables organized by Juris North and Yale's Academics Stand Against Poverty (ASAP) in 2020, amid the COVID-19 pandemic. Featuring multidimensional perspectives from scholars and activists across continents—including Argentina, China, Brazil, the US, UK, Italy, Spain, and the Netherlands—it addresses crises through a lens of pluralism, examining human dignity and climate change as interconnected themes exacerbated by the pandemic. The book critiques unidimensional approaches to global issues like pandemics, territorial disputes, terrorism, trafficking, and environmental degradation, advocating a multidimensional approach that encompasses the "pluralism of pluralisms" characteristic of crises to foster cooperative, effective solutions without eroding sovereignty. Part I explores the vulnerabilities of human dignity in health emergencies, Indigenous rights, and ethical responsibility, highlighting inequalities in marginalized groups. Part II analyzes climate governance issues, ranging from regulating greenhouse gases in the US and Brazil to BRICS responses and community innovations in water management amid COVID-19 disruptions. Dedicated responses to these contributions synthesize lessons for the development of multiscalar, equitable strategies, bridging local actions and global justice to protect vulnerable populations and promote sustainable recovery in a polycrisis era.

1.1 Introduction

The chapters in this book are drawn from papers presented at the online roundtables organized by Juris North in collaboration with Yale's Academics Stand Against Poverty (ASAP) between April and December 2020. Established in 2010, ASAP is a non-partisan, independent global organization aiming to eradicate severe poverty

J. E. Núñez (✉)
Manchester Law School, Manchester, UK
e-mail: J.Nunez@mmu.ac.uk

© The Author(s), under exclusive license to Springer Nature Switzerland AG 2026

J. E. Núñez (ed.), *Perspectives on Crises*,
https://doi.org/10.1007/978-3-032-23836-8_1

worldwide. Established in 2015, Juris North is a legal and political discussion group led by chairs of academic institutions in Aberdeen, Durham, Hull, Lancashire, Liverpool, Manchester, Newcastle, Surrey, and Westminster. Juris North was launched in 2015 and now has over 2,000 members worldwide. The online roundtables featured speakers from virtually every corner of the world, from Australia to Canada and from Argentina to China, including contributions from Brazil, the United States, the United Kingdom, Germany, India, China, Sweden, Italy, Russia, Spain, and the Netherlands.

This collection brings together original research by academics and activists in order to present, explore, and discuss worldwide perspectives and views related to crises by means of a multidimensional dialogue. Current events such as the COVID-19 pandemic, the ongoing Israel–Palestine difference, terrorism, the socio-political crisis in Venezuela, Russia's relationship with neighboring states, and Brexit are a few examples of domestic, regional, and international multi-layered crises. With the pandemic as the frame of reference, the book provides an informed platform for debate over some key issues, which have been thematically grouped into two categories: human dignity and climate change. The individual chapters range between exploring particular case studies and considering their global impact.

There are several ongoing global issues that are negatively impacting societies in the local, regional, and international contexts. Although COVID-19 took the center stage a few years ago, there are now even more global issues, including territorial disputes; other pandemics; arms, drug, and human trafficking; terrorism; the flow of refugees; disputes, conflict, and war. These issues have a particular feature: their solution requires a collaborative, coherent, and cohesive approach. In order to develop a better understanding of global issues, a global and interdisciplinary assessment is of central relevance. At present, the scholarly literature and consequent governmental actions on these issues are unidimensional because they are particular to a state or a scientific discipline. Two important consequences of this unidimensional focus are that global issues are not examined in their whole complexity and that elements common to many of them are not identified. This book addresses both these gaps in existing research.

By accepting that any community or population consists of people who are different in many senses, it is possible to acknowledge that pluralism is a permanent societal feature. Similar to civil society, the international community includes several agents of very different natures (sovereign states, pseudo-states, failed states, cultures, subcultures, religions, communities, individuals). People in civil societies may be weak or strong, wealthy or poor, classed as abled or disabled, and so on, while the international arena includes developed and non-developed nations, democratic and non-democratic legal systems, populated and not populated territories, sovereign states, pseudo-states, quasi-states, and other forms of governance. In the case of civil societies and the international community, the respective national and international agents both recognize some inter-subject rules of conduct.

In any circumstances in which there are agents of different kinds, such as individuals, communities, and states, their interrelations will introduce identity issues and conflicts of interest. As a result, some criteria are needed for choosing the principles that can guarantee decision-making impartiality and the fairness of the outcome. Arguably, in the case of civil societies, many national legal orders already offer rules and mechanisms to secure impartiality, normatively and effectively, in the way in which different people are considered and with a certain degree of fairness (or at least, the ability to challenge unfair situations). The global order is very different. Although there are international authorities, procedures, and rules that in principle acknowledge the equality of states and give central roles to non-governmental organizations and, to an extent, people (for example, European Union law), realpolitik shows clearly that impartiality in the way different international agents are considered is scattered (for example, there are some states that are "more equal" than others in the decision-making procedures of international organizations such as the United Nations) and therefore, the fairness of the current world order is highly questionable.

The tension in the global order between what the law says and what happens in realpolitik is more evident in times and situations of crises. Clearly, leaders and organizations around the world are failing to address the pandemic's ramifications in terms of human dignity and climate change issues in a coordinated and efficient manner. In a similar vein, scholars in legal and political sciences and international relations are presenting dead-end arguments, with futile hermeneutical, technical, conceptual, and theoretical discussions, and seem oblivious to the urgency the crises present. The urgency relates to the direct impact of COVID-19 as well as the exacerbation of pre-existing conditions. For instance, to name a few, key issues include the impact on legal and sociopolitical inequalities; the economic ramifications of the pandemic and the prospect for recovery depending on places and social characteristics such as gender, ethnicity, age, skill levels, local government support, etc.; and the effects on the environment.

Simply put, the book fills a major gap in scholarly literature by providing multidimensional perspectives or views on crises by means of an interdisciplinary analysis of selected thematic areas (human dignity and climate change). Furthermore, the global nature of the response is represented by the contributors who are academics and activists from different disciplines and who come from a wide range of backgrounds in terms of, for example, geographical location, gender, and ethnicity.

The key problem this book focuses on is connected with the current fragmented way in which crises are tackled by different states and academic disciplines locally, regionally, and internationally. More precisely, because of the different local laws and policies in place, global issues are dealt with differently by local stakeholders and their relevant local actions which, unsurprisingly, results in very different levels of failure and success. In a globalized society, as the pandemic is self-evidently showing, the negative results in one or a few local areas have a negative impact elsewhere in the world. Consequently, the book's main aim is to provide a sample of perspectives and views on local law and policy relevant to local stakeholders' action toward the same global issue (COVID-19) in light of specific thematic areas (human dignity and climate change).

In line with this aim, this volume has the following key objectives: to develop and consolidate an existing multidisciplinary and international forum for the exchange of knowledge, discussion, and research of global issues in order to deal with these issues locally in novel ways (i.e., in that sense, this work is multidisciplinary and the main disciplines are: law, political science, international studies); to identify, compare, contrast, and evaluate current law and policy applicable to different states with regard to the same global issue in order to test local tools, actions, and techniques already proven to be effective in crisis management; to disseminate key findings to academics, policy makers, and stakeholders through a summary report. The main long-term objective (the book's local-to-global aspect) is to draw on the foundation knowledge gained across the chapters and to make recommendations about local law and policy that offer the most efficient way to tackle global issues, by considering the effective local law and policy initiatives already implemented elsewhere.

Considering the multidimensional approach,[1] the current fragmented analyses of the pandemic and the selected thematic issues, and the overall aim and key objectives outlined above, this volume has two central working hypotheses:

1. The global order can progress from a pluralism to a pluralism of pluralisms that is widely sharable—i.e., it is evident that the current world order is not equally hospitable to all states, communities, and individuals.
2. Sovereign states can cooperate together and accept limitations without sacrificing their sovereignty. Similarly, other international agents can cooperate together and accept limitations without compromising their freedom.

At the level of the individual and at the level of the state, sovereignty implies there is an ultimate lawmaker and law interpreter for a determined group of people in a defined territory. Despite the fact that politics shows that states are able to cut across legally defined jurisdictions and take intergovernmental decisions, as in the case of the European Union, such legal frameworks still acknowledge Member States (i.e., sovereign states in this volume) have exclusive sovereignty unless a given power has been conferred in law (e.g., EU law principle of conferral, art. 5.2 TEU). In that sense, legally, there is still a global multiplicity of different legal systems of various natures or, more accurately, a pluralism of pluralisms. In law, each sovereign state has its own peculiarities in terms of the creation and application of the law (i.e., pluralism of legal systems). Equally, each of these sovereign legal systems may share some features in terms of the law-creation and law-application rules and authorities (formal validity) but differ in terms of their content and nature (material validity) that have to do with a variety of agents (individuals, communities, and states) in several contexts (local, regional, and international). This myriad of sovereign legal systems is multi-agent and multi-contextual and, therefore, is a pluralism of pluralisms.

The challenge is to present a version of pluralism that is widely sharable when no world order can be equally hospitable to all agents including states,

[1] For details about dimensional understanding including uni- and multidimensionality see Núñez (2023).

communities, and individuals. Such a version of pluralism should, therefore, facilitate the means to coordinate this plurality of rules, procedures, concepts, and characterizations. This coordination should be able to embrace domestic, regional, and international legal orders that may include, for example, democratic and non-democratic regimes. It is relatively easy to recognize that democratic and non-democratic states may deal differently with communities and individuals within. For instance, a democratic legal regime may accept freedom of expression with certain limitations while a non-democratic regime such as one ruled by an authoritarian single ruler may opt for the complete elimination of individual liberties. However, even democratic regimes have several differences, such as the way in which they define legal concepts and respective legal attributes in relation to adults, minors, gender-based issues, and controversial themes like the death penalty, abortion, and organ donation. Consequently, this collection understands any arrangements that enable the global coordination of different legal systems must welcome the a priori assumption they will be different in several ways regardless of their political status.

1.2 Unidimensional Perspectives on Crisis or Multidimensional Perspective on Crises

To develop a widely acceptable version of pluralism that can embrace different legal and political systems is challenging. In order to share an understanding of notions such as "law," or "human dignity," or "crises" and, consequently, their conceptual or normative and substantive or factual implications, a context of discussion must be shared; a shared platform of certain presuppositions must be agreed. Social sciences are sciences of realities in the sense they are sciences of experience. To be more precise, disciplines like law and political science are human-made[2] and centered on human interaction and, therefore, they are sciences of human cultural experience and not of natural or caused experience. However, it is often the case that each of these disciplines have fragmented perspectives or views about the same issue. The famous Indian story "The Blind Men and the Elephant" illustrates metaphorically this unidimensional disciplinary perspective or view. John Godfrey Saxe's (1816–1887) version[3] of the story follows:

> It was six men of Indostan,
> To learning much inclined,
> Who went to see the Elephant
> (Though all of them were blind),
> That each by observation
> Might satisfy his mind.

[2] The author uses intentionally gender-neutral language. The introduction does not include discussions about natural law theories and how or by whom law is created.

[3] Saxe (1872).

The *First* approach'd the Elephant,
And happening to fall
Against his broad and sturdy side,
At once began to bawl:
"God bless me! but the Elephant
Is very like a wall!"

The *Second*, feeling of the tusk,
Cried,—"Ho! what have we here
So very round and smooth and sharp?
To me 'tis mighty clear,
This wonder of an Elephant
Is very like a spear!"

The *Third* approach'd the animal,
And happening to take
The squirming trunk within his hands,
Thus boldly up and spake:
"I see,"—quoth he—"the Elephant
Is very like a snake!"

The *Fourth* reached out an eager hand,
And felt about the knee:
"What most this wondrous beast is like
Is mighty plain,"—quoth he,—
"'Tis clear enough the Elephant
Is very like a tree!"

The *Fifth*, who chanced to touch the ear,
Said-—"E'en the blindest man
Can tell what this resembles most;
Deny the fact who can,
This marvel of an Elephant
Is very like a fan!"

The *Sixth* no sooner had begun
About the beast to grope,
Then, seizing on the swinging tail
That fell within his scope,
"I see,"—quoth he,—"the Elephant
Is very like a rope!"
And so these men of Indostan
Disputed loud and long,
Each in his own opinion
Exceeding stiff and strong,
Though each was partly in the right,
And all were in the wrong!

MORAL,
So, oft in theologic wars
The disputants, I ween,
Rail on in utter ignorance

Of what each other mean;
And prate about an Elephant
Not one of them has seen!

The above story metaphorically reveals how any issue is explored by different scientific disciplines. From such partial perspectives or views (e.g., *only* legal, *only* political, *only* sociological, *only* disciplinary), any issue is analyzed, studied, and described according to particular disciplinary methodologies, concepts and conceptions, and a priori assumptions. Even when taken individually, each discipline can itself offer different partial perspectives and views about the same issue without necessarily acknowledging these different departing assumptions. For example, in legal science there are two clearly distinguishable accounts of law: a factual conception of law in which law could be seen as human conduct, and a conceptual conception of law in which law could be seen as legal norms.

In this disciplinary context, the multidimensional theory used in this book as applied to law differs from both rationalism and empiricism. Rationalism maintains that the object to be known by the jurist is the norm and that positive law is intuited or captured differently, not by our five senses but by our reason or intellect. For this view, legal science would be a science of ideal objects because norms are known by using our intellect (as we do with the objects of mathematics) but they are not perceived by our five senses. Empiricism opposes this ideal view of law and accepts its inter-socio and psychological reality. Consequently, legal knowledge is based on what the sociological or psychophysical experience reveals. Empiricism does not recognize any other contact with experience than that by means of sensible intuition. This way of knowing helps in understanding the nature with which legal knowledge dissolves the distinction between the knowledge of data by reference to another event that occurs. These facts may refer to the rules they originate from or the rules they apply to. For instance, by interpreting the law it may be possible to know the real intention of those who are sanctioned based on the mere link of existence present between the fact and the law. Consider judges and their decisions. For rationalism, the law is a norm in all its possible significance (e.g., a negative sanction applied by the judge to a particular case). For empiricism, however, the law is a psychological fact based on its circumstantial socio-environmental relationship. In that sense, this collection acknowledges that any issue may present different perspectives or views.

The multidimensional analysis proposed in this book, as applied for example to law, accepts that norms and facts are not at odds. The object to be known by the jurist is not the norm or the naked fact, but the human behavior center of imputation of legal norms. The view focuses on a particular angle in the same way that the object of knowledge of the astronomer is the stars and not the relevant laws of the universe. This does not mean that, for example, Newton's laws are not of use to the astronomer. These laws are concepts, intellectual constructions by which it is possible to know the stars. Similarly, for legal science the object of knowledge of the jurist is not the norm but human behavior in its interference or interrelation with others, because legal norms are only concepts with which that conduct is known.

Norms are, therefore, simply the concepts with which the legal scholar thinks and understands that behavior. Just as natural experience puts into physics something that does not come from the mere logical structure of knowledge of nature, the science of law as a science of realities contains a difference from the merely logical side. The difference comes directly and immediately from human experience. More broadly, contrary to legal empiricism, a multidimensional view considers human behavior is an object of experience radically different from that of natural objects. While natural objects constitute an experience of necessity governed by the relationship between cause and effect, human behavior constitutes an experience of freedom where the creation of something axiologically original emerges at every moment. In that vein, this book will outline an account of the same global issue (COVID-19) according to which different "ontological" statuses are recognized but, as it is explained, these different meanings of the same issue remain related, and are indeed synergetic.

While the perspectives and views in the following chapters are multidimensional because they have to do with different disciplines or different angles within the same discipline, the approach also applies to particular issues concerning the pandemic. More precisely, the book addresses issues related to human dignity and climate change that, on the surface, may seem to have little in common. Yet by applying a common lens, such as the COVID-19 pandemic, the similarities become apparent. In this book, the pandemic has a double function: thematically, it is the main subject of study and, methodologically, it offers all the selected sub-themes and participating scholars a common, more focused, and magnified view. The methodological focus is supported by the fact that, as will be shown in detail in each chapter, the pandemic makes pre-existing deep-rooted issues more evident, and these are now difficult to hide by local, regional, and international authorities and governments by, for example, playing with biased or partial statistics, using polarized mass or social media, or blaming an external foe as a way to distract from internal turmoil.

Global extreme poverty kept on rising in 2020 and 2021 to levels not seen since the Asian financial crisis in the 1990s.[4] Statistical data shows that Latin America is one of the regions most affected by the pandemic and, specifically, with regard to poverty.[5] COVID-19 has exacerbated already existing differences such as social mobility, income, and inequalities. Related to gender issues, crisis does not occur in a vacuum. One of the key observations from women's groups and others working on gender-based issues during the COVID-19 pandemic is that the crisis exacerbated already existing issues and inequalities. The burden of responding to this crisis has not fallen equally. The inequality of this burden is both a political choice and a result of structural inequalities that have deep historical roots. As such, among many other things, crises—including the COVID-19 crisis—expose also the fragility of the frameworks, systems, and conceptual paradigms through which we understand our relationships with others, with society, and with the material world. The pandemic

[4] United Nations (2021).

[5] Economic Commission for Latin America and the Caribbean (ECLAC) (2022).

has had more impact on women and jeopardizes years of work against gender inequalities.[6] Women are disproportionally impacted by poverty, gender-based violence keeps on rising, and challenges in employment including job security, lower social protection, and pay are some of the most noticeable examples.[7] However, the fact that the burden of the COVID-19 crisis has often been demarcated by gender was not a product of the crisis itself—these inequalities were in place long before the first reported infections, laying the groundwork for the gendered differences in experiences of 2020 and of crisis. These gendered differences are multiscalar: from interpersonal relationships, to households, to municipalities, cities, and states, gender plays a role in how we understand our interconnections and inequalities.

Taking into consideration issues pertaining to poverty, gender, and other situations that were directly and indirectly influenced by the pandemic, the chapters in Part I on human dignity bring a variety of views. Despite the different perspectives, it is possible to identify at least three common ideas in the papers of this section: all of them, firstly, focus on the crisis and challenges caused by the COVID-19 pandemic and, secondly, trace their discussion back to the fundamental concept of human dignity and, thirdly, pay special attention to vulnerable human beings in concrete conditions. Therefore, they amount to a cooperative contribution that enables the shaping of the "new normality" with respect to human dignity as well as protection of its vulnerability.

Part II brings together a group of experts on climate change to explore the particularities that the pandemic brought to the subject. The main conclusion is that there are more similarities than differences between the two global threats and that most of the main environmental problems were already there before the pandemic and were made more blatant. In brief, issues pertaining to climate change require multi-stakeholder collaboration and global efforts but, while efforts to tackle climate change still lack such urgency, if correctly designed, public policies to face the pandemic can also bring permanent benefits to the climate.

1.3 The Contributions in this Book

This section briefly presents the collection of research-based contributions that address the intertwined crises of climate change and their profound implications for human dignity. The book is divided into two thematic parts. The first set of chapters (Part I, Chaps. 2–4) explores the theme of human dignity, examining how global crises, including pandemics and socioeconomic inequalities, challenge fundamental human rights and necessitate innovative legal and social responses to ensure equity and justice. The second set (Part II, Chaps. 6–8) focuses on climate change, analyzing legal, policy, and community-driven approaches across diverse global contexts,

[6] UN Trade and Development (UNCTAD) (2021).

[7] International Monetary Fund (Fiscal Affairs) (2022).

from the US and Brazil to BRICS nations and local communities in India and Costa Rica. A dedicated response to these crises is offered in both sections (Chaps. 5 and 9), emphasizing the need for coherent, multiscalar strategies that integrate lessons from the past and from ongoing challenges to foster sustainable and equitable solutions, protecting vulnerable populations and promoting human flourishing in an era of polycrisis.

Chapter 2: A Legal Ethics of the Vulnerability of Human Beings: Human Dignity and Responsibility to Rethinking the Present Time. José-Antonio Santos proposes a legal ethics of vulnerability, emphasizing responsibility and human dignity in the context of the COVID-19 pandemic. The paper critiques the limitations of legal positivism, advocating an external legal perspective to address the fragility of vulnerable populations. Santos explores how the pandemic exposed the need to rethink concepts like suffering, compassion, and medical ethics, arguing that responsibility, rather than compassion, should guide legal and bioethical frameworks. By examining the dehumanization in medical practices and the ethical dilemmas of end-of-life care, the study underscores the necessity of protecting human dignity through equitable legal norms. This contribution enriches the volume's multidimensional approach by offering a philosophical and legal lens on vulnerability, urging coordinated, justice-oriented responses to global crises that prioritize the human rights of the most fragile, aligning with the book's aim to bridge local and global perspectives.

Chapter 3: Human Dignity, Right to Health, and Balancing: With Special Focus on Vulnerability in a Public Health Emergency. Wei Feng and Jingshu Wang explore the interplay between human dignity and the right to health during public health emergencies like COVID-19, emphasizing the vulnerability of marginalized groups. The paper delineates human dignity's dual dimensions—individual and social—rooted in equality and personality, drawing on Mencius, Kant, and Radbruch. It addresses four key tensions—hierarchy doubts, naturalistic fallacies, triage dilemmas, and social determinants—using the International Covenant on Economic, Social and Cultural Rights (ICESCR) framework to advocate for a balanced, inclusive right to health. The authors propose four proportionality criteria—availability, accessibility, acceptability, and quality—to guide equitable policy responses. Focusing on China's COVID-19 response, they highlight vulnerabilities of groups like pregnant women and medical personnel. This contribution enriches the book by offering a legal-theoretical perspective on balancing dignity and health rights, advocating for non-discriminatory, globally coordinated measures to protect vulnerable populations.

Chapter 4: Indigenous Dignity Under Threat in the Brazilian COVID-19 Pandemic. Jairo Lima and Andrei Domingos Fonseca examine the erosion of Indigenous human dignity in Brazil during the COVID-19 pandemic, highlighting the government's anti-Indigenous policies under President Jair Bolsonaro. The paper traces the historical marginalization of Indigenous peoples through colonization and state actions, culminating in intensified violations during the pandemic, including underreporting of Indigenous deaths, inadequate health measures, and exploitation of Indigenous lands. It critiques the dismantling of protective institutions like Fundação Nacional do Índio (FUNAI) and Secretaria Especial de Saúde Indígena (SESAI), which resulted in economic interests being prioritized over Indigenous rights. The authors emphasize Indigenous resistance, notably through the landmark lawsuit ADPF 709, which challenged state inaction in the Brazilian Supreme Court. This contribution underscores the collection's focus on human dignity by exposing systemic violations and advocating for coordinated legal and policy responses to protect vulnerable Indigenous communities, aligning with the book's call for a pluralism of pluralisms.

Chapter 5: Response to Part I: Human Dignity in Times of Crisis: A Contested Concept. Natalina Stamile and Kay Lalor provide a critical response to the book's human dignity section, exploring the complex interplay between crisis, emergency, and human dignity during the COVID-19 pandemic. They underscore dignity's foundational yet contested role in human rights law, emphasizing its fluidity and institutional function in navigating legal tensions. The pandemic is framed as a "magnifying glass" that exposed and exacerbated societal inequalities, disproportionately impacting vulnerable groups. The response engages with the chapters in Part I, highlighting themes of dignity and responsibility, and dignity and inequality, particularly in healthcare settings. It emphasizes the relational nature of dignity, shaped through interactions and resistance, as seen in Indigenous struggles. This contribution enriches the book by synthesizing philosophical, legal, and social perspectives, advocating for a reimagined approach to dignity that addresses global interdependence and structural inequities in times of crisis.

Chapter 6: Regulating Greenhouse Gases as Criteria Pollutants in the United States and Brazil. Oswaldo Lucon examines the urgent need to regulate greenhouse gases (GHGs) as criteria pollutants to mitigate climate change, comparing the United States and Brazil. The chapter highlights how climate change exacerbates pandemics, conflicts, and economic crises, threatening human dignity through impacts on health, food security, and ecosystems. It traces the US Clean Air Act's influence on global pollution control, noting setbacks in GHG regulation due to Supreme Court rulings and political shifts. In Brazil, despite constitutional environmental protections, GHGs remain unregulated as pollutants, hindering Paris Agreement commitments. Subnational efforts in both countries, like the US "We Are Still In" campaign and Brazil's state-level initiatives, show promise but face legal and practical barriers. This contribution underscores the book's focus on human dignity by advocating for robust, legally enforceable climate policies to protect vulnerable populations, emphasizing global cooperation and regulatory alignment.

Chapter 7: BRICS Response to Climate Governance Crisis in Pandemic Times. Douglas de Castro and Danielle Mendes Thame Denny analyze the BRICS countries' responses to the climate change crisis, exacerbated by the COVID-19 pandemic, emphasizing vulnerabilities in the Global South. Drawing on virtual roundtables from 2020, the paper critiques the inefficacy of international climate regimes, highlighting how the pandemic intensified inequalities and strained global cooperation. Using content analysis of BRICS declarations (2017–2021), it reveals a focus on economic development over environmental sustainability, despite shared vulnerabilities in land use and forestry. The authors propose that the ideational alignment of BRICS countries could enhance climate governance through cooperation, yet national interests often prevail. China's ecological civilization model is noted as a potential influence. This contribution enriches the book by linking climate inaction to threats against human dignity, while advocating for stronger multilateral governance to protect vulnerable populations and promote equitable, sustainable development in crisis contexts.

Chapter 8: Repairing Water in the Face of Climate Change: A Tale of Two Communities. Gabriela Cuadrado-Quesada examines how climate change affects water quantity and quality, exacerbating socio-environmental injustices, particularly in the Global South, as highlighted during the COVID-19 pandemic. Through empirical analysis of two communities—Santa Cruz, Costa Rica, and Hivre Bazar, India—the paper explores civic innovations addressing water scarcity and pollution. Drawing on the hydro-social cycle and Donna Haraway's "staying with the trouble," it frames community actions like aquifer monitoring, reforestation, and equitable water governance as creative responses to climate impacts. These efforts promote sustainability and social repair, empowering vulnerable populations. The study critiques the hydrological cycle's limitations, proposing a hydro-socio-logical perspective to reflect human–nature interconnections. This contribution enriches the book by linking water justice to human dignity, advocating for community-driven solutions to complement inadequate governmental responses, fostering equitable and sustainable practices in crisis contexts.

Chapter 9: Response to Part II: Global Perspectives from Law and Policy on the Climate Crisis. Carla-Leanne Washbourne synthesizes legal and policy responses to the climate crisis, drawing parallels with the COVID-19 pandemic to highlight governance challenges in a polycrisis era. Analyzing cases from the US and Brazil, BRICS countries, and local communities in India and Costa Rica, the chapter examines how environmental legislation, like the US Clean Air Act, and civic innovations shape climate action. It emphasizes the need for coherent, multiscalar governance to address interdependent social-environmental challenges, noting tensions between economic development and sustainability. The chapter underscores how climate change disproportionately impacts vulnerable populations, threatening human dignity. By advocating for policy learning from past crises and local initiatives, it proposes integrating diverse knowledge systems to foster equitable, resilient responses. This contribution enriches the book by linking legal and policy frameworks to human dignity, urging cohesive global–local strategies to protect vulnerable communities in ongoing and future crises.

Chapter 10: Conclusion. Natalina Stamile, Rafael González Muños, Marlène Sam, and Yarina Amoroso bring together conclusive remarks pertaining to the collection's multidisciplinary exploration of human dignity and climate governance amid the COVID-19 pandemic, framing crises as magnifiers of structural inequalities and governance failures. The conclusion critiques unidimensional, state-centric responses, advocating a "pluralism of pluralisms" for coordinated diversity that respects sovereignty while fostering cooperation. Part I rethinks dignity through vulnerability, responsibility over compassion, health rights balancing, and

Indigenous resistance in Brazil. Part II examines climate inaction in the US and Brazil, and BRICS, alongside community innovations in water justice in India and Costa Rica. Converging on ethics of care, polycentric governance, rights of nature, and hybrid epistemologies, the chapter calls for adaptive, justice-oriented frameworks integrating local knowledge and global interdependence. Ultimately, crises threaten dignity yet also reveal its potential as an ethical compass for resilient, equitable reconstruction in a polycrisis era.

1.4 Toward a Sketch of Global Justice

Justice is a value with multiple facets (e.g., social, political, legal, and moral) and, as such, it plays a major role in any human interrelation. Different agents such as states, communities, and individuals involve different genders, ethnicities, religions, and beliefs as well as social, legal, political, and financial interrelations, i.e., the world is a mixture of different diversities, it is a pluralism of pluralisms. Justice and fairness enable these different agents who belong to diverse groups to live together in civil and international societies. There are different theories that try to explain why and how people come together at a certain point of their evolution and decide to be part of a community. The leading explanation for centuries has been the contractual theory, of which Hobbes, Locke, Rousseau, Kant, and Rawls offer some examples.[8] In order to live together in concord a minimum mutual acceptance is required among members of any societal organization, which establishes a sort of invisible net that makes them part of the same conglomerate (i.e., a nation).

In line with this theory, a pluralistic environment implies various values. These values may be autonomous (e.g., peace, security, and solidarity) or heteronomous (e.g., power, order, and cooperation) and all of them, ideally, are related, coordinated, and/or guided by one core principle: justice. The values that are labeled as autonomous are considered so because they have to do with a unit of concern[9] or a person; the ones that are heteronomous refer to a societal or communal coexistence. Thus, each value can have an excessive or defective form, similar to the Aristotelian idea of virtues as a balance between deficiency and excess (e.g., power as a value can be excessive resulting in oppression, or defective bringing about impotence; order as a value can imply in excess a ritualism and, in deficit a state of disorder).

More specifically, in terms of the variety of values in a plural society, in this book there are several different conceptions of justice. A brief but enlightening explanation of some different conceptions of justice is given by Hans Kelsen in *What is*

[8] Pogge (2007), in partic. pp. 60 ff.

[9] Often, in global justice literature, units of concern are human beings or persons. See Pogge (1992). However, while cosmopolitans like Barry, Beitz, Nussbaum, O'Neill, and Pogge center on units of concern in terms of individuals, Rawls focuses on "peoples." For a more detailed analysis about the differences between Rawls and cosmopolitans see Caney (2002), pp. 98–99. See also Kuper (2000).

Justice?[10] A more contemporary model of justice and fairness was created by John Rawls in his *A Theory of Justice*.[11] Rawls' thinking on international justice can be found in *The Law of Peoples*. Unsurprisingly, Rawls's *Law of Peoples* became the seed for different models of global justice.[12]

This book does not claim to follow Rawls or to bring together a global justice response to crises. More humbly, the chapters that follow present a myriad of selected issues at the level of the individual and at the level of the state that have a negative impact on civil and international societies, and they showcase several examples in which global justice is lacking or in question. Unfortunately, for different reasons, individuals, communities, and states choose to center on their differences rather than their affinities. The result is the spread and ongoing nature of issues such as pandemics, terrorism, territorial disputes, climate change, poverty, and violations to human dignity. Several voices have been raised to try to find global solutions to these pervasive problems. Despite their good intentions, such solutions have the tendency to refer to ideal ways to tackle real problems. Hence, they fail by default because of their lack of applicability.

These pages sketch a reconceived way of understanding the relationship between individuals, communities and states. Accepting the fact that states will not give up their sovereignty (at least not at this point in history) and acknowledging that individuals should have a minimum set of guarantees protected by law regardless of their individual circumstances (e.g., country of nationality, country of residence, income level, gender, cultural background, ethnicity), the book proposes to embrace coordination by means of learning from different national legal and political orders and international law. By means of coordination it is possible to effectively respect both state sovereignties and units of concern in law and policy.

Indeed, coordinating different legal systems is a task that deserves further exploration. This volume takes the first steps in creating that path. The complexity that state sovereignty presents seems difficult to deal with. The arrangements should embrace all agents (individuals, communities, and states) and accept the existence of several contexts (local, regional, and international) as well as a variety of legal systems. One of the crucial lessons is to design the arrangements with reference to different laws and policies while being mindful that sovereignty, the pandemic, and the issues discussed in the book are multi-subjective, multi-contextual, multifaceted, and multidimensional. Any coordination of legal and political systems must accommodate these particularities without disregarding any of them if it aims to work in practice in different domestic, regional, and international jurisdictions. Consequently, what is of importance in this book is to stress that an option in law and policy should guarantee state sovereignties as well as units of concern without giving any of them a position of privilege in relation to the other.

---

[10] See Kelsen (1973), Chap. 1.

[11] The design of this chapter is mainly inspired by Rawls (1999a), Chap. 3.

[12] Rawls (1999b); Brock (2023).

Obviously, to create substantive and procedural universal law and policy goes beyond the scope of this book. Accordingly, the conclusions are partial and only aim to give a blueprint of what is possible and realistically achievable in law and policy. The next steps must recognize not a pluralism but a pluralism of pluralisms. This acknowledgment implies that sovereign states and units of concern should not be considered alone, but in parallel with all agents (individuals, communities, and states) and the different ways they interrelate with each other. Moreover, these agents act on several contexts (local, regional, and international) and their interrelations bring about many views (legal, political, philosophical, and non-scientific ones).

Cooperation in the form of collaboration offers all participants the opportunity to learn from existing law and policy already applied elsewhere to the same situation. For example, measures applicable in relation to low-income women and vulnerable young adults and children in Brazil during the pandemic may have proven to be effective in dealing with poverty and gender-based issues elsewhere, and could be replicated successfully by other states. Conversely, domestic law and policy that have proven to increase the likelihood of violations to human rights and human dignity (e.g., unequal access to water, food, shelter, and vaccines) or to aggravate climate change situations like global warming in several areas around the world may help demonstrate the necessity of intergovernmental or supranational regional and international institutions, such as a global health fund.

To reiterate, the following chapters are a modest testament of the way in which different individuals from different backgrounds and jurisdictions are able to work together by cutting across state sovereignties and disciplinary boundaries and being open to knowledge interchange. Ultimately, any national, regional, or international arrangements that intend to bring lasting methods to tackle crises must acknowledge the pluralism of pluralisms present in fact and in law. In a similar vein, if existing understandings in terms of sovereignty and units of concern continue, they will only perpetuate a status quo and maintain legal and political uncertainty, thereby obstructing efforts to tackle efficiently any global justice issue.

References

Brock G (2023) Global justice. Available via Stanford Encyclopedia of Philosophy. https://plato.stanford.edu/entries/justice-global/. Accessed 1 Apr 2022

Caney S (2002) Cosmopolitanism and the law of peoples. J Polit Philosophy 10(1):95–123

Economic Commission for Latin America and the Caribbean (ECLAC) (2022) Press Release: Extreme poverty in the region rises to 86 Million in 2021 due to the deepening of the social and health crisis prompted by the COVID-19 pandemic. Available via https://www.cepal.org/en/pressreleases/extreme-poverty-region-rises-86-million-2021-due-deepening-social-and-health-crisis. Accessed 11 Sept 2025

International Monetary Fund (Fiscal Affairs) (2022) Gender equality and COVID-19: Policies and institutions mitigating the crisis. https://blog-pfm.imf.org/en/pfmblog/2021/07/gender-equality-and-covid-19-policies-and-institutions-for-mitigating-the-crisis. Accessed 11 Sept 2025

Kelsen H (1973) Essays in legal and moral philosophy. D. Reidel Publishing Company, Dordrecht

Kuper A (2000) Rawlsian global justice: beyond *the law of peoples* to a cosmopolitan law of persons. Polit Theory 28(5):640–674

Núñez JE (2023) Cosmopolitanism, state sovereignty, international law and politics: a theory. Routledge, Taylor & Francis Group, London and New York

Pogge T (1992) Cosmopolitanism and sovereignty. Ethics 103:48–75

Pogge T (2007) John Rawls: his life and theory of justice. Oxford University Press, Oxford

Rawls J (1999a) A theory of justice, Revised edn. Oxford University Press, Oxford

Rawls J (1999b) The law of peoples. Harvard University Press, Cambridge, MA

Saxe JG (1872) The blind men and the elephant. Available via *All About Philosophy*. https://www.allaboutphilosophy.org/blind-men-and-the-elephant.htm. Accessed 11 Sept 2025

UN Trade and Development (UNCTAD) (2021) COVID-19 threatens four 'lost decades' for gender equality. https://unctad.org/news/covid-19-threatens-four-lost-decades-gender-equality. Accessed 11 Sept 2025

United Nations (2021) COVID-19 has led to the first rise in extreme poverty in a generation. In: The Sustainable Development Goals Report 2021. https://unstats.un.org/sdgs/report/2021/goal-01/. Accessed 11 Sept 2025

Part I
Human Dignity

Chapter 2
A Legal Ethics of the Vulnerability of Human Beings: Human Dignity and Responsibility to Rethinking the Present Time

José-Antonio Santos

Abstract The purpose of this chapter is to develop a legal ethics of the vulnerability of human beings given what happened in the COVID-19 pandemic crisis, by building up a legal and philosophical framework related to responsibility and human dignity concepts. Assessing the present alongside the burden of the past, however, requires a sensible view of the past aligned with the political equity of all human beings. The study examines a particular definition of human dignity from an ethical and legal point of view to advocate for the value and principle of responsibility as an epistemic tool to rethink the vulnerability of human beings. The role of this legal ethics is analyzed in the face of changes in medical ethics and the concepts of suffering and compassion for vulnerable people.

2.1 Conceptual Approach to A Legal Ethics of Vulnerability

Any approach to a legal ethics of vulnerability can be impartial, with its character being determined by the existential biography and the social context of the individual who develops it. However, this starting point requires some conceptual clarifications to understand this proposal. Legal ethics cannot be understood as *simply ethics*, but as a discipline with its own thematic entity that tries to explain the law with the help of ethics. This explication is not exempt from difficulty, because on more than one occasion both scopes seem opposed and the need to relate them inevitably generates some confusion. Legal ethics raises a fundamental question of which law is just, and it has a sufficient thematic entity and development to be considered as an autonomous legal discipline. In the same way, it is possible to observe the autonomy obtained by the philosophy of law with respect to philosophy and the sociology of law with respect to sociology, until both became legal disciplines.

J.-A. Santos (✉)
Faculty of Law and Political Sciences Rey Juan Carlos University, Madrid, Spain
e-mail: joseantonio.santos@urjc.es

© The Author(s), under exclusive license to Springer Nature Switzerland AG 2026

J. E. Núñez (ed.), *Perspectives on Crises*,
https://doi.org/10.1007/978-3-032-23836-8_2

These interdisciplinary approaches are *frontier disciplines*, i.e., disciplines that border on other subjects, which makes it difficult to distinguish the strictly legal contents from those that are not.

As a starting point, the perspective of "external legal judgment" is adopted in search of a "criterion of justice," rather than an "internal legal judgment" more typical of "legal dogmatics." In other words, the so-called *positive* law is centered on different types of legal norms and decisions that are valid or applicable[1] at a specific moment. The legal dogmatics is sometimes insufficient to offer a satisfactory response to the current problems on which the law must decide, leaving aside more comprehensive perspectives than those represented by legal positivism in the strict sense of the term. The fact of adopting an external legal perspective means delving precisely into a more comprehensive vision, typical of the legal philosopher, and not a more restrictive one such as that of the legal theorist. This statement does not imply taking as a starting point the approach of the plain philosopher, and much less that of the moralist thinker, for a "legal system that morally wants more, actually gets less. Force what you are not authorized to force, succumb to material moralization."[2]

Reflection on the legal ethics of vulnerability takes on new importance and intensity as a result of the COVID-19 pandemic crisis, which makes it more evident that it is impossible to reflect on it, from an ethical and legal point of view, without keeping in mind concepts such as compassion, weakness, fragility, vulnerability, or more specifically, by disregarding the presence of the vulnerable or weak. According to Ausín, "the vulnerability is related to the possibility of suffering, to the disease, to pain, to fragility, to the limitation, and finally to death."[3] The COVID-19 pandemic has highlighted the need to rethink the present time in relation to vulnerability and to rethink concepts such as fragility and weakness, in order to give them greater specific weight. All this is within a context marked by a growing utilitarianism that "continues to encounter resistance." For this reason, the "health crisis has become the catalyst for a necessary reaction [...] against a growing social utilitarianism [...] closer to the Anglo-Saxon world than to our own philosophical and cultural heritage."[4]

The crisis of the COVID-19 pandemic shows that weakness must be met with responsibility toward the human being in a situation of fragility. The term *weak* is understood in a very broad sense as a human being who has physical, mental, or moral disabilities that may or may not be reversible, but who presents a condition seen with some empathy by the rest of the members of the community. The definition of the concept of weakness arises from a previous condition of scarcity or deficiency regarding the physical, mental, or moral condition of the subject; however, vulnerability arises from a possibility, although it is similar to weakness.

---

[1] von der Pfordten (2011), p. 1.

[2] Höffe (1990), p. 89.

[3] Ausín (2019), p. 138.

[4] Albert (2020), p. 192.

The protection of children or elderly persons is legally understood as protection for the weak. In this approach, equity plays a relevant role in relation to the weak or vulnerable: "It is essential to the exercise of the right to protection of the weak and the asymmetric rebalancing that occurs in social relations. Lawyers should feel especially interested in the validity of equity in the allocation of health resources. This is a question of law, and not of medical science."[5] It is crucial not to confuse what is legal and what is not, so that jurists are aware of a broader legal conception than the strictly positivist position.

The concept of being vulnerable or vulnerability is more encompassing and inclusive than that of being weak or weakness, and its use in the field of applied ethics and political philosophy is more extensive. Vulnerability implies that a human being can be physically or morally injured, but that it requires ethical recognition by other individuals, and the promulgation of legal norms by the State that protect individuals. All these legal norms and decisions position human dignity as a fundamental value, which serves as a brake on the different violations of human beings. Vulnerability requires alterity, which means understanding the subject in its cultural and pandemic context to create a "we" that includes and respects the vulnerable human being. On the other hand, weakness does not necessarily present the characteristic of alterity. In addition, the concept of weakness is normally accompanied by a pejorative meaning (e.g., having little strength or resistance), making it difficult for weak human beings to be properly included in society. However, it is easy to imagine the impossibility of a world without vulnerable subjects in times of pandemic. Any individual can be considered weak from this perspective at some point in his life. The issue becomes more complex when that weakness is permanent or its reversibility is slight over time.

2.2 Legal Ethics of Vulnerability Facing the Transformation of Medical Ethics

The legal ethics of vulnerability is also a practical ethics of duties. One of its highest duties is *to do justice*, for which purpose it is necessary to offer reasons and arguments about the protection of the vulnerable. The legal ethics of vulnerability, in its task of doing justice, finds its similarity with the legal ethics of the oppressed in an important claim— the right for a common space for the vulnerable human being to be treated with respect and as equal—despite presenting an *ideological* character that is less marked. This practical legal ethics must be applied to the specific context of health.

Just as legal ethics and deontology are linked, so are medical ethics and deontology. Both disciplines analyze the principles and rules of conduct that must be observed for the practice of their respective professions to show a medical model as

[5] Albert (2020), p. 199.

professional. Through this approach, medical professionalism can be understood as the correct performance of the professional activity. A civilized society must be decent, stable, and responsible. An affirmation of such significance is incumbent on doctors and jurists in pursuing a minimally decent, lasting, and responsible society.[6]

There is no single definition of the concept of medical professionalism. Blackmer highlights the difficulty of this term, which

> describes the skills, attitudes, values and behaviours common to those undertaking the practice of medicine. It includes concepts such as the maintenance of competence for a unique body of knowledge and skill set, personal integrity, altruism, adherence to ethical codes of conduct, accountability,[7] a dedication to self-regulation, and the exercise of discretionary judgment. Professionalism is also the moral understanding among medical practitioners that gives reality to what is commonly referred to as the social contract between medicine and society. This contract in return grants the medical profession a monopoly over the use of its knowledge base, the right to considerable autonomy in practice and the privilege of self-regulation.[8]

Both of these definitions of medical professionalism contribute to an understanding of the virtuality of this social contract. The problem is that the concept of medical professionalism has acquired such a degree of complexity that it is difficult to specify its hallmarks in a globalized world where technology, economy, and law play significant roles. Medical professionalism cannot be understood in a restrictive sense as the bridge that unites medicine with civil society, while ignoring its potential as a social contract.

Medical professionalism has three central elements that can be understood as a whole and not separately: "Devotion to service, profession of values and negotiation within society." These elements can help preserve "the decency and stability that are essential to civilized society."[9] These features can be reached from any profession in its deontological aspect, which takes a relational character. According to Ollero, any social norm that favors fraud must be rejected. For this reason, the expectations of others on how the subject is to behave are key in the professional context, which will depend on notions such as responsibility and trust.[10]

Returning to medical ethics, according to Pellegrino the deterioration of the sphere of medicine as a moral community has had serious consequences for the profession and society. The author highlights how the refusal of the medical community to act as a moral community is self-defeating, because physicians are retreating into a kind of self-protective moral atomism that puts personal survival before moral purpose. No leadership is provided to defend the care of the sick as a primary

---

[6] Wynia et al. (1999), p. 1615.

[7] Blackmer uses the concept of accountability. In English, responsibility and accountability are sometimes used as synonyms but they can also be differentiated as the word responsibility has a connotation of assigning a duty. In other languages such as German (*Verantwortung*), French (*responsabilité*) or Italian (*responsabilità*) the question does not raise a major problem.

[8] Blackmer (2007), p. 58.

[9] Wynia et al. (1999), p. 1615.

[10] Ollero (2003), p. 59.

concern or to stand for the just distribution of healthcare or to counter the dominance of the market ethos.[11] As Jonas points out, "we should be open to the idea that the natural sciences do not tell the whole truth about nature."[12] Jonas' principle of responsibility appears as a categorical imperative that has more in support for Kant than against him. An important fact is that the title of the English edition of Jonas' book is *The Imperative of Responsibility*.[13] In the field of contemporary German philosophy, there is an interest in labeling, based on a false dichotomy, the authors as Kantian or Hegelian.

Scientific humanism that is based exclusively on technological advances cannot prosper because otherwise the doctor–patient relationship would be of no use. It is necessary to take into account that, according to Román, knowledge, science, and technique will never be sufficient and this is not only due to the continuous need for expansion that the vocational attitude of a profession requires, but also due to its indispensable complementary relationship with the ethics that all human activity requires.[14] A society cannot be based almost exclusively on technoscience, since in every political community a multitude of *frontier problems* arise in which ethics and law have much to say, but, unfortunately, the law does not always have the most satisfactory answers to bioethical questions. The analysis of bioethical problems involves a process of legal reflection with a philosophical background. The human approach and scientism should not be incompatible, even though arduous and complicated situations are generated that, on many occasions, pose ethical and legal dilemmas for health personnel.

This legal ethics of vulnerability does not pursue an ethical maximum such as the ethics of virtues, but rather an "ethical minimum"[15] that implies responsibility for and toward other people, without prejudice to the fact that legal ethics, like the ethics of virtues, presents a character of commitment to society. The legal ethics of vulnerability and the ethics of virtues reaffirm a necessary relationship with biolaw and bioethics respectively based on a position that does not pretend to be aseptic or impartial, but rigorous. Legal ethics gains importance in its relationship with bioethics and biolaw approaches that pose complex ethical and/or legal dilemmas to the health professional, such as triage in the COVID-19 pandemic, where decision--making is usually irreversible.

Bioethics is a branch of ethics that focuses on providing guiding principles for the actions of human beings in relation to life, which is different from medical ethics that focuses on the rules of behavior applied to medical praxis. Biolaw, understood from an integrating perspective, consists of a "branch of the legal system characterized by its attention to respect and protection of life from conception to the

[11] Pellegrino (1990), pp. 224, 225.

[12] Jonas (1979), p. 35.

[13] Böhler (2017), p. xlvi.

[14] Román (2013), p. 20.

[15] Ollero (1996), p. 313.

end."[16] Given these definitions of bioethics and biolaw, one can easily see how the content of both has varied considerably, making it quite difficult to establish their contours. Bioethics and biolaw must meet two characteristics from the perspective of the legal ethics of vulnerability: they should not falsify reality in their analysis and must be committed to the present time. On the one hand, when it is said that they should not falsify reality, this means that issues of vulnerability must be approached rigorously and as closely as possible to reality, knowing the limitations, complexity, and different perspectives that are presented. This position makes us think that apodictic and closing arguments cannot be offered. On the other hand, the legal ethics of vulnerability must be committed to the present time, which implies looking at the integral protection of vulnerable groups. Vulnerable human beings must be respected and treated as a member of the human species, which means recognizing the importance of ensuring their human dignity.

It is necessary to advocate for a relationship model between the health professional and the patient that adequately combines the autonomy of the patient's will with the correct pre-understandings of the health professional. Consequently, individualism emphasizes the right to autonomy of the subject, a position from which the patient will be able to carry out at all times the clinical decision of how long they want to live. This utilitarian perspective prioritizes individual self-determination over the right to life. John Stuart Mill made it very clear: "The principle of freedom cannot require that he should be free not to be free. It is not freedom to be allowed to alienate his freedom."[17]

It is a fact that each individual has a wide margin of action in the exercise of his/her freedom, as the subject is a free and autonomous being able to make his/her own decisions at the end of life. A different matter is that the participation of a third party is required to end or help end the life of a patient, as happens in euthanasia and assisted suicide. From this point of view, autonomy is based on a concept of freedom that allows the person to decide on death. Thus, Dworkin postulates that "we insist on freedom, and we place the right of conscience at its center." And then he adds: "It matters as much that we live up to our freedom as that we have it. Freedom of conscience presupposes a personal responsibility of reflection, and it loses much of its meaning when that responsibility is ignored. A good life need not be an especially reflective one; most of the best lives are just lived rather than studied."[18] This does not mean that there may be a life plan and certain planning for its realization.

Currently immersed in a context of crisis and precariousness in the labor market, health professionals have greater difficulty in detecting and treating these end-of--life issues, together with the fact of a growing dehumanization of medicine. Actually, according to Haque and Waytz, "dehumanization is endemic in medical practice."[19] This situation is, among other factors, due to excessive technification based on mod-

[16] Ollero (2006), p. 19.

[17] Mill (1903), p. 80.

[18] Dworkin (1994), pp. 239–240.

[19] Haque and Waytz (2012), p. 176.

ernizing procedures and devices or facilities without the existence sometimes of duly qualified personnel to implement said procedures and/or manage these devices. This panorama hinders adequate medical assistance for the benefit of a *medicine of options*, based on the principle of a patient's autonomy. The patient will choose the option that suits him or her best, with the acquiescence of the doctor in scrupulous compliance with the legal system to avoid problems. Sometimes, doctors will opt for the *easiest decision* and that on more than one occasion will coincide with the one to which the legal system leads them for fear of civil or criminal liability, even though medical negligence must be duly proven and not by mere inference. This panorama also clearly shows a dehumanization of law. It would be desirable to strengthen the training of health professionals, and above all those working in the field of palliative care, with the aim that the good judgment of the medical specialist prevails in line with the best medical tradition.

Compliance with informed consent and protocols to create legal certainty in the performance of the professional activity by doctors must be harmonized with the closeness between the patient and the doctor, especially at the end of life. The provision of informed consent in patients at the end of life is problematic, due to the simple fact that their autonomy is altered by their situation of vulnerability and fragility, which modifies their ability to make decisions. In contrast to this situation, there arises a problem for the health professional: the realization of defensive medicine instead of a humanized medicine. The first approach, defensive medicine, consists of departing from the usual medical practice as a safeguard against possible litigation when applying the different knowledge and techniques used for the prediction, prevention, diagnosis, and treatment of human diseases. In other words, it means deviating from the proper procedure of the doctor in fear of possible lawsuits that may be filed by third parties in relation to the performance of the professional activity. Humanized medicine consists of applying that knowledge and using techniques for the prediction, prevention, diagnosis, and treatment of diseases, taking up axiological concepts such as responsibility—bringing them from the past to the present—in order to protect and care for human beings in vulnerable situations.

Defensive medicine dilutes compassion and responsibility toward the patient to the point of causing a distance between doctor and patient, a situation in which both have been harmed. Doctors spend part of their time gathering proof and evidence to shield themselves from possible civil and/or criminal liability, while in reality they are people who have to take care of people. A classic study conducted by researchers at Harvard Medical School concluded that most doctors in various specialties tended to adopt a defensive professional culture when faced with the pressure of being sued for medical malpractice.[20] This is an attitude, on the part of doctors, that has been increasing over time and spreading to many countries, in particular the United States. Defensive medicine benefits neither doctors nor patients, and the

---

[20] Kessler and McClellan (1996), pp. 355, 388.

adverse effects, according to Sekhar and Vyas, are not limited to the increased cost of medical care but also affect the overall quality of the healthcare system.[21]

Defensive medicine is an increasingly common area of conflict and must be subject to the prudent and committed attitude of the doctor with the patient, an approach which is not incompatible with the recognition of the patient's will. It was thought that perhaps naively offering a range of decision possibilities could help citizens to know what is most correct for them at the end of life in the COVID-19 pandemic. The problem is that "what is done with human life concerns us all, it cannot be a merely private matter."[22] It is not a merely individual situation, but it contains within it a kind of marked collectivism.

From this perspective, it could be thought that the autonomy of the patient should prevail. However, if the doctor senses that the patient is not prepared to accept the harsh reality, they may not tell them the whole truth, so that the latter thinks that he or she is going to improve, even if only emotionally. Hence, the meaning of the term "bearable truth" refers to the information that is transferred to the patient, considering their disposition and the degree of bearability to receive it. Thus, according to Espinosa at al., doctors must not lie but must not put too much pressure on their patients. Patients usually give us clues about how much they want to know and when they would like to know it. Giving them that information is a process that begins in the first interview and ends at the moment of death.[23] Providing fair information is crucial, so all available data should not be given at once. Too much information can impair the patient's ability to cope with bad news and make the decision more difficult. This was especially the case during the COVID-19 pandemic in which even the healthcare professionals did not know what was medically most appropriate for each patient. Espinosa at al. convey the idea of a *bearable* truth that fits with an idea of a patient's trust in the doctor. The relationship of trust is bidirectional between the two. It is a frequent routine developed in hospitals. According to Schroth, the relationship must be based on trust between the two, but also on solidarity. This fact causes the formalization of the doctor–patient relationship, which leads to a loss of solidarity but enhances the subject status of the patient. This formalization assumes that the patient has to be involved, especially when making decisions in conditions of insecurity.[24]

This situation has led to a blurring of the doctor–patient relationship, by excessively prioritizing the interest of patients to the detriment of good medical practice. To explore this deeper, it can be said that "causing well is also a legal duty of health professionals who are qualified of not only theoretical knowledge, skill, and technical ability by the protocols and the *law of the skill*, but also the right intention to benefit the patient."[25] The application of guidelines and protocols must have an eye

---

[21] Sekhar and Vyas (2013), pp. 295–296.

[22] Camps (2001), p. 49.

[23] Espinosa et al. (1994), p. 811.

[24] Schroth (2011), p. 483.

[25] Vidal (2016), p. 93.

on medicine that is closer to the patient, based on the experience of the doctor in similar cases. This process is not only intuitive but also supported by scientific evidence, considering that it is necessary to listen to the patient and to know the origin of their pain. This means going beyond the purely pragmatic and emotional mentality and paying special attention to the protection of the subject in a situation of weakness or vulnerability. To achieve this purpose, vulnerability and human dignity must be inseparable in a pandemic context, that is, intentional physical or moral damage to a human being supposes an attack on their human dignity. It is an invitation to the rehumanization of ethics and, above all, of law to aim for a utopian outcome and achieve a world in peace.[26] According to Bloch, the common point between social utopias and so-called natural law theories is the achievement of a more humane society. However, there are some differences relating to the greater significance assigned to issues in the past than today: The social utopia was designed in advance for situations in which the *overwhelmed* and *oppressed* cease to exist, while Natural Law constructs situations in which the *humiliated* and *offended* cease to exist.[27] Both disciplines share a pacifying task, even though ethics places emphasis on its meliorative capacity in relation to people and the law on its capacity to measure people's actions so that they do not harm each other. Such an approach does not mean ignoring the benefits of personalized medicine that allows, thanks to technology, a more accurate and early diagnosis. However, the fact of extolling the benefits of technology should not mean isolating the patient or, that is, dehumanizing them.

2.3 Suffering in the Context of Human Rights

It is a reality that academic legal literature has little interest in the question of suffering. This circumstance causes perplexity given that, according to Andorno and Baffone, "human rights have to a large extent emerged in the midst of the twentieth century as a response to human suffering." Traditionally, suffering has not been considered "as a *legal* concept," but only "as the implicit *psychological* underpinning of human rights violations."[28] Legal ethics takes suffering into account because it considers it as an injustice that human beings suffer. This obviousness makes us rethink the fact of taking measures so that human beings do not suffer but, at the same time, it is necessary to know suffering more deeply so as to work better with it in the field of human rights. One of the moral duties of medical ethics is to prevent suffering, but this is not the case in the legal field itself, the purpose of which is prevention through the protection of human rights.

---

[26] The meaning given to rehumanization is a "hermeneutic key for the philosophy of history to come, open to the utopia of a world in peace." Cañas Fernández (2000), p. 172.

[27] Bloch (1961), p. 13.

[28] Andorno and Baffone (2014), p. 185.

Suffering is not a concept of law but one about law, which shows how any philosophy of human rights must be, to a greater or lesser extent, concerned with those who *suffer*, that is, with those who are in a disadvantaged position in society, and who must enjoy added protection against possible violations. More broadly, suffering can be connected to human rights, understood as "a social response to human suffering."[29] The concept of suffering takes on a special role due to its constant presence at the end of life. It is not easy for a health professional to gauge the suffering of a human being. What is sometimes forgotten is that suffering is always present in different parts of life, so it may be appropriate to try to work with it, learn to live with some pain, and reflect on the proximity of death at the end of life. It is possible to think of the existence of an ethical and legal duty to care for the pain and suffering of others for the duration of the COVID-19 patient's life.

What is intended is that the patient's death is calm, serene, and of quality, although all of these outcomes are immeasurable characteristic notes, especially the last one. The approach to understanding quality at end of life depends on internal factors (correct diagnosis, listening to the patient's preferences, listening to the opinions of relatives and caregivers, generating a climate of intra-family peace, etc.) and external factors (social and economic environment of family members, care for the patient's caregiver, etc.). A death without suffering at the end of life is not always usual, but a death without pain, agony, or special shocks, together with an acceptable quality of life, should be pursued. It is also necessary to be aware that to a greater or lesser degree death always generates anguish since it is difficult to be educated about dying. Hence, to *die with dignity*, first of all, it is necessary to *know how to die*. The concept of dying with dignity does not cease to cause perplexity because, in the opposite sense, one could die without dignity.

The concept of human dignity is a quality of merit inherent to the human being, regardless of their capacity for action; it is neither gained nor lost, but is guaranteed, recognized, violated, etc. In short, "it is about being aware of the objective dignity of the human person, that man" (understood as a human being) "cannot be treated at the discretion of power and society."[30] The retrospective nature of dignity makes the human being valued for his or her belonging to humanity; specifically, a person is valued for what they have been and for what they are: a human being. From this perspective, "humanity is not only made up of present human beings but also past and future human beings; humanity is connected not only through collective action but also through narrative and word. Humanity is past, present, and future."[31] One can only speak of human dignity "if the recognition of universality and the demand for non-exclusion are accepted as a premise."[32] It is an idea perfectly compatible with a legal ethics of vulnerability, while a different question is that, in practice, dissonances are observed in the characterization of universality and non-exclusion:

---

[29] Andorno and Baffone (2014), p. 183.

[30] Hervada (1991), pp. 226–227.

[31] Santos (2021), p. 226.

[32] Aparisi (2013), p. 215.

Is it possible to make the claim of universality of human dignity feasible in certain situations by end of life in the COVID-19 pandemic crisis, even when the person does not want that universality? What if the person is the one who is excluded and is thought of as not worthy of that human dignity?

As a general rule, no one wants to die, unless one finds oneself with sources of pain or without the will to live, that is, with physical, psychological, or moral suffering. The problem is the fear of dying held by most human beings, and not being prepared for death. Even some individuals who say that they are prepared for death can be afraid that a critical illness may strike them. All these circumstances entail a process of teaching the patient to live and die, which involves accompanying people in the process of dying. Discerning death requires first elucidating the ins and outs of life, that is, being aware that death implies knowing how to discern the truly important things that life holds.

Suffering in relation to serious or terminal illness is a matter of value and degree. The signs of identification of suffering have varied considerably to the point of being able to affirm that, at present, its effects can be increasingly controlled, although the difficulty in delimiting its contours remains evident. Sometimes, in the case of patients at the end of life, more than physical suffering is evident, where existential suffering is concerned, understood as a crisis in which the individuals question the reason for their existence, the meaning of their life, or the reasons for continuing or not living, among others. For example, the patient may ask: What am I doing here in my situation? What is the point of continuing like this? Why have I lost hope? When this happens, it can help to empathize and perform an exercise in otherness, putting oneself in the other's place, considering their wishes but also explaining the best arguments to give meaning to the life of that person in a situation of vulnerability or weakness. A good start might be to look the patient in the eye, call them by their name, and ask how to be of help. Most of the time, patients need things as simple as being listened to, accompanied, cared for, treated with affection and empathy, sharing with them, talking to them, etc. Assertive communication is important in this regard, despite the simplicity of carrying out these actions in theory. On many occasions, these actions are complicated by the context in which they have to be developed.

The suffering can be double: for the patient and the relatives or professional caregivers. It must not be forgotten that, on occasions, family members act as caregivers at the same time, which complicates their coexistence with the patient on an emotional level. Both have in common, among other things, that they do not want to feel alone: one being cared for and the other or others caring. Care practices are of interest in relation to healthcare and are an act of justice toward human beings in a situation of vulnerability or weakness, although this does not mean that they cannot be applied to the construction and improvement of democratic or friendly relations. In care practices, prudence, communication skills, or empathy take on important dimensions, which are exercised and developed in the context of the vulnerability of the subject who suffers, but not without reciprocal responsibility in the COVID-19 pandemic crisis. In the etymological sense, empathy means being *within the suffering* but coming out affected, marked and, above all, aware. It refers to the participation by a person in the feelings and ideas of another and becoming aware of their physical, mental, and existential situation. In care practices, the role of doctors and nurses is of special interest, without ignoring the different functions performed by the rest of the health professionals to create a climate of trust.

Learning to live with suffering means understanding it from a perspective closer to Stoicism than to Augustinianism. The pedagogical task of working with suffering implies teaching how to live with the disease. This means understanding that illness and health have an evaluative component, a circumstance that allows the patient to give different weight to each of them in their daily lives. Without going any further, one is born with suffering and, many times, it happens that one dies with suffering, be it physical, psychic, or existential, although this is not the most desirable and convenient experience. Just remember the baby's first cries at birth as a sign of good health!

From the point of view of legal ethics, it is not a matter of creating martyrs prepared to suffer, but, rather, citizens are to be aware of their limitations and the non-linearity of life. This awareness is not resignation, but responsibility to lead a life, although this life is not in certain moments always close to fullness. Therefore, it is difficult to understand the reason why people (particularly those in favor of euthanasia) do not prepare a legal advance directive with which they would be able to avoid the suffering that certain care or treatments can cause, with regard to their health at the end of life, in order not to fall into therapeutic obstinacy or situations of unwanted discomfort.

2.4 Compassion Toward the Other at the End of Life

According to the Oxford English Dictionary, compassion is defined as "the feeling or emotion, when a person is moved by the suffering or distress of another, and by the desire to relieve it; pity that inclines one to spare or to succour."[33] Feelings such as sorrow or tenderness emerge to help put into practice a type of empathy that helps (or at least tries) to better understand the sufferer. At the starting point, compassion may be minimally adequate for the caregiver to empathize with the sufferer. The true suffering that a subject has at a certain moment is only going to be truly felt by him or her because the suffering is subjective. Attempts to objectify suffering are to a certain extent useless, except that they can be accompanied with some episode of quantifiable pain. The rhetoric of compassion generates an undesirable situation for the other as unequal, both at the point of departure and that of arrival, although it is true that compassion plays a more important role in the field of ethics than it can (or rather should) play in law. It is a concept that functions as a value within medical ethics, but that should not have a relevant role in legal ethics above all because of

[33] "Compassion" in Oxford English Dictionary (2025). https://www.oed.com/dictionary/compassion_n?tab=meaning_and_use#8805967.

how pernicious this concept can be in law. The sustained proposal is that legal ethics must work with responsibility understood as a central value concerning the problems related to vulnerability in the COVID-19 pandemic crisis.

Compassion has been seen as "the virtue of well-used disappointment, that is, it tempers the impotence that arises after the experience of failure."[34] That is to say, it occurs only "just after the experience of incapacity, after the failure of the attempt to fully realize justice in the world; but it is unjustifiable as a program to replace the fight against injustice or to temper the conflict resulting from inequalities."[35] That is where the law makes its special sense: Not only when compassion fails, but also as a mechanism to reduce inequalities. Compassion plays a determining role in the terminological configuration of terminal illness characterized by great suffering, be it physical, mental, or moral, on the part of the patient as well as his immediate family and, on occasions, other relatives. It comes to light in situations of agony, understood as the state that precedes death and in which life is gradually extinguished, despite not occurring in all patients. With respect to COVID-19 patients in a situation of special vulnerability, the state must opt, at the starting point, for the protection of the patient's life, although at the point of arrival it must not fall into the temptation of protecting actions that fall into obstinacy therapeutics with futile treatments that suppose an unnecessary lengthening of the life of the patient (sometimes mistakenly wanted by the members of the family), despite having received adequate medical information. Certainly, a deliberate shortening of the patient's life is also problematic when assessing correct medical practice. The implementation of palliative care is ethically indicated and considered as correct from a legal point of view, provided that it is by the *law of the skill* and is carried out proportionately with the aim of "relieving symptoms (among which pain usually plays a major role) that cause suffering and deteriorate the quality of life of the patient in a terminal situation," and provided that the "analgesics or sedatives" are used "in the dose necessary to achieve the therapeutic objectives, although it could indirectly cause an advance of death."[36] For this reason, it is necessary to reconcile the principle of nonmaleficence with that of beneficence, characterized by trying to achieve a reasonable benefit for the patient.

Avoiding therapeutic obstinacy is crucial in order not to carry out a life extension when there are no real possibilities for improvement. One question is related to a thought that patients have, especially in their terminal phase: the idea of a *bad death*. In other words, the problem is not so much the tragic outcome itself, but death with suffering, in medical terms, with pain. Patients want to die without pain and in a peaceful situation, which means that they do not fall into a situation of abandonment and at least are provided with nutrition and hydration by mouth at the end of life. Both are perfectly indicated care. A different and more complex issue is the clear determination of their proportionality in certain cases. However, it is easy to fall into

---

[34] Innerarity (1994), n.p.

[35] Altisent (2003), pp. 145–146.

[36] Gómez (2016), n.p.

the dichotomy between quantity and quality of life to opt for one or the other. The key lies in establishing a fair proportion between the two concepts, although reaching a truly conclusive argument is almost impossible as each patient has a different awareness of their own situation and the ability to endure suffering over time. A life of quality supposes a life in which one does not fall into therapeutic obstinacy with futile treatments.[37]

According to Revel, "the word *compassion* sometimes conjures up in the West a notion of condescending piety, of commiseration, which supposes a distance about the one who suffers."[38] Compassion, particularly toward the loved one, does not benefit either the patient or their relatives, since it can mean an argument to end the patient's life, by which the patient is surely the one who loses the most, unless there is a conception especially transcendent of life, according to which non-existence could be better than existence. In this context, it is necessary to ask about the meaning of life. A first approximation involves assessing the meaning of present life through an analysis-balance of life as experienced in its entirety and not as isolated individual events, giving special relevance at the end of life to the small moments formed as a whole, which make life, on more than one occasion, truly profitable. A responsible attitude requires a reflective life in which one has a life plan. If one does not have a life project, it is difficult to achieve happiness. Life is not improvised, so planning for the future in which everyone knows where they want to go is healthy. This life plan is always unfinished since there are always new goals to fulfill. Finding meaning in life implies finding meaning "in our actions. The question of responsibility is first of all dictated by the vocation to continue loving the world and, therefore, it is supposed to be common to those who ask and those who respond. Asking and answering is a commitment against the great enemy, despair, which leaves us alone and opens the door to narcissism."[39]

From positions contrary to euthanasia, it is admitted, on many occasions, that life is a supernatural gift and consequently inviolable. In many moments, these conceptions appear to consider much more compassion than responsibility, as is the case sometimes with the defenders of euthanasia, even though they often resort to defending the freedom of the individual to organize their life plan in the final stage. In the field of ethics, charity plays an important role if it is understood as a kind of horizontal solidarity with a dose of altruism, projected as a manifestation of compassion and respect for the dignity of the human being. A compassionate attitude is plausible above all in the bioethical debate and not so much in the biolegal one, despite the fact that it is sometimes shown in this type of discourse when addressing the concept of human dignity. The law cannot be governed by compassion, nor should it act for charitable reasons, but with responsibility and justice. Therefore, it is conceivable that the law does not pretend to be compassionate and even less so in exceptional situations. The law aims to make interpersonal relationships fairer.

---

[37] Santos (2014), p. 177.

[38] Revel and Ricard (1997), p. 232.

[39] Villacañas (2007), p. 69.

Compassion and responsibility, as well as human dignity, are catch-all terms for defending a wide range of courses of action regarding euthanasia and assisted suicide of vulnerable people in the COVID-19 pandemic crisis. It is necessary to differentiate compassion from responsibility. A compassionate attitude toward the pain of others, especially toward the loved one at the end of life, does not benefit the patient or his family members and may even be an argument to end his life. In more than one case, intermediate courses of action may fail by opting for the *easiest decision*. Supporters of euthanasia are favorable, according to Hendin, to ideals such as compassion or autonomy, although they promote rules that, despite their good intentions, will only end in coercion and cruelty. Thus, they will influence the dehumanization of the elderly as much or more than the indiscriminate use of medical technology. This is so much the case that it can lead to common points emerging between the defenders of euthanasia and therapeutic obstinacy: Both are incapable of accepting death as being part of our lives that are not subject to our control.[40]

In the context of euthanasia and assisted suicide, the ethical and legal pointillism of extreme cases often resorts to dramatic, conflicting, and occasionally tearful cases, which tend to blur the macro debate of ideas by falling into the realm of exceptional hard cases. Most of the cases are resolved without any conflict because the patient either does not request euthanasia or it is simply prohibited by the legal system in question. The strategy consists of refuting a general rule based on some exceptional or marginal cases. They are the borderline cases that outline shadows, rather than shed light on problems. There could also be cases of individuals who, although subject to certain renunciations and restrictions, can develop a meaningful and fruitful life project. Borderline cases unleash a strong emotional charge and in turn generate compassion for those who listen to these stories.

Compassion is derived from macro-stories and micro-stories, although the former are the ones that capture the attention of the media and, curiously, their variety is not great. These moments are riddled with particularisms that appear exposed in the media to society as macro-stories when there are cases every day in hospitals and residences of micro-stories that have, at least, the same relevance and whose daily experiences are not counted. Microhistory helps to reveal an understanding that small facts—no matter how insignificant they may seem today—can help explain the importance of historical time. Moreover, it is reasonable to think that some of the cases were not correctly managed from a medical and legal point of view.

From a perspective contrary to euthanasia and assisted suicide, it is easy to think that overestimating the hard cases and legislating in the sense of their regulation could lead to a slippery slope in legislative matters, together with the fact that the general rule is that decisions are invested on exceptional cases. The slippery slope consists of the progressive expansion from assisted suicide to euthanasia, from terminally ill to chronically ill patients, from voluntary to involuntary euthanasia, from

---

[40] Hendin (1997), pp. 290–291.

physical illness to mental suffering,[41] and from euthanasia in the elderly to euthanasia in minors,[42] etc. The defenders of this position fear that if certain controlled medical practices begin to be accepted at the end of life, others such as assisted suicide will end up being legalized. It may be the case—as has happened in the Netherlands and Belgium—that euthanasia is admitted to people who cannot request it or who are not suffering unbearably. Keown says that, in its empirical form, the slippery slope argument asserts that "even if a line can in principle be drawn between voluntary and non-voluntary euthanasia, a slide will occur in practice because the safeguards to prevent it cannot be made effective."[43]

Now, in "pluralist democracies today, there is understandable reluctance to be associated with Nazi ideas and practices. Racist eugenics are condemned, though one comes across discreet allusions to the burden and futility of sustaining the severely mentally handicapped. Much more popular is the conception that some sorts of life are not worth living; life in such a state demeans the patient's dignity, and maintaining it (otherwise than at the patient's express request) insults that dignity; proper respect for the patient and the patient's best interests requires that his life be brought to an end."[44] To understand the present and be able to look optimistically toward the future, it is necessary to understand the past.

This situation has led to problems related to the end of life being seen as something harmful, annoying, uncomfortable, and even negative. The issue acquires greater notoriety when rethinking the following statement by Jonas: "Modern thought which began with the Renaissance is placed in exactly the opposite theoretic situation: death is the natural thing, life the problematic."[45] This is the case where reflecting on life at certain times has a negative consideration, which is not an obstacle to agreeing that therapeutic obstinacy can border on torture to the point that suffering no longer makes sense. This fact means that palliative sedation, administered in proportionate doses, may be convenient to reduce or eliminate pain in a patient who presents a set of differentiated refractory symptoms. Intentionality plays a fundamental role as the result of that death is not pursued, so the indicated sedation is not euthanasia.

---

[41] The slippery slope argument is exemplified, to cite one of the most relevant cases of comparative law, in the Judgment of the Supreme Court of the Netherlands of June 21, 1994. HR 21-06-1994, NJ 1994, 656, Chabot.

[42] It is enough to remember the cases of euthanasia in minors in Belgium and the Netherlands.

[43] Keown (1995), p. 408.

[44] Finnis (1995), p. 24.

[45] Jonas (1977), p. 28.

2.5 Responsibility as a Value and Principle at the End of Life

The ethics of responsibility and the legal ethics of vulnerability converge in that both are ethics of *emergency*, although the former has a more markedly pessimistic, ontological, and dichotomous accent marked by the alternative of being or not being of human existence. The legal ethics of vulnerability has a marked legal, but fundamentally deep, accent since it describes and, above all, prescribes a way of philosophizing, which at this point of biolegal criticism resembles Jonas' ethics of responsibility as both unfold in an *emergency* context with its struggle to preserve human existence. The legal ethics of vulnerability connects very well with constitutional law, especially in its guaranteeing function, and with applied ethics in its function of a fire warning. Being a fire announcer (*Feuermelder*[46]) is a public task that should be advocated to any author committed to the present time. According to Jonas and Habermas, some approaches can be detected that could be called bioconservative,[47] in terms of what could be beneficial for bioethics and biolaw, but which have in common their interest in *saving human existence*. According to Habermas, the "reference to the human species would mark the border between the natural teleology of Jonas or Spaemann and the philosophy of history of Adorno and Horkheimer."[48] The underlying thread of this chapter is found on that same border, which is influenced by Jonas' principle of responsibility[49] as well as a call not to endanger the existence of humanity. Jonas' affirmation that "all traditional ethics is anthropocentric"[50] is not an obstacle here as, from the legal ethics described and with the help of the philosophy of history, this paradigm is revisited to temper its marked ontological and metaphysical character. Legal ethics is largely anthropocentric due to its interest, in this context, in the basic realities of human events such as life and death.

In linguistic terms, the word responsibility comes from the Latin *responsum* which means response and which in turn derives from the verb *respondere* (to respond). Hence, the concept of responsibility supposes a response to an abstract commitment contracted by the subjects with society. This obligation implies recommitting to an emergency such as the treatment of a vulnerable human being at the end of life. Therefore, responsibility understood as a value and principle serves as a two-sided criterion to offer indications of how to act in the field of ethics and law. It is logical to think that it can harbor an idealistic character, which aims to preserve a better future for the coming generations.

---

46 Benjamin (1972), p. 122.

47 This is perhaps because of the meaning that could be given to their thinking as life preservers, that is, because they advocate preserving existence, despite the differences between the two thinkers.

48 Habermas (2002), p. 86.

49 "Act so that the effects of your action are compatible with the permanence of genuine human life on Earth," Jonas (1979), p. 36.

50 Jonas (1979), p. 22.

The legal concept of responsibility can be understood as a legal principle that entails an optimization requirement of a specific legal nature. In the constitutional sense, the idea of "responsibility for future generations can be found today as a principle that characterizes the entire constitutional public order."[51] Responsibility functions as an inspiring value of the legal system and as a principle understood as an optimization requirement that implies a commitment by the part of the individual, according to factual and legal possibilities, regarding the performance of acts or decisions that affect humanity. The concept of responsibility helps to build and trace a sustainable present and a more hopeful future, knowing that the law alone will not solve the problems related to the vulnerability of human beings. For this reason, the responsibility of oneself toward others (self-responsibility) is necessary from the commitment understood as another ethical and legal obligation, and the responsibility of individuals as an integral part of citizenship and also that of governments (hetero-responsibility).

From a legal perspective, Schubert points out the virtuality of the principle of responsibility in relation to the consideration of "a general intuitive consensus on the guarantee of the *Dasein* of humanity."[52] The obligation to maintain "the *Dasein* of humanity" is configured as a "categorical legal imperative." In this sense, humanity is understood in an absolute way: "It is, or it is not, it cannot be proportional, optimal or minimal."[53] Here a weaker ontological presupposition of the principle of responsibility is subscribed, despite emphasizing the importance of preserving humanity and its consideration as an obligation of legal-political category based on an ethical-legal plane. The strong or absolute ontological presupposition of the existence of humanity can be tempered with Muguerza's criticism of Jonas' principle of responsibility: "As for ethics, nothing worse could happen to it [...] than its subordination to ontology, as Jonas' claim to *base on 'is' all 'ought'*, because the first *duty* that the principle of responsibility would then impose would be to preserve at all costs, that is *at any price*, the otherwise desirable *prevalence of 'is' over the nothing*."[54]

Humanity is not properly understood without humanizing healthcare in connection with technology. Humanizing is taking up axiological concepts such as responsibility, and bringing them from the past to the present, in order to protect human beings in situations of vulnerability.

---

[51] Schubert (1998), p. 271.

[52] Schubert (1998), p. 334.

[53] Schubert (1998), p. 275.

[54] Muguerza (2007), p. 45.

2.6 Conclusion

The legal ethics of vulnerability understands the human being as a historical subject that *is* thanks to what it *was*. Human beings must take responsibility as historical subjects by being aware of the commitment made with future generations to build a better future. A legal ethics of vulnerability seeks to overcome the purely pragmatic and emotional mentality to protect the individual in a situation of vulnerability. This starting point should serve to try to understand bioethics and biolaw from a basis of intellectual honesty that supposes a non-distortion of reality and a commitment to the present time.

It is necessary to change the mentality of societies and to promote a revitalization (or better, a recovery) of the best tradition of the medical profession in relation to law, ethics, and technology. That means to take advantage of technological advances without dehumanizing the patient, considering that the law is born with the vocation of doing justice through the protection of vulnerable human beings in the COVID-19 pandemic crisis. This conception requires respect for the human rights of these individuals and consideration of them as equal to the rest of the members of their species.

The value of responsibility is a specific principle of justice, which influences the way of understanding and deliberating about care practices, protecting the human rights of all people in vulnerable situations. A vision of the value and principle of responsibility focuses on dialogue with the individual in a situation of vulnerability, which consists of seeing in the other what is of one's own. It is an alterity, in the field of legal ethics, to give a key role to responsibility as opposed to compassion, which means committing oneself and not pitying. There is a misunderstanding in the desire to apply charity and compassion to the legal field, when in reality prudence and responsibility should prevail. It is pertinent to assume the existence of various concepts of responsibility, which in turn contain different conceptions. The responsibility principle exceeds the borders of care practices, but it is in the health field where its relationship with human rights can be more easily seen.

The patient, as well as the relatives, must rethink the end of life in the COVID-19 pandemic, considering that compassion and love, as part of mercy, can become disturbing elements in the philosophy of law. The compassionate reasoning that, theoretically, should be outside the legal debate, in practice ends up mistakenly—on more than one occasion—introduced into the law. Caring should not be a compassionate act, but an act of responsibility toward vulnerable people. The task of caring for the pain and suffering of a vulnerable human being requires objectivity in the consideration of values, dialogue, prudence, and patience. Pain and suffering must be understood as life experiences that one must learn to work with. However, both sensations must be seen from an inclusive and not exclusive attitude of the vulnerable human being, to develop an awareness in thinking about the future that is being left to the coming generations.

In the context of legal ethics, responsibility arises as a primary obligation, so it is convenient to assess the meaning of life through an analysis of life experienced in its entirety and not as isolated individual facts, giving special relevance to the small moments. It is a vision that highlights our responsibility as historical subjects for the construction of a better future.

Acknowledgments This work has been supported by the Alexander von Humboldt Foundation during my stay as a Senior Researcher at the University of Göttingen in Germany.

References

Albert M (2020) Vulnerabilidad y atención sanitaria. Cuadernos de Bioética 31(102):183–202

Altisent R, Rodeles del Pozo R, Aguilar AG et al (2003) Declaración sobre la eutanasia de la Sociedad Española de Cuidados Paliativos. Cuadernos de Bioética 14(50):144–151

Andorno R, Baffone C (2014) Human rights and the moral obligation to alleviate suffering. In: Green RM, Palpant NJ (eds) Suffering and bioethics. Oxford University Press, Oxford, pp 182–200

Aparisi A (2013) El principio de la dignidad humana como fundamento de un bioderecho global. Cuadernos de Bioética 24(81):201–221

Ausín T (2019) The public dimension of care: Towards a public ethics of care. In: Vallverdú J, Puyol A, Estany A (eds) Philosophical and methodological debates in public health. Springer, Dordrecht, pp 137–148

Benjamin W (1972) Einbahnstraße. In: Rexroth T (ed) Gesammelte Schriften. Suhrkamp, Frankfurt am Main, p. 122

Blackmer J (2007) Professionalism and the medical association. World Med J 53(3):58–74

Bloch E (1961) Naturrecht und menschliche Würde. Suhrkamp, Frankfurt am Main

Böhler D (2017) Einleitender Kommentar. Das Prinzip Verantwortung im Kontext. In: Böhler D, Herrmann B (eds) Kritische Gesamtausgabe der Werke von Hans Jonas. Philosophische Hauptwerke, vol 1/2: Tragweite und Aktualität einer Zukunftsethik. Rombach, Freiburg, Berlin, Wien, pp xvii–lix

Camps V (2001) Una vida de calidad. Reflexiones sobre bioética. Ares y Mares, Barcelona

Cañas Fernández JL (2000) La idea de rehumanización, clave existencial para la filosofía de la historia futura. Anales del Seminario de Historia de la Filosofía 17:167–194

Dworkin R (1994) Life's dominion: An argument about abortion, euthanasia, and individual freedom. Vintage Books, New York

Espinosa E, Zamora P, González Barón M (1994) Letters to the editors. New England J Med 331(12):811

Finnis J (1995) A philosophical case against euthanasia. In: Keown J (ed) Euthanasia examined: ethical, legal and clinical perspectives. Cambridge University Press, Cambridge, pp 23–35

Gómez M (ed) (2016) Atención Médica al final de la vida: Conceptos y definiciones, elaborated by the Working Group on Medical Care at the End of Life of the Collegiate Medical Organization (OMC) and the Spanish Society of Palliative Care of Spain. https://www.colmedjaen.es/images/2018/conceptos_definiciones_omc_secpal(1).pdf. Accessed 2 Oct 2025

Habermas J (2002) Die Zukunft der menschlichen Natur. Auf dem Weg zu einer liberalen Eugenik? 4th edn. Suhrkamp, Frankfurt am Main

Haque OS, Waytz A (2012) Dehumanization in medicine: causes, solutions, and functions. Persp Psychol Sci 7(2):176–186

Hendin H (1997) Seduced by death: Doctors, patients, and the Dutch cure. W W Norton & Co, New York

Hervada J (1991) Los derechos inherentes a la dignidad de la persona humana. Humana Iura: Suplemento de derechos humanos 1:223–256

Höffe O (1990) Kategorische Rechtsprinzipien. Ein Kontrapunkt der Moderne. Suhrkamp, Frankfurt am Main
Innerarity D (1994) Poética de la compasión. Comunicación y sociedad 7(2):n.p
Jonas H (1977) Das Prinzip Leben: Ansätze zu einer philosophischen Biologie. Suhrkamp, Frankfurt am Main
Jonas H (1979) Das Prinzip Verantwortung: Versuch einer Ethik für die technologische Zivilisation. Insel, Frankfurt am Main
Keown J (1995) Euthanasia in the Netherlands: Sliding down the slippery slope. Notre Dame J Law Ethics Public Policy 9(2):407–448
Kessler D, McClellan M (1996) Do doctors practice defensive medicine? Quart J Econ 111(2):353–390
Mill JS (1903) On liberty. Watts & Co, London
Muguerza J (2007) ¿Convicciones y/o responsabilidades? Tres perspectivas de la ética en el siglo XXI. In: Aramayo RR, Guerra MJ (eds) Los laberintos de la responsabilidad. Plaza y Valdés y CSIC, Madrid, pp 21–51
Ollero A (1996) ¿Tiene razón el derecho? Entre método político y voluntad científica. Congreso de los Diputados, Madrid
Ollero A (2003) Deontología jurídica y derechos humanos. In: AA.VV. Ética de las profesiones jurídicas. Estudios sobre deontología, vol 2. Quaderna Editorial, Murcia, pp 53–72
Ollero A (2006) Bioderecho. Entre la vida y la muerte. Thomson-Aranzadi, Cizur Menor
Pellegrino ED (1990) The medical profession as a moral community. Bull New York Acad Med 66(3):221–232
Revel JF, Ricard M (1997) Le moine e le philosophe. Le bouddhisme aujourd'hui, NiL éditions, Paris
Román B (2013) Para la humanización de la atención sanitaria: los cuidados paliativos como modelo. Medicina Paliativa 20(1):19–25
Santos JA (2014) Los olvidados del nacionalsocialismo. Repensar la memoria. Centro de Estudios Políticos y Constitucionales, Madrid
Santos JA (2021) Das Gedächtnis als epistemisches Element zum Verständnis der Menschenwürde. In: Neumann U, Tiedemann P, Liu SI (eds) Menschenwürde ohne Metaphysik, vol 165. ARSP, Beiheft, pp 219–229
Schroth U (2011) Medizin-, Bioethik und Recht. In: Kaufmann A, Hassemer W, Neumann U (eds) Einführung in Rechtsphilosophie und Rechtstheorie der Gegenwart, 8th edn. C.F. Müller, Heidelberg, pp 459–484
Schubert J (1998) Das "Prinzip Verantwortung" als verfassungsstaatliches Rechtsprinzip: rechtsphilosophische und verfassungsrechtliche Betrachtungen zur Verantwortungsethik von Hans Jonas. Nomos, Baden-Baden
Sekhar MS, Vyas N (2013) Defensive medicine: a bane to healthcare. Ann Med Health Sci Res 3(2):295–296
Vidal E (2016) Bioética(s), derechos, crisis, principios. In: Santos JA, Albert M, Hermida C (eds) Bioética y nuevos derechos. Granada, Comares, pp 79–104
Villacañas JL (2007) Responsabilidad y esferas de acción. In: Aramayo RR, Guerra MJ (eds) Los laberintos de la responsabilidad. Plaza y Valdés y CSIC, Madrid, pp 53–75
von der Pfordten D (2011) Rechtsethik, 2nd edn. Beck, München
Wynia MK, Latham SR, Kao AC et al (1999) Medical professionalism in society. New England J Med 341(21):1612–1616

Chapter 3
Human Dignity, Right to Health, and Balancing: With Special Focus on Vulnerability in a Public Health Emergency

Wei Feng and Jingshu Wang

Abstract In a public health emergency caused by a pandemic—including but not limited to COVID-19—human dignity and the right to health reveal themselves as more vulnerable than ever, and fierce tensions also arise between them and various other fundamental rights and values. Human dignity has dual dimensions, i.e., regarding the individual and social human beings. Nevertheless, both dimensions reserve the equality of person, so that the concept of human dignity has a necessary connection with that of personality. There are four groups of crucial questions on the balancing of human dignity and the right to health in public health emergencies: the hierarchy doubt, the naturalistic fallacy, the triage dilemma, and the social determinants. The concept of the right to health in the context of the ICESCR is characterized by its inclusiveness with public health as well as its progressive realization by applying the four concretized criteria of the proportionality test: availability, accessibility, acceptability, and quality. In the process of preventing, treating, and controlling infectious diseases, mankind in general—and pregnant women, medical personnel, elderly persons, and persons with other disabilities in particular—are all vulnerable, and their health rights should not be discriminatorily constrained in public health emergencies.

W. Feng (✉)
China University of Political Science and Law,
Beijing, China

University of Kiel, Kiel, Germany
e-mail: wei.feng@cupl.edu.cn

J. Wang
China University of Political Science and Law,
Beijing, China

© The Author(s), under exclusive license to Springer Nature Switzerland AG 2026
J. E. Núñez (ed.), *Perspectives on Crises*,
https://doi.org/10.1007/978-3-032-23836-8_3

3.1 Introduction

The novel coronavirus that emerged from Wuhan in late 2019 (COVID-19) changed the world from a place of legal certainty into a public health emergency. The uncertainties around scientific proof, public information, and methods of effective protection[1] were all deemed to threaten the health and life of every individual. One may wonder whether there has yet been a strong normativity in any possible situation of a "new normality." It is assumed that there is one candidate for a strong normativity: human dignity. However, human dignity in general and the protection of the right to health in particular are confronted with greater challenges, especially regarding vulnerable or marginalized groups. The concept of human dignity has been criticized as being either too thick or too thin.[2] Nevertheless, this chapter aims to demonstrate that the image of the human in law has dual dimensions, that is, both as an individual being and as social beings.

Concerning the right to health, the very first question is how to define the concept of "health" and its meanings. More specifically, there is a need to consider how to balance the dual goals, namely, the health of individuals and the health of the public environment. To strike the appropriate balance, an inclusive concept of the right to health in the context of international human rights law should be adopted in the policymaking process, both at the national and the international levels. Moreover, in a pandemic, the right to health will probably be restrained or not fully realized in terms of its degree, speed, and scope. However, any limitations and delays of realization should be carefully controlled so as to comply with the principle of human dignity and that of non-discrimination. Otherwise, with the shortage of resources and without purposive measures of pandemic control, any vulnerable groups would be faced with disproportionate difficulties.

In this chapter, we will first clarify the dual dimensions of human dignity (Sect. 3.2). Then we will continue with a preliminary discussion of the four crucial questions on the balancing of human dignity and the right to health when facing COVID-19 and other pandemics, namely: the hierarchy doubt, the naturalistic fallacy, the triage dilemma, and the social determinants (Sect. 3.3). To solve these problems in detail, we will further analyze the concept of the right to health in the context of the International Covenant on Economic, Social and Cultural Rights (ICESCR), emphasizing its concern with inclusiveness in public health as well as its progressive realization by applying the four concretized criteria of balancing: availability, accessibility, acceptability, and quality (Sect. 3.4). Based on all the above analyses, we will aim to illustrate the criteria of the right to health, emphasizing vulnerability in various aspects, so as to better handle the prevention and control of pandemics (Sect. 3.5).

---

[1] See Drosten et al. (2022); Frankenberg (2020).

[2] For controversies on absoluteness and relativity, inability and ability of balancing, necessity and contingency of human dignity, see Neumann (1998), pp. 153–166; Alexy (2002), pp. 62–64; Alexy (2015), pp. 83–96; Gröschner and Lembcke (2009); Brandhorst and Weber-Guskar (2017).

3.2 Dual Dimensions of Human Dignity

3.2.1 Dignity of Individual Human Beings and Its Institutionalization

The meaning of "human dignity" varies from author to author. Not all of them acknowledge the notion of human dignity in a strong sense, nor do they concentrate, with full awareness, on the dignity of individual human beings. Hence, we would like to emphasize three examples here, all of which are undoubtedly concerned with the absolute dignity of human beings as individuals.

The first example is Mencius (372–289 BC) from ancient China, who came closest to an absolute concept of the dignity of the individual, since he already summarized humanity (*ren*), righteousness (*yi*), propriety (*li*), and wisdom (*zhi*) under the concept of "dignity gifted from heaven" (*tian jue*, as opposed to "dignity acquired from man," *ren jue*) and described "good eminence" (*liang gui*) as being that which "all human beings (*ren ren*) have in themselves."[3] The second example comes from the Talmud in which, regarding prohibitions by rabbinic law, there is a principle that states: "*Great is human dignity, as it overrides a prohibition in the Torah.*"[4] These two examples, as one may see, are from entirely different cultures, and are illuminating in terms of the quest for a universalizable image of human dignity that can overcome the religious and cultural backgrounds of both East and West.[5]

The third example is a definition by Immanuel Kant from early modern Germany, which identifies human dignity as autonomy and the intrinsic value of all rational beings, including human beings.[6] Kant's method in his *Groundwork of the Metaphysics of Morals* is essentially analytical; namely, the three key concepts of "good will," "duty," and "law" are analyzed step by step based on the "common rational moral cognition." Accordingly, good will is the only "intrinsic unconditional value."[7] However, since human beings always have other natural inclinations, the good will then requires acting "from duty," which differs from merely acting "in conformity with duty."[8] Furthermore, Kant understands duty as "the necessity of an action from respect for the law," the latter of which means the "categorical imperative," i.e., unconditional normative requirements for action.[9] Based on that understanding, he *discovers* the famous "categorical imperative," which would be

---

[3] Ivanhoe (2009), Mencius, Book 6A, 16 and 17 (emphasis added); see also Höffe (2002), p. 60; Höffe (2007), p. 40.

[4] Steinsaltz (2012), Talmud, Shabbat: 94b (original emphasis). We would like to thank Kenneth Ehrenberg for his suggestion of the Talmud.

[5] See Höffe (2002), p. 64; Alexy (2013), p. 13; Lee (1994), pp. 93–103; Lee (2018), pp. 47–197; Schaefer (2013), p. 186; also see Feng (2022), p. 4, footnote 6.

[6] See Kant (1785) Ak 4, p. 434; English translation: Kant (1996), p. 84.

[7] Kant (1785) Ak 4, p. 393; English translation: Kant (1996), pp. 49–50 (trans. altered).

[8] Kant (1785) Ak 4, p. 397; English translation: Kant (1996), pp. 52–53.

[9] Kant (1785) Ak 4, pp. 400, 413–420; English translation: Kant (1996), pp. 55, 67–73.

recognized by every rational being. The relevant extract reads: "So act that you use humanity, whether in your own person or in the person of any other, always at the same time as an end, never merely as means."[10] On this basis, Kant confirms the "idea of the dignity of a rational being."[11] Only that which is not replaceable by an equivalent, has no price, or has not merely a relative value, can then have an intrinsic, unconditional, incomparable value that is, namely, dignity.

Nevertheless, the above analysis does not yet answer the question of how the categorical imperative—as well as human dignity—is possible.[12] To reconstruct Kant's justification of human dignity appropriately, it is crucial to shed light on his differentiation between *homo noumenon* and *homo phaenomenon*, that is, between personality and human beings, between the humanity in the human person and the physical existence of the human.[13] In light of this idea, Kant's "categorical imperative" in its juristic use[14] is then the "right of humanity." According to Kant, the right in the "right of humanity" includes the right of humanity in his own person on the one hand and the right of other human beings on the other hand. The former corresponds to the juristic duty to oneself, the latter to the juristic duty to others, while both are "indirect-ethical" duties.[15]

Due to the influence of the above-mentioned ideas as well as other philosophical thoughts and cultural traditions from all over the world, it is possible to observe the institutionalization of human dignity both at the international and the national levels. One can then read of the "dignity and worth of the *human person*" in the Preamble of the Charter of the United Nations of 1945 (UN Charter)[16] and see all human beings described as "born free and equal in dignity and rights" in Article 1 of the Universal Declaration of Human Rights of 1948.[17] At the national level,

---

[10] Kant (1785) Ak 4, p. 429; English translation: Kant (1996), p. 80. I should like to thank Jorge Emilio Núñez for his suggestion that Kant did not discover the categorical imperative in the empirical sense, but, rather, he created, designed, thought about, etc. the categorical imperative. According to Núñez, the verb "discover" would make the sentence mean something that it is not. In reply, we would say that this is precisely the sense of the Kantian categorical imperative, which can be recognized and hence obeyed by all rational beings, primarily human beings. In Kant's phrase, it is the self-lawgiving of a rational being, but not an imperative given by any philosopher such as Kant himself. See Kant (1785) Ak 4, p. 431; English translation: Kant (1996), p. 81. Whether this self-lawgiving or autonomy could be possible is another question, as explained in the following paragraphs.

[11] Kant (1785) Ak 4, p. 434; English translation: Kant (1996), p. 84.

[12] See Kant (1785) Ak 4, pp. 449–450; English translation: Kant (1996), pp. 96–97.

[13] See Kant (1797) Ak 6, p. 239; see also Feng (2021), pp. 37–39.

[14] See Dreier (1979), p. 294; Alexy (2005), pp. 103–105.

[15] See Kant (1797) Ak 6, p. 240. We would like to thank Jorge Emilio Núñez for raising the point that the three examples discussed here (Mencius, Talmud, and Kant) could be conceived as randomly selected notions of human dignity. However, as we state above, the very task of our article is to answer the question: how can we give strong justifications—both secular and trans-religious, both Indigenous and trans-cultural—for a universalizable value, such as human dignity? For authors who share a similar intent, see Höffe (2002), p. 56; Alexy (2013), p. 13.

[16] The Preamble of UN Charter (1945), 1 UNTS XVI (emphasis added).

[17] Article 1 UDHR (1948), UNGA Res. 217 A (III), A/810, 10 Dec 1948.

human dignity is "untouchable" according to Article 1(1)(1) of German Basic Law;[18] the "[d]ignity of the individual and unity and integrity of the Nation" are assured by the principle of fraternity in the Preamble of the Indian Constitution; and the US Supreme Court has also emphasized human dignity in its standing adjudications until recently.[19] These are only examples of various constitutions and their judicial practices in post-World War II developments.

In the current Chinese Constitution of 1982, the conception of "dignity of the *human person* of citizens" has also been incorporated as a positive norm into Article 38(1) in order to overcome the past events of the so-called Cultural Revolution that occurred between 1966 and 1976 in China. This was the intent of the constitutional drafters and there is already a common academic opinion on this point among Chinese constitutional scholars.[20] Furthermore, the above dignity clause in Article 38(1) in combination with another clause on "human rights" in Article 33(3), which was incorporated into the Chinese Constitution through the Amendments in 2004, provides a coherent understanding of the diverse images of "citizens," "people," "mankind," and "human as such" in the Chinese Constitution. Finally, it is important to emphasize that the drafters of the Chinese Constitution of 1982—just as those of the UN Charter—had originally understood the concept of dignity and that of *personality* as having a necessary connection[21] and constructed the freedom of the person, the general right of personality, and the idea of human dignity in a progressive relationship.

3.2.2 *Dignity of Social Human Beings*

All the above concerns, at least at the first glance, are often considered as only referring to the dignity of individual human beings. What about, however, the dignity of social human beings? As explained by Gustav Radbruch in twentieth-century Germany, the images of the human in law are only fictive constructions created during different legal epochs, and include not only the human as individual, but also the human in community and the human in society,[22] or—as reformulated later—the concepts of individualism, supra-individualism, and transpersonalism, which are

[18] See Herdegen (2020), pp. 14–15.

[19] See, e.g., Obergefell v. Hodges, 576 U.S. 644 (2015), p. 10 and p. 13; Masterpiece Cakeshop, Ltd. v. Colorado Civil Rights Comm'n, 584 U. S. ___ (2018), pp. 9–10.

[20] See Lin (2008), p. 52. We would like to thank Prof. Dayuan Han for pointing out the historical background of the current Chinese Constitution of 1982. Jimmy Chia-Chin Hsu's question on this point also provided an opportunity for further clarification.

[21] This necessary connection between the concept of human dignity and that of personality can be justified by Kant. See Kant (1797) Ak 6, p. 239; see also Alexy (2015), pp. 88–91; and Feng (2021), pp. 37–39.

[22] See Radbruch (1927), p. 8; Reprint: Radbruch (1993) GRGA 2, p. 470; English translation: Radbruch (2020), p. 675 (trans. altered).

then understood as standing in a relation of "antinomy."[23] Partly due to the influence of Radbruch and other authors, some scholars distinguish between "an internal and an external perspective" of human dignity[24] or between the action and interaction—and hence socialization as well as enculturation—of human beings.[25] Furthermore, according to the German Constitutional Court, for example, there is at least the right to resocialization[26] and the guarantee for minimal existence.[27] For this reason, we will concentrate specifically on the concept of person in the narrative on legal epochs developed by Radbruch in connection with human dignity.

3.2.2.1 The Image of the Human (in Law) as Fictive Construction

The first insight provided by Radbruch is about the "periodization" of legal development according to different images of the human, that is, the transition from patriarchal-communal law through liberal-individualistic law to organized social law.[28] Accordingly, if we consider the human being as the subject motivated by law, then we can observe the transition from the human in the community through the human as an individual to the human in society or collective human being. If we consider the human being as the author of law, then we can summarize the transition from the unconscientious spirit of people through the conscientious will of the state to the conscientious will of the people. The second insight is that all the images of the human above are only "fictive constructions," and are not empirical average types of human being.[29] The main feature of the organized social law is the transition from the "isolated perceived individual lacking individuality" to the "concrete and socialized human being."[30]

If we take a closer look at the personality as a purported subject of legal norms, according to Radbruch's works in the later period of the German Weimar Republic, then we can find the three worldviews or values above—appearing in the final version of his theory as "individual human personalities," "total human personalities," and "human works" respectively—are not in a chronic relation anymore, but in an "antinomy" relation without absolute preference given to one or another.[31] Hence,

[23] Radbruch (1932), p. 51; Reprint: Radbruch (1993) GRGA 2, p. 279; English translation: Radbruch (1950), pp. 92–93 (trans. altered).

[24] Höffe (2002), p. 67.

[25] See Brugger (2008), pp. 56–62.

[26] See BVerfGE 35, 202 (235) – Lebach (1973); see also Feng (2017), pp. 52–71.

[27] See BVerfGE 45, 187 (228) – Life Imprisonment (1977).

[28] See Radbruch (1927), pp. 5–18; Reprint: Radbruch (1993), GRGA 2, pp. 467–476; English translation: Radbruch (1950), pp. 672–681.

[29] See Radbruch (1927), p. 8; Reprint: Radbruch (1993), GRGA 2, p. 470; English translation: Radbruch (2020), p. 675 (trans. altered).

[30] Radbruch (1930), p. 37; Reprint: Radbruch (1993) GRGA 2, p. 486.

[31] See Radbruch (1932), p. 51; Reprint: Radbruch (1993), GRGA 2, p. 279; English translation: Radbruch (1950), p. 92 (trans. altered).

their importance depends on current interest conflicts and a process of balancing, or in other words, on the democratic procedure.[32] For example, all men with individual personalities organize themselves as a society. Meanwhile, the transpersonalistic culture of humans could establish itself as a community.

One may wonder whether we can draw a juristic relation between moral change and human dignity in every transformative society in the post-World War II era. To answer this question, firstly, we need to be aware of what we mean when we talk about "morals." Morality as such will not change, but is the eternal, the highest criterion. The "categorical imperative" introduced by Kant above is a very good example.[33] On the contrary, only "practical morals" or ethical convictions will change from time to time. Secondly, we should continually emphasize that the three worldviews or values do not exist in a straight line of historical improvement, but in a relation of antinomy.[34] To this extent, the conflicts between different ethical convictions will remain in every society.

3.2.2.2 The Human in Social Law: A New Concept of Person?

Now we can reconsider Radbruch's concept of social law and social human beings. The crucial question is whether these terms represent an entirely new concept of person, or just some adjustments to it. Three points should be mentioned here. (1) The social law is *NO LONGER in contradiction* to the individualistic law. It is only necessary to emphasize that both are different from the supra-individualistic-conservative standpoint.[35] In this context, Radbruch mentions "social individualism" in comparison to "demo-liberal individualism" or the "individual-social" standpoint.[36] (2) According to Radbruch, the work of *individualizing construction*, alongside two other works of interpretation and systematization, is still the core work of doctrinal legal science.[37] (3) The concept of *person* is still a fictive *equal* concept,[38] which means that equality is contained in both individual and social human beings as fictive, artificial legal concepts. Finally, social law cannot change the equal concept of person at all.

---

[32] We would like to thank Zubair Khan for raising this question.

[33] See Kant (1785) Ak 4, pp. 388, 401; English translation: Kant (1996), pp. 43, 56.

[34] See Radbruch (1932), p. 51; Reprint: Radbruch (1993) GRGA 2, p. 279; English translation: Radbruch (1950), p. 92.

[35] See Radbruch (1932), p. 66; Reprint: Radbruch (1993), GRGA 2, p. 298; English translation: Radbruch (1950), p. 154 (trans. altered).

[36] See Radbruch (1932), p. 64; Reprint: Radbruch (1993), GRGA 2, p. 296; English translation: Radbruch (1950), p. 103 (trans. altered).

[37] See Radbruch (1932), pp. 119–121; Reprint: Radbruch (1993), GRGA 2, pp. 354–357; English translation: Radbruch (1950), pp. 149–151 (trans. altered).

[38] See Radbruch (1932), p. 127; Reprint: Radbruch (1993), GRGA 2, p. 363; English translation: Radbruch (1950), p. 156.

Of course, there are possible doubts concerning the dual dimensions of human dignity. Firstly, one may think that there is no such clause relating to "social human beings" in some constitutions. Taking the Indian Constitution as an example, it assures "the dignity of the individual" in the Preamble, but without mentioning social human beings, even though it does contain some community rights in Articles 25(2)(b), 38(1), 43(1), and 46.[39] More specifically, according to the research of Sougata Talukdar, the right to health in India includes healthcare "yet goes beyond it to embrace the broader social dimensions"[40] of the individual and population well-being.

In addition, one may still be concerned about the possible primacy of the social human being. According to Radbruch's understanding as stated above, however, social human beings are not huge, collective, invisible entities. They are still individuals but with social roles, rather than individuals without concrete characteristics.

3.3 Human Dignity in Tension and Balancing During a Public Health Emergency

Given the dual dimensions of human dignity, as well as the circumstances set out by COVID-19, human dignity and a variety of fundamental rights and values not only become urgent, but their relations are also in tension during public health emergencies. Citizens and governments are balancing interests in a very limited time,[41] sometimes without confirming whether those results of balancing are sufficiently justified or reasonable. Here, we could single out at least four groups of tension or collision of rights and values: (1) One can easily encounter the question of whether the right to life as such, and the right to health, enjoy an unconditional preference to any other rights, such as the freedom of travel, religion, and communication. This issue can be called the hierarchy doubt. (2) Can one still claim to experience life and living with dignity, when life involves all kinds of limitations or even living in a persistent vegetative state? This difficulty reveals the naturalistic fallacy between human life and human dignity. (3) How can patients be equally treated when the capacity problem faced by hospitals and medical personnel is alarming? There is also the problem of triage with insufficient life-saving equipment for a rising number of patients. Or, to put the question simply, which patient can be equipped with the ventilator first to keep him- or herself alive?[42] This challenge could be symbolized as the triage dilemma. (4) Finally, given the fast-developing pace of digital

[39] We would like to thank Pritti Ramani for sharing her opinion about human dignity in the Indian Constitution.

[40] Talukdar (2022), pp. ix, 6.

[41] See Marco (2020).

[42] See Marco (2020); Lübbe (2020); Fateh-Moghadam and Gutmann (2020).

technology, can the once negative function of the right to self-determination of information[43] cope with the pandemic, by simply ignoring the significant positive function of data for social reliance, donation, participation, and, finally, solidarity? Besides this relative abstract information, even the resistance against wearing masks in public areas[44] as well as that against injection of vaccines[45] cannot be solely left to personal arbitration. These last issues concern the social determinants of rights in collision.

In trying to solve these four groups of crucial issues for balancing human dignity—and the right to health—during a public health emergency, we should not only shed light on the concept of absolute human dignity in its strong sense and hence its dual dimensions, as well as the systematic combination of human rights and human dignity, but also understand the concept of human dignity in its analytical connection with the concept of personality.

3.3.1 The Hierarchy Doubt—Rights to Life as Such and Rights to Health in Balancing

The doubt about the "hierarchy" of values arose from the beginning of material value-ethics as a subject of study.[46] Actually, the "objective value system" is not hierarchically determined as usually assumed, even when such usage exists in a "hierarchy of values."[47] One of the leading figures in this field, Max Scheler, understands the value system, based on the perception of preference and disfavor, as something given phenomenologically or as *a priori but material*.[48] However, it is not yet decided which concrete value is to be preferred or disfavored. The values correspond only to the "ideal objects."[49] In other words, the values in the system can and also need to lend themselves to *balance*. If we turn the axiological system into the deontological one, following Robert Alexy, then we can recapture the "ideal object"—as well as its need to be realized into the "real ought" or "personal-individual ought"[50]—through the "principle/rule-model."[51] According to this model, all values and fundamental rights are understood as principles, namely "optimization requirements," one of which can then be balanced against other colliding

[43] See Fährmann et al. (2020a); Fährmann et al. (2020b); Klafki (2020a).

[44] See Mangold (2020); Wolff (2020).

[45] See Kießling (2020); Tonti (2020); Klafki (2020b).

[46] See Scheler (1916), p. 1.

[47] Scheler (1916), p. 2.

[48] Scheler (1916), p. 49.

[49] Scheler (1916), p. 164.

[50] Scheler (1916), pp. 241, 509.

[51] Alexy (2002), pp. 80–86; see also Feng (2017), p. 64.

principles and, if it succeeds, some rules can be constructed, namely "definitive commands."[52]

In this sense, even human dignity has two levels, that is, human dignity as principle and human dignity as rule.[53] The significance of the *principle* of human dignity is extremely epistemically certain, usually enjoying priority against other fundamental rights, which then implies a definitive *rule* of human dignity.[54] Therefore, contrary to what is usually assumed or criticized, the preference of the principle of human dignity is not absolute at all. During a public health emergency, the right to life, as such, and the right to health based on human dignity, are both of national[55] and international concern.[56] They are acknowledged as highly certain to be protected, even at very high costs. Nevertheless, other rights, such as that of travel,[57] religion,[58] voting,[59] and demonstration[60] are also essential to the freedom and integrity of individual human beings. There may well be a high degree of urgency for the right to life and health within determined time limits, but the costs are neither absolute nor permanent—rather they lend themselves to balance.[61] A similar logic applies to the relation between the right to health and the interest of public health.[62] To this extent, we should have not only a "plan of lockdown" to protect the lives and health of individuals, but also an exact "plan of exit" to satisfy all other essential rights and values. Therefore, the quest is not for a determined hierarchy of rights and values but to acknowledge the significance of rights in concrete circumstances.

3.3.2 The Naturalistic Fallacy—Life as Such and Life with Dignity

The existential dilemma of triage reveals a more sophisticated question. This is because the relationship between human dignity and the right to life, health, and even all the rights that are essential for a decent life would sometimes be understood in the following way: Physical as well as psychological existence and integrity are

[52] Alexy (2002), pp. 47–48.

[53] Alexy (2002), p. 64.

[54] Alexy (2002), pp. 62–63.

[55] See Habermas and Günther (2020).

[56] See Han (2020), pp. 11–19; Wang (2020), pp. 71–82.

[57] See Fischer-Uebler (2020); Elsuwege (2020).

[58] See Heinig (2020).

[59] See Binder and Drnovsky (2020).

[60] See Gutmann and Kohlmeier (2020); Gusy (2020); Hong (2020b).

[61] See Wagner (2020). Besides, Kluge criticizes generally the use of "merit" as an "unacceptable" criterion for judging which individual's right enjoys the priority. See Kluge (2022), pp. 80–81.

[62] For the connection between the right to health and public health, see below in Sect. 3.4.1.

the natural foundations for the abstract claim to human dignity, which leads to the consequence that either there are only concrete essential rights in the end with merely some rhetoric of human dignity, or there exists a human dignity but without natural foundations, which is assumed as a mysterious "tyranny" of value.[63] In particular, there would also be a similar fallacy concerning the relation between the right to health on one side and the interest of public health on the other side. The interest of public health against infectious diseases, usually in the name of the lives of the population, may well be considered as the natural foundation for every single member in this society to enjoy the right to health against other diseases.[64]

This criticism of the "naturalistic fallacy" is widespread in discussions of human dignity.[65] These naturalistic claims may reduce human dignity to a minimum and only emphasize the right to life and health being realized in a possibly undiscriminating way. This also reflects the doubt about the value system above purely a natural existence. The only way out is precisely to refute the naturalistic strategy of human dignity, and instead to justify the normativity of human dignity appropriately. There should be differentiation between life as such and life with dignity,[66] and it should be emphasized that the concept of human dignity and that of personality are necessarily connected. The personality, in turn, is not only *homo noumenon* but also combines the *homo phaenomenon*.

3.3.3 The Triage Dilemma—Life with Equal (Medical) Treatment

As stated above, the capacities of hospitals and medical personnel in every country are tested and under continuous pressure in public health emergencies.[67] In principle, incapacity is to be avoided. When it happens, however, the dilemma of triage and the use of life-saving equipment become a challenging "existential" question, as we have witnessed in several countries or areas. In some regions during the COVID-19 pandemic, e.g., in Italy and France, they applied a simple criterion of age, which is arbitrary and traumatic.[68] In other medical or legal communities, e.g., in Germany, they suggested differentiated standards, such as the possibility of being saved.[69] Eike-Henner W. Kluge from Switzerland criticizes the use of age, describing

---

[63] See Schmitt (1967); Somek (2020a); Somek (2020b).

[64] For the rights of persons with disabilities or other sicknesses during the COVID-19 pandemic, see below in Sect. 3.5.4.

[65] See Neumann (1998), pp. 153–166; Feng (2021), p. 60. For Neumann's latest reply, see Neumann (2022), pp. 138–139, footnote 63.

[66] See Volkmann (2020b); Kube (2020).

[67] See Marco (2020); Prem et al. (2020).

[68] See Marco (2020).

[69] See Lübbe (2020); Fateh-Moghadam and Gutmann (2020).

it as an "unacceptable" criterion for allocation of medical resources, while he suggests life-saving, rather than quality-enhancing, factors should be considered as "ethically relevant criterion."[70] Under all these circumstances, one is actually striking a balance, but the methods or criteria in use should satisfy the proportionality test. That means, one should make judgments both on the factual possibilities—namely the test of "suitability" and that of "necessity"—and the legal or normative possibilities—namely the test of "proportionality in the narrow sense."[71] Besides, one might well develop more *concretized* criteria of balancing concerning the concrete rights and circumstances.[72]

The triage dilemma is much tougher since professional judgments need to be taken in a very limited time and sometimes with insufficient scientific evidence. Hence, the situation of "stalemate" concerning the empirical epistemic certainty of these judgments cannot be eliminated.[73] In extremely hard situations, such as the temporary collapse of the hospital system, preventing every loss of life is beyond the *factual possibilities*, that is, the test of suitability as well as that of the necessity of measures.[74] One may accept that there could be only compensations for patients' families afterward.

Nevertheless, the especially strong requirement of human dignity still has control over the *normative possibilities* to prevent extremely disproportionate treatments of dying patients. For example, the doctor should not take triage away from one dying patient just to save another newly arriving patient who is assumed to better fulfill the criteria, whether it be by age or the possibility to be saved.[75] Once again, there is no such thing as an absolute limit for balancing—as someone may assume[76]—of life against life, or "dignity against dignity."

3.3.4 *The Social Determinants—Digitalization, Vaccine, and the Vulnerability of the Social Human Being*

The less sophisticated but fragmented controversies that arise in pandemic situations involve the collision between liberal, negative rights and the various positive demands, such as digital, economic, medical, and environmental measures. The

[70] See Kluge (2022), pp. 79–80.

[71] Alexy (2002), pp. 66–69.

[72] For the "concretization thesis" of balancing, see Alexy (2019), p. 219. Specifically, for the concretized criteria of balancing concerning the right to health, see below Sect. 3.4.3.

[73] Alexy (2019), p. 410.

[74] Kluge also emphasizes the "impossibility grounded in the lack of societal resources" as an ethical criterion, e.g., in the case of preventing infectious diseases. See Kluge (2022), pp. 85–86. For the more concretized criterion of availability regarding the right to health, see below in Sect. 3.4.3.1.

[75] See Hörnle (2020).

[76] See Hong (2020a).

warning against a retreat to the so-called "police state" or the status of "legality without legitimacy *qua* constitutionality" was heard on internet blogs and virtual meetings during the COVID-19 pandemic.[77] To this extent, besides the demand for strong political leadership and sufficient medical facilities,[78] a stable economy and the necessary social care are also needed to "flatten the curve" of a pandemic and, at the same time, to ensure the vulnerable groups as social human beings are protected from discriminatory treatment.

Taking digitalization as a good example, personal information including PCR test results becomes significant for decision-making during a public health emergency, triggering the debate about digital surveillance or "donation."[79] Nevertheless, digitalization does provide benefits, if it is not overwhelming, exclusive, and permanent. Hence, as the result of balancing, it is better to let individuals decide to voluntarily donate their personal health information, rather than to interfere with their everyday activities without limitation. There are plenty of examples of such practice, such as the "Corona-Warn-App" or "Corona-Datenspende-App" in Germany,[80] as well as the widely used "Green Code" in China and other countries in East Asia. Still, we would always be cautious of possible misuses of the one-sided, arbitrary labeling of the so-called "Red Code"[81] or "Yellow Code."[82]

Furthermore, despite the social distancing required during a public health emergency, there is a chance of resocialization through digitalization. Digital communication, shopping, working, and schooling are substituted methods for in-person social activities. Particularly, for some vulnerable groups, e.g., pupils living in poor areas, the digital facilities are tools to help improve their participation in education and reduce the fact of their unequal situation, which can help to prevent the tendency of fragmentation of society and contribute to the goal of solidarity.[83]

The vaccine is another example here. The continuing research on vaccines against COVID-19 provided hope for the ending of the pandemic. Nevertheless, the question of whether vaccines can be sufficiently and equally distributed, either globally or just domestically, became a real task for an already fragmented global society. The related problems are: Whether a vaccine should be "free of charge for all." Whether a vaccine should be compulsorily injected, in order to protect the special vulnerable groups from being infected, or whether the injection could only be voluntary since there are possible side effects. Once again, to find the solutions to these questions, we might well consider the distribution and injection of vaccines as

---

[77] See Lepsius (2020), Kumm (2020), Cahill (2020).

[78] See Prem et al. (2020); Pils (2020).

[79] See Robert Koch-Institut (2022).

[80] As at 28 June 2022, there were 547,569 donors and 470,201,424 pieces of donated data. See Robert Koch-Institut (2022).

[81] See Han (2022).

[82] See Ma (2022); see also the criterion of acceptability below in Sect. 3.4.3.3.

[83] See Liu (2020); see also the criterion of availability and that of accessibility below in Sects. 3.4.3.1 and 3.4.3.2.

one of the "social determinants" of the right to health, as the Committee on Economic, Social and Cultural Rights (CESCR) puts it.[84]

Therefore, all of this concerns the connection between the negative and positive functions of fundamental rights, which could also be enhanced by the dual dimensions of human dignity and, specifically, by the inclusiveness of the right to health, which will be further explored in Sect. 3.4. There is only left to add that, although each of the four crucial problems concerning the pandemic above might be handled against different theoretical backgrounds, we should not assume in advance a single holistic view to solving these problems all at once.

3.4 Right to Health: Its Inclusiveness and Progressive Realization

In the public health emergencies caused by COVID-19 and other pandemics, the protection of the right to health encountered challenges in many aspects. Threats to the individual right to health, as well as those to the healthy public environment necessary to the realization of this right, arise not only from the infectious diseases themselves but also from the limited conditions of public health services and the (in)effectiveness of responses. Hence, it is necessary to clarify the connotation and scope of the right to health, so as to avoid the emergency response from disproportionately constraining the right to health as well as violating other fundamental rights.

After World War II, the right to health as a human right has been acknowledged and incorporated into international law.[85] The UN Charter refers to the role of the United Nations as to include promoting solutions for health problems;[86] and the Constitution of the World Health Organization of 1946 (WHO Constitution) defines the concept of health in its Preamble and states that "the enjoyment of the highest attainable standard of health is one of the fundamental rights of every human being without distinction of race, religion, political belief, economic or social condition";[87] moreover, Article 12 of the ICESCR of 1966 acknowledges the right to health, which is further recognized and concretized in other conventions.[88] China signed the ICESCR in 1997, and the 20th Session of the Standing Committee of the National People's Congress (NPC) of China ratified the ICESCR in 2001.[89] Up until 2019, China had submitted three reports on its implementation to the CESCR. Therefore,

[84] See CESCR (2000), General Comment No. 14, para 16; see also the criterion of acceptability and that of quality below in Sects. 3.4.3.3 and 3.4.3.4.

[85] See Tobin (2012), pp. 8–9.

[86] See Article 55(2) UN Charter (1945).

[87] The Preamble to the WHO Constitution (1946).

[88] See Gaffney (2018), pp. 178–181; Wang and Rao (2019), p. 22.

[89] See Chen and Wu (2013), p. 160; Qiu (2014), p. 103.

it is also in line with the actual situation in China, based on the ICESCR, to discuss the protection of the right to health during the public health emergencies caused by COVID-19 and other pandemics, which would help China to better fulfill its human rights protection obligations.

3.4.1 Dual Dimensions of Right to Health in Connection with Public Health

According to the structure of Article 12 of the ICESCR, the concept of the right to health contains dual goals: one is that individuals enjoy the right to health, and the other is that the states parties have the obligation to take steps, by creating healthy public environments, to achieve the full realization of the right to health. The latter means that the individual right to health requires the state to provide healthcare services and guarantee "the underlying determinants of health."[90] To this extent, the CESCR then points out in its General Comment No. 14 that the right to health is an inclusive right, including the right to enjoy adequate sanitation, healthy occupational and environmental conditions, access to health-related education and information, as well as the participation of the population in all health-related decision-making at the community, national, and international levels.[91] Besides, it highlights the "social determinants of good health"[92] such as environmental safety, education, economic development, and gender equality. All of these elements reflect the right to health as both a liberal and a social right. Furthermore, the WHO Constitution states in its Preamble that "[h]ealth is a state of complete physical, mental and social well-being and not merely the absence of disease or infirmity."[93] It is to this extent that John Tobin, on the one hand, admits human dignity as having an "overlapping consensus"[94] in including the worth of individuals and, on the other hand, tries to develop "a social interest theory of rights" to health beyond individualism.[95] Therefore, a healthy public environment is to be included in the concept of the right to health.

This *inclusiveness* of the right to health may, however, complicate the realization of the right in concrete situations. The dual goals of the right to health would probably appear inconsistent or even in conflict with each other, since states may often constrain the right to health or other individual rights with the motivation to

---

[90] CESCR (2000), General Comment No. 14, para 11.

[91] CESCR (2000), General Comment No. 14, para 11.

[92] CESCR (2000), General Comment No. 14, para 16.

[93] The Preamble to the WHO Constitution (1946). Kluge suggests defining health as "a state of homeostatic balance that allows the organism to survive, mature and function in a specific-specific manner in the environment in which they are embedded." See Kluge (2022), p. 21.

[94] Tobin (2012), pp. 56–57.

[95] Tobin (2012), pp. 9–10, 54–55 and 57–59; see also Talukdar (2022), p. 10.

guarantee public health or other public interests. For example, measures such as compulsory quarantining, compulsory medical treatment, and travel control may constrain the rights of individuals to health, personal freedom, and movement; moreover, the allocations of anti-pandemic materials may impact the healthy workplace environment of medical personnel. Recognizing these dual dimensions of the right to health in its conceptual connection with public health, and given the possible tension between these dimensions, the decision-making during a public health emergency should then promote, but not disproportionately constrain, the right to health as including dual goals. Hence, it is necessary to discuss the conditions and reasons for constraining the right to health, so as to evaluate the proportionality of relevant measures.

3.4.2 Conditions and Reasons for Constraining the Right to Health

Concerning whether the rights guaranteed by the ICESCR can be constrained, the Covenant makes a general provision in Article 4 that "the State may subject such rights only to such limitations as are determined by law only in so far as this may be compatible with the nature of these rights and solely for the purpose of promoting the general welfare in a democratic society." [96] Under the drafting background of the Covenant, the core objective of Article 4 is to prevent states from arbitrarily constraining the rights guaranteed by the ICESCR.[97] Article 4, in combination with Article 5(1) of the ICESCR, provides general guidance for balancing individual rights and the public interest within the framework of the ICESCR.[98] Specifically, it emphasizes that the purpose of limitations is to promote the "general welfare in a democratic society." Accordingly, state parties are allowed to impose limitations on rights for reasons such as national security, public order, public health, or public morals. However, the limitations are also required not to harm the democratic functioning of society.[99] This then reflects the proportionality of limitations, according to which the least harmful limitations must be taken when there are multiple ways of limiting.[100]

Furthermore, Article 12(2)(c) of the ICESCR on the prevention, treatment, and control of epidemic, endemic, and other diseases can be understood as a special

[96] See Saul et al. (2014), Article 4.

[97] See UNGA 3rd Committee (1962), Draft International Covenants on Human Rights, para 24.

[98] See CESCR (2000), General Comment No. 14, para 28.

[99] See Limburg Principles (1987), paras 53 and 54.

[100] This understanding is also reflected by the CESCR in its General Comment No. 21 since it refers to this criterion to assess limitations on the right to participate in cultural life. See CESCR (2009b), General Comment No. 21, para 19.

restriction on the right to health itself.[101] In order to prevent and control infectious diseases, it would be permissible to take measures that constrain individual rights, such as compulsory quarantining and compulsory treatment for those confirmed or suspected to be infected with diseases. However, there is space for further discussion on the proportionality of such limitations in specific circumstances. For example, we can question whether the criteria for judging who should be subject to compulsory quarantining are discriminatory, or whether the freedom of the infected persons to control their health and body and their right to informed consent are still guaranteed during their treatment. Therefore, even if the state limits a right based on a treaty obligation, the limitation is not to be arbitrary and unconditional, but should at any time lend to balancing with the claims to protection of other rights.

Finally, considering the possibility of insufficient resources, Article 2(1) of the ICESCR then stipulates the principle of *progressive realization* of the rights of the Covenant, that is, state parties can gradually achieve the full realization of the rights recognized in the Covenant to the maximum of its available resources, committing to taking steps and adopting all appropriate measures. Meanwhile, Article 2(1) of ICESCR also points out that such limitations should be overcome through various efforts. Furthermore, the CESCR in its General Comment No. 3 considers Article 2(1) of the ICESCR as imposing both "obligations of conduct" and "obligations of result" on state parties.[102] Accordingly, the purpose of the principle of progressive realization of the rights is to require state parties to guarantee rights of the Covenant even in the case of limited resources, rather than allowing the delay of obligation to guaranteeing rights.

3.4.3 Proportionality Concretized in Progressive Realization of the Right to Health

Since the state's obligation to realize the right to health may only be fulfilled gradually due to resource shortages, the CESCR points out in its General Comment No. 14 that the realization of the right to health is subject to some essential elements, which provide us with the following four guiding criteria for evaluating the degree of protection to the right to health. In essence, these criteria may well be understood as the concretization of the proportionality test for balancing the right to health in its progressive realization.

[101] See Saul et al. (2014), Article 12.

[102] See CESCR (1990), General Comment No. 3, para 1.

3.4.3.1 Availability

The first criterion provided by the CESCR in its General Comment No. 14 is availability, stating that "[f]unctioning public health and health-care facilities, goods and services, as well as programs, have to be *available in sufficient quantity* within the state party."[103] Availability is directly related to the issue of resources, since the extreme shortage of resources and their unreasonable allocation would restrict the achievement of availability standards. For example, the limited investment in public health facilities at the local level would result in insufficient medical services in rural and remote areas; the lack of effective storage plans for medical equipment, protective materials, and medicines may not adequately guarantee the need for health prevention and treatment in a public health emergency. According to Kluge's understanding, this criterion of availability is included in the more general criterion of effectiveness in the sense of cost/effectiveness considerations.[104]

3.4.3.2 Accessibility

The second criterion is accessibility, which demands that "[h]ealth facilities, goods and services have to be *accessible to everyone without discrimination*, within the jurisdiction of the state party."[105] More precisely, this availability has four overlapping dimensions, namely, (1) non-discrimination, in law and in fact, on any of the prohibited grounds; (2) being within safe physical reach; (3) economic affordability; and (4) the right to "seek, receive and impart" information and ideas concerning health issues without impairing the right to have personal health data treated with confidentiality.

To this extent, accessibility can be considered as the effect of the *non-discrimination* obligation of rights protection, especially by taking active measures to protect the rights of vulnerable groups.[106] For example, "the principle of equity [...] demands that poorer households should not be *disproportionately* burdened with health expenses as compared to richer households."[107] More precisely, the CESCR in its General Comment No. 20 provides a definition of discrimination, which constitutes "any distinction, exclusion, restriction or preference or other differential treatment that is directly or indirectly based on the prohibited grounds of discrimination and which has the intention or effect of nullifying or impairing the recognition, enjoyment or exercise, on an equal footing, of Covenant rights," and

---

[103] CESCR (2000), General Comment No. 14, para 12 (emphasis added); see also Tobin (2012), pp. 159–167.

[104] See Kluge (2022), pp. 59–69.

[105] CESCR (2000), General Comment No. 14, para 12 (emphasis added); see also Tobin (2012), pp. 167–172.

[106] See CESCR (2000), General Comment No. 14, para 12. For the legal and factual equality and its relation to the non-discrimination obligation, see also Feng (2025), pp. 40–41.

[107] CESCR (2000), General Comment No. 14, para 12 (emphasis added).

which also includes "incitement to discrimination and harassment."[108] Accordingly, discrimination consists of both direct and indirect discrimination. Indirect discrimination refers to laws, policies, or practices which appear neutral at face value, but have a disproportionate impact on the exercise of Covenant rights as distinguished by prohibited grounds of discrimination.

In a public health emergency, the measures implemented for prevention and control of diseases contain many restrictive elements. For example, traffic control and the suspension of public transportation in the city make it very difficult for the disabled, the elderly, pregnant women, and other vulnerable groups with limited mobility to seek medical treatment or even purchase daily necessities. Without effective transportation aids or exceptional supporting plans, these restrictive policies would discriminatorily affect these groups, reducing access to healthcare.[109] However, non-discrimination is still "an immediately and cross-cutting obligation,"[110] which is the core obligation of state parties throughout the Covenant. Article 2(2) of the ICESCR stipulates that state parties shall guarantee that the Covenant rights will be exercised without discrimination. This Article 2(2) is in parallel with Article 2(1), which stipulates the principle of progressive realization. Therefore, non-discrimination and equal treatment shall not be constrained on the grounds of limited resources. Even in the progressive realization of rights, there should be no discrimination.[111] Concerning *de facto* discrimination due to a lack of resources or otherwise, the state party should bring it to an end as speedily as possible,[112] and the state party should give due priority to the realization of Covenant rights in the use of the available resources.[113]

3.4.3.3 Acceptability

The third criterion is acceptability. Accordingly, "[a]ll health facilities, goods and services must be *respectful of medical ethics* and *culturally appropriate*, i.e., respectful of the culture of individuals, minorities, peoples, and communities, sensitive to gender and life-cycle requirements, as well as being designed to respect confidentiality and improve the health status of those concerned."[114] This means that even with available and accessible resources, the ethical, cultural, or other subjective aspects of the measures may be so unacceptable that the relevant persons have to give up access to resources. For example, negligence in protecting personal health

[108] CESCR (2009a), General Comment No. 20, para 7.

[109] See also below in Sects. 3.5.2 and 3.5.4.

[110] CESCR (1990), General Comment No. 3, para 1; and CESCR (2009a), General Comment No. 20, para 7.

[111] See CESCR (2001) Concluding Observations: Japan, para 12.

[112] See Limburg Principles (1987), para 38.

[113] Limburg Principles (1987), para 28.

[114] CESCR (2000), General Comment No. 14, para 12 (emphasis added).

information or other privacy, and the lack of action to ensure non-discrimination of the patients confirmed to be infected, may lead people who are suspected to be infected or those who are at risk of infectious disease to become reluctant to report information truthfully, resulting in damage to the rights to health of themselves and the public. Nevertheless, based on the above characteristics that demonstrate the right to health includes both a liberal and a social right, the acceptability of public health measures will help to obtain the subjective cooperation and efforts of individuals so that the relevant measures can be better realized.

3.4.3.4 Quality

The fourth criterion concerns quality, which requires that the above health facilities, goods and services must also be scientifically and medically appropriate and of good quality, including "skilled medical personnel, scientifically approved and unexpired drugs and hospital equipment," etc.[115] Merely achieving availability cannot fully guarantee the realization of the right to health. For example, even if the authorities at the county level are equipped with health stations and other facilities, the lack of adequately trained medical personnel and qualified medical supplies would still lead the medical services to not be able to function in a public health emergency. Another example concerns new types of diseases as if the scientifically approved drugs, vaccines, and other methods are not authorized for treatment, the patient's health would be damaged due to the ineffectiveness or major side effects of the drugs.

Under the guidance of the concretized criteria of the proportionality test concerning the right to health outlined above, state parties should then establish a system guaranteeing medical care and satisfactory public health in ordinary situations. Meanwhile, they can monitor the performance of such a system in preventing and controlling infectious diseases and, hence, can make corresponding improvements. Therefore, by applying these criteria, we can properly evaluate the proportionality of the measures and relevant policies of pandemic control, especially concerning the issue of vulnerability in a public health emergency.

[115] CESCR (2000), General Comment No. 14, para 12. However, Tobin understands the criterion of acceptability and that of quality as being subordinated to that of accessibility. See Tobin (2012), pp. 172–173.

3.5 Vulnerability of the Right to Health During Prevention, Treatment, and Control of Infectious Diseases

Now we can summarize vulnerability in more than one sense: (1) One can comprehend the vulnerability of mankind as *homo phaenomenon* facing a public health emergency, e.g., caused by COVID-19 as well as other diseases.[116] (2) A second observation is the vulnerability of certain groups as social human beings. In demanding non-discriminatory medical services, certain vulnerable groups such as pregnant women and persons with disadvantages or other sicknesses are more likely to be neglected due to unreasonable distribution of health facilities, goods, and services. Besides, the medical personnel and their interest in healthy workplace environments would be harmed in the event of a resource shortage. (3) Furthermore, there would also be the vulnerability of certain fundamental rights or human rights. Those rights, which are closely related to and dependent upon the realization of the right to health, e.g., the rights to equality, privacy, access to information, and movement, are all vulnerable to disproportionate restraints during a public health emergency.[117] All these understandings of vulnerability require then respect for human dignity.

The prevention and control of infectious diseases is an important aspect of guaranteeing and realizing the right to health. Article 12(2) of the ICESCR is directly related to public health emergencies, which, with the interpretation of the CESCR in its General Comments No. 14, prescribes that the state shall take steps to ensure (a) the right to maternal, child, and reproductive health; (b) the right to healthy natural and workplace environments; (c) the right to prevention, treatment, and control of diseases; and (d) the right to health facilities, goods, and services.[118] In the following subsections, we will discuss all these rights in detail, and according to their relations to the above aspects of vulnerability.

---

[116] See Santos, Chap. 2 in this volume.

[117] See CESCR (2000), General Comment No. 14, para 3. Similarly, Kluge finds that the "need-sensitivity" or the "time-sensitivity" would make a difference in judging whether to carry out an intervention concerning the right to health. See Kluge (2022), pp. 86–87.

[118] See CESCR (2000), General Comment No. 14, paras 14–17. The old formulations in ICESCR Article 12(2) are: "The steps to be taken by the States Parties to the present Covenant to achieve the full realization of this right shall include those necessary for: (a) The provision for the reduction of the stillbirth-rate and of infant mortality and for the healthy development of the child; (b) The improvement of all aspects of environmental and industrial hygiene; (c) The prevention, treatment and control of epidemic, endemic, occupational and other diseases; (d) The creation of conditions which would assure to all medical service and medical attention in the event of sickness." See ICESCR Article 12(2). For another listing of vulnerability concerning the right to health, see also MacDonald (2007), p. 1.

3.5.1 The Right to Prevention, Treatment, and Control of Diseases

The right to prevention, treatment, and control of diseases reflects the vulnerability of mankind as *homo phaenomenon* against diseases. Respectively, the right to prevention of diseases requires state parties to establish prevention and education programs for behavior-related health concerns; the right to treatment of diseases includes the creation of a system of urgent medical care and the provision of disaster relief and humanitarian assistance in emergencies; finally, the right to control of diseases refers to the individual and joint efforts of states parties to make available relevant technologies, using and improving epidemiological surveillance and data collection on a disaggregated basis, as well as other strategies of infectious disease control.[119]

According to the Infectious Diseases Prevention and Control Law of China (IDPCL), the state has established a monitoring system for infectious diseases, and the disease prevention and control agencies of cities with districts and those of counties are responsible for the monitoring and reporting of epidemics and public health emergencies in the region.[120] In the Third Report on the Implementation of ICESCR submitted by China to the CESCR in 2019, China mentioned that it had established "the largest direct network reporting system for infectious diseases and public health emergencies, with an average reporting time of *four* hours."[121] Regarding the early warning system for infectious diseases, the health administrative department of the State Council and the governments of provinces, autonomous regions, and municipalities are responsible for issuing early warnings of infectious diseases based on the prediction of the occurrence and prevalence of infectious diseases.[122] Regarding the system of information announcement for infectious diseases, the health administrative department of the State Council is responsible for announcing information on the epidemic situation to the public, and may authorize the health administrative departments of the governments of provinces, autonomous regions, and municipalities to publish this information in the relevant region.[123]

In the case of the COVID-19 pandemic, the Wuhan Municipal Health Commission (MHC) released the first notification on the "novel pneumonia" in Wuhan on its official website on December 31, 2019, reporting the number of patients, the clinical symptoms, etc., while it said that "no obvious human-to-human transmission is found, and no infection of medical personnel is found" and "the disease can be prevented and controlled." Meanwhile, it reminded the citizens, as preventive advice, to reduce visiting public places and to wear masks. The subsequent official

---

[119] See CESCR (2000), General Comment No. 14, para 16.

[120] See Article 17 Infectious Diseases Prevention and Control Law of China (2013).

[121] China, Third Periodic State Party's Report on the Implementation of the ICESCR (2019) the part written by the Central Government of China, E/C. 12/CHN/3, p. 22 (emphasis added).

[122] See Article 19 Infectious Diseases Prevention and Control Law of China (2013).

[123] See Article 38 Infectious Diseases Prevention and Control Law of China (2013).

notices did still not clearly indicate whether the "novel pneumonia" was an infectious disease and whether a corresponding emergency plan was activated. On the morning of January 20, 2020, the State Council held its executive meeting and, with its approval, the National Health Commission (NHC) of China announced its decision to include pneumonia infected by COVID-19 as a Category B infectious disease stipulated in the IDPCL of China and to take measures of prevention and control for Category A infectious diseases.[124] It was only on January 21, 2020, that the Hubei Provincial Government then issued a notice to initiate a level II response to the public health emergency. The notice mentioned relevant measures, such as strengthening the quarantining, but did not announce a more detailed emergency response plan.[125]

The problem is that there are ambiguities and conflicts in the provisions of the IDPCL of China and those of the Emergency Response Law (ERL) of China on mechanisms and authorizations of infectious disease response. On the one hand, Article 19 of the IDPCL of China prescribes the early warning only in a general way, i.e., "disclosure according to the situation."[126] The precise conditions and contents of the early warning, however, are not stipulated. Besides, the authorized levels are restricted to "the health administrative department of the State Council and the people's governments of provinces, autonomous regions and municipalities." Accordingly, local organizations of disease prevention and control and governments at all local levels should report to the higher authorities within a very short period of the disease first emerging. However, the competence to identify some new diseases as belonging to certain types of infectious diseases and then to announce them to the public are reserved for the health administrative department of the State Council.

On the other hand, according to the ERL of China, the local governments at or above the county level shall, in accordance with relevant laws, administrative regulations, and the competences and procedures prescribed by the State Council, issue warnings of corresponding levels, and decide and announce that the relevant areas have entered the early warning period.[127] However, only when it is determined, according to the IDPCL of China, which type of infectious disease is involved, can the above department then be empowered by the IDPCL of China to carry out the emergency response measures. These rules of empowerment, to a certain extent, restrict local governments from releasing information to the public in the first place

[124] This was the case until December 26, 2022, when the Joint Prevention and Control Mechanism of the State Council in Response to COVID-19 then changed the name "pneumonia infected by coronavirus" to "infection by coronavirus" and announced that, from January 8, 2023 onwards, this disease would be re-classified as a Category B infectious disease with measures of prevention and control for Category B infectious diseases. See Joint Prevention and Control Mechanism of the State Council in Response to COVID-19 (2022), Lian Fang Lian Kong Ji Zhi Zong Fa [2022] No. 144.

[125] See Hubei Provincial Government (2020) E Zheng Fa [2020] 4.

[126] Article 19 Infectious Diseases Prevention and Control Law of China (2013).

[127] See Article 43 of the Emergency Response Law of China (2017).

and taking flexible prevention and control measures based on local disease development.

Since both of the above laws are enacted by the Standing Committee of the NPC of China, there is no obvious hierarchy between them: from one side, Article 19 of the IDPCL of China would be interpreted as a special law, if only regarding the level of authorization to release warnings and information on a public health emergency such as an infectious disease; from the other side, given the generality of Article 19 of the IDPCL of China, the ERL of China can also be understood as a special law on early warning and emergency response mechanisms.

In a broader sense, however, the right to prevention, treatment, and control of diseases demands the institutional guarantee, on the part of public authorities and organizations, for protecting the dignity and the right to health of mankind. It is then necessary for China to organize the relevant legal rules more systematically and to reconsider the setting of legal authorization levels between infectious disease prevention and emergency response, so as to authorize governments at lower levels to take more timely measures and to respond promptly, ensuring the public's right to know the information concerning the public health emergency.

3.5.2 The Right to Maternal, Child, and Reproductive Health

The right to maternal, child, and reproductive health includes access to family planning, pre- and post-natal care, emergency obstetric services, and access to information and required resources.[128] Negligence of this right, failure to make plans and allocate specific resources, or a lack of open and transparent information, would lead to a great threat to the right to maternal, child, and reproductive health. Hence, this concern reveals both the vulnerability of certain social human beings and that of specific fundamental rights.

For example, during the COVID-19 outbreak in 2019, numerous hospitals in Wuhan were re-designated as fever clinics and hospitals for COVID-19, resulting in a situation where those hospitals originally designated for obstetric examination and reproductive health were unable to provide punctual maternity medical services for pregnant women. In addition, pregnant women with fever symptoms encountered more severe conditions, since ordinary fever clinics did not accept them. The designated hospitals recommended by the government to receive pregnant women had insufficient beds, while private maternity hospitals required proof of not being infected with COVID-19, i.e., a negative result of a PCR test. On February 1, 2020, more than a month after the COVID-19 outbreak, the relevant reproductive medical service information was still not transparent and updated on time.[129]

[128] See CESCR (2000), General Comment No. 14, para 14.

[129] See Wu and Song (2020).

On February 6, 2020, the MHC Wuhan released a list of 44 midwifery institutions with service content and contact information. Accordingly, a pregnant woman with a fever needed to go to the health service center at the community level first for screening, and if she was suspected or confirmed to be infected with COVID-19, she could then only visit five designated hospitals to receive maternity care services.[130] Nevertheless, due to the limited capacity of the PCR test, it took a long time to apply to the community for screening. Furthermore, the above-mentioned announcement did not inform patients of the hospitals' reception capacity or provide a comprehensive guide on their level of obstetrics and neonatology. On February 8, 2020, Hubei Province and the State Council also issued policies on the guarantee of medical services for pregnant and postpartum women, proposing that "the PCR testing institutions should give priority to test pregnant and postpartum women, and all designated hospitals for COVID-19 treatment should implement green channel for referral of pregnant and postpartum women who are confirmed or suspected to be infected with COVID-19."[131] Even so, some pregnant and postpartum women still faced situations such as being unable to obtain emergency services promptly.

Under these circumstances, social welfare organizations played an important role. The WeChat group of "Pregnant Women Left behind in Wuhan" was spontaneously set up by five volunteers, with 400 pregnant women in Wuhan joining the group. This WeChat group also invited professional doctors, drivers, social workers, etc. to provide online consultation, psychological counseling, vehicle borrowing, hospital communication, and other assistance.[132] Nevertheless, these 400 pregnant women accounted for only a small proportion of the number of pregnant women in Wuhan during the lockdown. According to the Hubei Provincial Statistics Bureau, there were 119,400 registered births in 2018 in Wuhan, with an average of nearly 10,000 births per month.[133] Therefore, approximately 10,000 pregnant and postpartum women were affected during the pandemic, and there was a considerable gap in medical services for them. To this extent, local governments still need to establish more open, transparent, and convenient access to information and effective coordination channels for help, which includes conducting online statistics on the needs of pregnant women in the local areas, updating the capacity of hospitals to receive and treat pregnant women and newborns, publishing the online consultation methods of maternity hospitals, and guaranteeing medical transportation and other services.

[130] See Wuhan Municipal Health Commission (2020).

[131] Hubei Provincial Health Commission, COVID-19 Epidemic Prevention and Control Headquarters (2020), p. 2; Joint Prevention and Control Mechanism of the State Council in Response to COVID-19 (2020a), Fei Yan Ji Zhi Fa [2020] No. 25.

[132] See She (2020).

[133] See Hubei Provincial Statistics Bureau (2019).

3.5.3 *The Right to Healthy Natural and Workplace Environments*

The right to healthy natural and workplace environments requires preventive measures concerning occupational accidents and diseases, the guarantee of access to safe water and basic sanitation, adequate housing and safe and hygienic working conditions, the prevention and reduction of the population's exposure to harmful substances, and an adequate supply of food and proper nutrition.[134] Persons engaging in pandemic prevention—especially medical personnel, hospital nurses, community workers, workers in construction, transportation, and funeral services, and journalists, etc.—should be provided with safe working environments. Meanwhile, when the pandemic is under a certain level of control, workers who are required to return to work should also be assured of safe and healthy workplace environments.

In the COVID-19 pandemic, up until midnight on February 11, 2020, the [mainland of] China reported a total of 1,716 confirmed cases of infected medical personnel, accounting for 3.8% of the total confirmed cases nationwide, of which six persons died, 0.4% of deaths nationwide. Hubei Province reported 1,502 confirmed cases of infected medical personnel, accounting for 87.5% of the total confirmed cases of medical personnel nationwide.[135] The infection of local medical personnel in Hubei widened the gap in treatment capacity. Until February 19, 2020, there had been 32,395 medical personnel from all over the country supporting the pandemic areas in Hubei Province.

In response to the infection of medical personnel in the COVID-19 pandemic, the NHC China issued some regulations for strengthening the protection of medical personnel during pandemic prevention and control. These regulations include requiring medical institutions to strictly implement rules of infection prevention and control, issuing guidelines for the use of protective medical equipment, conducting infection control training for all medical personnel, arranging schedules scientifically to keep medical personnel reasonably rested, providing showering and bathing facilities to ensure that the medical personnel can meet the hygiene requirements when they leave the isolation ward, strengthening the health monitoring and infection reporting of medical personnel, and treating the infected medical personnel.[136] At the same time, the temporary hospitals built in Huo Shen Shan and Lei Shen Shan designated for COVID-19 also facilitated dormitories for medical personnel to ensure that they enjoyed appropriate living conditions.

[134] See CESCR (2000), General Comment No. 14, para 15.

[135] See in detail Joint Prevention and Control Mechanism of the State Council in Response to COVID-19 (2020b).

[136] See NHC China (2020), Guo Wei Ban Yi Han [2020] No. 146.

3.5.4 The Right to Health Facilities, Goods, and Services

The scope of the right to health facilities, goods, and services includes the following: The state should not only provide everyone with equal and timely access to basic preventive, curative, rehabilitative health services and essential drugs, but also improve and strengthen the participation of the population, such as the organization of the health sector, the insurance system and, in particular, participation in political decisions to the right to health taken at both the community and national levels.[137] To this extent, the interpretation of this right by the CESCR in its General Comment No. 14 explicates the close connection between the right to health and other human rights, including the right to non-discrimination and equality, the right to access information, and the right to social security.[138]

In the COVID-19 pandemic, however, people with disabilities and patients who cannot take care of themselves have been at higher risk.[139] If they cannot be provided with equal medical care in a public health emergency, the state parties will not be able to meet the requirements of the above obligation.

For example, in the COVID-19 pandemic in Huajiahe Town, Hong'an County, Hubei Province, Mr. Yan was confirmed to be infected by COVID-19. His 16-year-old son, who had been a patient with cerebral palsy, had close contact with him. Although Mr. Yan entrusted his relatives, village cadres, and village doctors to take care of his son, his son did not receive adequate care but was further transferred to the observation center of Huajiahe Town for quarantining and treatment. On January 29, 2020, however, the son of Mr. Yan was confirmed dead in his room.[140]

Besides, elderly people in nursing homes are also easily neglected in public health emergencies. Due to the isolation measures in the community as well as the lengthy screening, monitoring, and waiting for a diagnosis, elderly persons who cannot be directly cared for by relatives are more affected by the restrictions of such pandemic prevention measures than ordinary people. Moreover, those elderly people with underlying diseases or relatively weak physical functions are more likely to develop into severe cases after being infected by COVID-19. If there are no additional measures to ensure equal treatment, the right to health services of such elderly people would not be equitably realized.

For example, "a nurse in the Wuhan Social Welfare Institute said that about 11 elderly people in the hospital died of repeated fever and respiratory failure and that medical personnel were also infected."[141] On February 13, 2020, an 85-year-old man in a nursing home in Wuhan had symptoms of fever and cough, and was suspected to be infected with COVID-19. His family members, however, were either

---

[137] See CESCR (2000), General Comment No. 14, para 17.

[138] CESCR (2000), General Comment No. 14, para 17.

[139] For the right of persons with disabilities to health as well as the "social model" of disability, see Weller (2013), pp. 17–37.

[140] See Ni (2020).

[141] Cao (2020).

far away abroad or quarantined due to the pandemic. The nursing home then provided the old man with an antipyretic to temporarily relieve the symptoms and, meanwhile, reported the situation to the community. But the nursing home was unable to send the old man to the designated hospital for diagnosis and treatment because he did not meet the medical conditions for "fever." Even the police and emergency services responded that they could not handle this situation. On February 19, 2020, the old man died suddenly.[142]

However, it is not only the elderly people, but also the less educated people, or people in areas with imperfect digital infrastructure, who are subject to greater restrictions in terms of obtaining information on pandemic control and medical treatment. Therefore, the state should adopt various means to enrich the channels of releasing public health information and try its best to enable these groups as social human beings to obtain pandemic prevention information in a convenient and timely manner. For example, the state can make use of mobile broadcasts, enhance information reporting on traditional media platforms such as radio stations, TV stations, and mobile phones, and provide simple contact methods such as hotlines.

3.6 Conclusion

The right to health is an inclusive fundamental human right in the framework of the ICESCR and related international conventions. Under the guidance of the concretized criteria of the proportionality test, i.e., those of availability, accessibility, acceptability, and quality, we can evaluate the level of fulfillment of obligations by state parties to respect, protect, and realize the right to health. When discussing in detail the measures that the state should take to realize the right to health in Sect. 3.5, this chapter mainly relies on the clear enumeration of Article 12(2) of the ICESCR, which is only intended to highlight several important aspects but not to exhaust the scope of the state's obligations, which also involve those rights interdependent and inseparable with the right to health, including the right to non-discrimination, the right to access information, freedom of association, and other fundamental freedoms and rights. This reminds us also of the connection and tension between the right to health and human dignity.

Given the public health emergency, some theories of "emergency" seem to have become popular again in academic circles and political forums.[143] These theories should be refuted after all as with rational discourse[144] we have returned to a sense of normality—a new normality is not an illusion, neither is the strong requirement of respect for human dignity.

[142] Cao (2020).

[143] See Volkmann (2020a); Möllers (2020); Daly (2020); Grogan (2020); Wolf (2020).

[144] See Bäcker (2020a, b).

We hold that human dignity deserves a place of strong normativity in the social distancing that arrived with the pandemic, and in the new normality of the future. Still, there are at least four key points to be re-emphasized here. Firstly, the analytical argument can justify the necessary connection between the concept of human dignity and that of personality. Secondly, the human dignity norm can be understood at two levels, namely both as *prima facie* principle and as definitive rule. Thirdly, social human beings should be acknowledged as one of the dual dimensions of human dignity. Fourth and last, employing Radbruch's terms, the individual dimension of human dignity is undoubtedly intrinsic, and the social dimension is not in contradiction with it, while both are contrary to the supra-individualistic understanding of human personality. To this extent, equality is still reserved for the concept of person and hence for human dignity.[145] In this era challenged by coronavirus, it is human dignity with a strong normative character that would lead to a post- and new normality.

References

Alexy R (2002) A theory of constitutional rights (trans: Rivers J). Oxford University Press, Oxford

Alexy R (2005) Ralf Dreiers Interpretation der Kantischen Rechtsdefinition. In: Alexy R (ed) Integratives Verstehen. Zur Rechtsphilosophie Ralf Dreiers. Siebeck, Tübingen, pp 95–109

Alexy R (2013) The existence of human rights. ARSP, Supplement 136:15–18

Alexy R (2015) Human dignity and proportionality analysis. Espaço Jurídico J Law 16:83–96

Alexy R (2019) Mart Susi's internet balancing formula. Eur Law J 25:213–220

Bäcker C (2020a) Corona in Karlsruhe: Eine Prognose. VerfBlog. https://doi.org/10.17176/20200325-123350-0

Bäcker C (2020b) Corona in Karlsruhe II. VerfBlog. https://doi.org/10.17176/20200409-032528-0

Binder C, Drnovsky A (2020) To vote or not to vote? An international human rights perspective on elections in times of the COVID-19 pandemic. VerfBlog. https://doi.org/10.17176/20200707-224811-0

Brandhorst M, Weber-Guskar E (eds) (2017) Menschenwürde. Eine philosophische Debatte über Dimensionen ihrer Kontingenz. Suhrkamp, Berlin

Brugger W (2008) Die Würde des Menschen im Licht des anthropologischen Kreuzes der Entscheidung. In: Härle W, Vogel B (eds) Begründung von Menschenwürde und Menschenrechten. Herder, Freiburg, Basel, Wien, pp 49–94

Cahill M (2020) Lockdown v. liberty: do we still believe in freedom? VerfBlog. https://doi.org/10.17176/20200520-133733-0

Cao WJ (2020) Multiple cases of suspected COVID-19 infection in Wuhan nursing homes (in simplified Chinese). Caixin.com, February 20. http://www.caixin.com/2020-02-20/101517851.html. Accessed 17 Oct 2025

CESCR (1990) General comment No. 3: The nature of states parties' obligations (Art. 2, para 1, of the ICESCR), E/1991/23, Dec 14, 1990, para 1

CESCR (2000) General comment No. 14: The right to the highest attainable standard of health (Art. 12 of the ICESCR), E/C.12/2000/4, Aug 11, 2000, paras 3, 11, 12, 14–17, 28

CESCR (2001) Concluding observations: Japan, E/C.12/1/Add.67, Sept 24, 2001, para 12

[145] For more on the dimension of equality of other constitutional rights and that of human dignity, see Feng (2025), pp. 38–39.

CESCR (2009a) General comment No. 20: Non-discrimination in economic, social and cultural rights (Art. 2, para 2, of the ICESCR), E/C.12/GC/20, Jul 2, 2009, para 7
CESCR (2009b) General comment No. 21: Right to everyone to take part in cultural life (Art. 15, para 1(a), of the ICESCR), E/C.12/GC/21, Dec 12, 2009, para 19
Chen PD, Wu D (2013) China's evolution in progressively realizing the right to health. In: Zuniga JM, Marks SP, Gostin LO (eds) Advancing the human right to health. Oxford University Press, Oxford, pp 159–171
China, Third Periodic State Party's Report on the Implementation of the ICESCR (2019) the part written by the central government of China, E/C. 12/CHN/3
Daly TG (2020) Democracy and the global emergency – shared experiences, starkly uneven impacts. VerfBlog. https://doi.org/10.17176/20200515-133624-0
Dreier R (1979). Zur Einheit der praktischen Philosophie Kants. In: Dreier R (1981) Recht – Moral – Ideologie. Suhrkamp, Frankfurt/Main, pp 286–315
Drosten C, Hennig K, Leif ES (2022) Coronavirus-Update, Folge 1–174, since 26 Feb 2020. https://www.ndr.de/nachrichten/info/coronaskript174.pdf. Accessed 5 July 2022
Elsuwege PV (2020) Lifting travel restrictions in the era of COVID-19: In search of a European approach. VerfBlog. https://doi.org/10.17176/20200606-013404-0
Fährmann J, Arzt C, Aden H (2020a) Ausweispflicht per Corona-Verordnung? VerfBlog. https://doi.org/10.17176/20200330-012927-0
Fährmann J, Arzt C, Aden H (2020b) Corona-Gästelisten – maßlose polizeiliche Datennutzung. VerfBlog. https://doi.org/10.17176/20200814-155220-0
Fateh-Moghadam B, Gutmann T (2020) Gleichheit vor der Triage: Rechtliche Rahmenbedingungen der Priorisierung von COVID-19-Patienten in der Intensivmedizin. VerfBlog. https://doi.org/10.17176/20200430-133550-0
Feng W (2017) The tension between constitutional rights and balancing adjudication. protection of general personality rights in the Lebach judgment in Germany as an example (in simplified Chinese). Shanghai Jiao Tong Univ Law Rev 22:52–71
Feng W (2021) Menschenwürde, Persönlichkeit und die verfassungsmäßige Kontrolle. Oder: starke Normativität ohne Metaphysik? In: Neumann U, Tiedemann P, Liu SI (eds) Menschenwürde ohne Metaphysik, vol 165. Archiv für Rechts- und Sozialphilosophie, Beiheft, pp 23–61
Feng W (2022) Dignidad Humana, Personalidad y Control de Constitucionalidad ¿Normatividad fuerte sin Metafísica? (trans: Santos JA, Salgado AFC, Mendiola JCM). UNIVERSITAS. Revista de Filosofía, Derecho y Política 37:2–50
Feng W (2025) Los derechos de igualdad como mandatos de optimización jurídicos y fácticos: problemas de discernimiento y acumulación debido a los principios formales (trans: Durán ADM). Chornancap Revista Jurídica 3(1):35–52
Fischer-Uebler A (2020) Wann kommt der Abschiebungsstopp? Unzureichender Schutz vor Abschiebungen in von der COVID-19-Pandemie betroffene Zielstaaten. VerfBlog. https://doi.org/10.17176/20200523-133316-0
Frankenberg G (2020) COVID-19 und der juristische Umgang mit Ungewissheit. VerfBlog. https://doi.org/10.17176/20200425-164854-0
Gaffney A (2018) To heal humankind: The right to health in history. Routledge, New York, London
Grogan J (2020) States of emergency. VerfBlog. https://doi.org/10.17176/20200526-133657-0
Gröschner R, Lembcke O (eds) (2009) Das Dogma der Unantastbarkeit. Siebeck, Tübingen
Gusy C (2020) Die Corona der Coronaleugner und das Versammlungsrecht. VerfBlog. https://doi.org/10.17176/20200827-183459-0
Gutmann A, Kohlmeier N (2020) Versammlungsfreiheit Corona-konform. VerfBlog. https://doi.org/10.17176/20200409-032733-0
Habermas J, Günther K (2020) "Kein Grundrecht gilt grenzenlos" Die Zeit, May 7, pp 43–44
Han DY (2020) The right to life. Its conflicts and balancing with other rights (in simplified Chinese). Human Rights 3:11–19

Han Q (2022) Bank depositors were labeled 'red code', who's behind it 'adding code' to the 'code'? (in simplified Chinese). Southern Weekend, June 15. https://mp.weixin.qq.com/s/0W-zGfwg4u1hp8ed-ychXQ. Accessed 17 Oct 2025

Heinig HM (2020) Gottesdienstverbot auf Grundlage des Infektionsschutzgesetzes: Verfassungsrechtliche Rechtfertigung und Grenzen. VerfBolg. https://doi.org/10.17176/20200318-003209-0

Herdegen M (2020) Kommentar zu Art. 1 GG. In: Maunz T, Dürig G (eds) Kommentar zum Grundgesetz, vol 1, 91st edn. C.H. Beck, München, pp 1–54

Höffe O (2002) Prinzip Menschenwürde. In: Höffe O, Medizin ohne Ethik? Suhrkamp, Frankfurt/Main, pp 49–69.

Höffe O (2007) Democracy in an age of globalisation (trans: Haubrich D, Ludwig M) Springer, Berlin

Hong M (2020a) Corona-triage and human dignity: on the limits of balancing life against life. VerfBlog. https://doi.org/10.17176/20200331-133213-0

Hong M (2020b) Coronaresistenz der Versammlungsfreiheit? Das Bundesverfassungsgericht ermöglicht eine Versammlung in Gießen. VerfBlog. https://doi.org/10.17176/20200417-182545-0

Hörnle T (2020) Dilemmata bei der Zuteilung von Beatmungsgeräten. VerfBlog. https://doi.org/10.17176/20200405-011200-0

Hubei Provincial Government (2020) Notice on strengthening the prevention and control of pneumonia infected by COVID-19 (in simplified Chinese), E Zheng Fa [2020] 4, Jan 25. https://www.hubei.gov.cn/zfwj/ezf/202002/t20200220_2142431.shtml. Accessed 17 Oct 2025

Hubei Provincial Health Commission, COVID-19 Epidemic Prevention and Control Headquarters (2020) Doing maternal epidemic prevention and protection (in simplified Chinese). Hubei Daily, Feb 9, 2020

Hubei Provincial Statistics Bureau (2019) Statistical bulletin of Wuhan's national economic and social development in 2018 (in simplified Chinese). http://tjj.hubei.gov.cn/tjsj/tjgb/ndtjgb/sztjgb/201910/t20191025_21403.shtml. Accessed 17 Oct 2025

Ivanhoe PJ (ed) (2009) Mencius (trans: Bloom I). Columbia University Press, New York

Joint Prevention and Control Mechanism of the State Council in Response to COVID-19 (2020a) Notice on strengthening maternal disease treatment and safe midwifery work during the prevention and control of COVID-19 (in simplified Chinese), Fei Yan Ji Zhi Fa [2020] No. 25. http://www.gov.cn/xinwen/2020-02/10/content_5476731.htm. Accessed 17 Oct 2025

Joint Prevention and Control Mechanism of the State Council in Response to COVID-19 (2020b) Press Conference (in simplified Chinese), Feb 14. http://www.gov.cn/xinwen/gwylflkjz12/index.htm. Accessed 17 Oct 2025

Joint Prevention and Control Mechanism of the State Council in Response to COVID-19 (2022) The overall plan for the implementation of treating the COVID-19 infection as 'category B infectious disease with measures for category B infectious diseases' (in simplified Chinese), Lian Fang Lian Kong Ji Zhi Zong Fa [2022] No. 144, Dec 26. https://www.nhc.gov.cn/xcs/zhengcwj/202212/8eaeef83bb7a4fdb851a3ae204295df1.shtml. Accessed 17 Oct 2025

Kant I (1785). Grundlegung zur Metaphysik der Sitten. In: Royal Prussian (later: German) Academy of Science (ed) (1903/1911/1973) Gesammelte Schriften (Collected Writings of Immanuel Kant), vol 4 (Ak 4). de Gruyter, Berlin, pp. 385–463. English edition: Kant I (1996) Groundwork of the metaphysics of morals. In: Kant I, Practical philosophy (trans: Gregor MJ). Cambridge University Press, Cambridge, pp 37–108

Kant I (1797) Metaphysik der Sitten. In: Royal Prussian (later: German) Academy of Science (ed) (1907/1914/1969) Gesammelte Schriften (Collected Writings of Immanuel Kant), vol. 6 (Ak 6). de Gruyter, Berlin, pp 203–493

Kießling A (2020) Coronavirus, Masern und die Grundrechte. VerfBlog. https://doi.org/10.17176/20200302-214914-0

Klafki A (2020a) Der Immunitätsausweis und der Weg zurück in ein freiheitliches Leben. VerfBlog. https://doi.org/10.17176/20200505-013642-0

Klafki A (2020b) Wer bekommt den knappen Covid-19-Impfstoff? Iustitia Distributiva und die rechtlichen Fallstricke medizinischer Priorisierungsentscheidungen. VerfBlog. https://doi.org/10.17176/20200922-223343-0

Kluge E-HW (2022) The right to health care: ethical considerations. Springer, Cham, Switzerland

Kube H (2020) Leben in Würde – Würde des Lebens. VerfBlog. https://doi.org/10.17176/20200403-041501-0

Kumm M (2020) Gegen obrigkeitsstaatliche Tendenzen in der Krise: Massive Freiheitseingriffe und deren Grundrechtliche Rechtfertigung. VerfBlog. https://doi.org/10.17176/20200420-182558-0

Lee MH (1994) Kant's ethics and reconstruction of Mencius' moral thinking (in traditional Chinese). Academia Sinica, Taipei

Lee MH (2018) Confucianism and Kant (in traditional Chinese), revised edn. Linking Publishing, New Taipei

Lepsius O (2020) Vom Niedergang grundrechtlicher Denkkategorien in der Corona-Pandemie. VerfBlog. https://doi.org/10.17176/20200406-131152-0

Limburg Principles on the Implementation of the ICESCR (1987) reproduced in UN Commission on Human Rights, Note Verbale dated 5 December 1986 from the Permanent Mission of the Netherlands to the UN Office at Geneva addressed to the Center for Human Rights, E/CN.4/1987/17, Jan 8, 1987, paras 38, 53 and 54

Lin LF (2008) Human dignity and personal dignity: on interpretation scheme of Article 38 of the PRC constitution (in simplified Chinese). Zhejiang Soc Sci 3:47–55

Liu YX (2020) The dilemma of rural online schooling under the epidemic: weak infrastructure and uneven quality (in simplified Chinese). Southern Weekend, Apr 16. https://new.qq.com/omn/20200416/20200416A0WL0200.html. Accessed 17 Oct 2025

Lübbe W (2020) Corona-Triage: Ein Kommentar zu den anlässlich der Corona-Krise publizierten Triage-Empfehlungen der italienischen SIAARTI-Mediziner. VerfBlog. https://doi.org/10.17176/20200316-002835-0

Ma XL (2022) Stamping the hand after PCR test: the epidemic prevention shall not offend the dignity of the residents (in simplified Chinese). The Beijing News, Jul 6. https://m.bjnews.com.cn/detail/1657101825168797.html. Accessed 17 Oct 2025

MacDonald TH (2007) The global human right to health: dream or possibility? CRC Press, Boca Raton, London, New York

Mangold AK (2020) Dürfen oder Müssen? Zur Maskenpflicht an Schulen und ihrer Verhältnismäßigkeit. VerfBlog. https://doi.org/10.17176/20200822-154707-0

Marco FD (2020) "It's like a war." The New York Times. March 17. https://www.nytimes.com/2020/03/17/podcasts/the-daily/italy-coronavirus.html?showTranscript=1. Accessed 17 Mar 2020

Möllers C (2020) Parlamentarische Selbstentmächtigung im Zeichen des Virus. VerfBlog. https://doi.org/10.17176/20200326-123121-0

Neumann U (1998) Die Tyrannei der Würde. Archiv für Rechts- und Sozialphilosophie 84:153–166

Neumann U (2022) "Gute" und "schlechte" Metaphysik bei der begründung der menschenwürde. In: Bäcker C (ed) Rechtsdiskurs, rechtsprinzipien, rechtsbegriff. Symposium zum 75. Geburtstag von Robert Alexy. Siebeck, Tübingen, pp 125–142

NHC China (2020) Notice on further strengthening the protection of medical personnel during epidemic prevention and control (in simplified Chinese), Guo Wei Ban Yi Han [2020] No. 146, Feb 18. https://www.nhc.gov.cn/wjw/c100175/202002/3228bd1532e94caa88f1b5d0944d4545.shtml. Accessed 17 Oct 2025

Ni YN (2020) A child with cerebral palsy died at home while his father was in quarantine. The Beijing News, Feb 1. https://www.bjnews.com.cn/detail/158052213715605.html. Accessed 17 Oct 2025

Pils E (2020) China's response to the coronavirus pandemic: Fighting two enemies. VerfBlog. https://doi.org/10.17176/20200525-133717-0

Prem K, Liu Y, Russell TW et al (2020) The effect of control strategies to reduce social mixing on outcomes of the COVID-19 epidemic in Wuhan, China: a modelling study. The Lancet 5:261–270

Qiu SN (2014) Equality and the right to health: a preliminary assessment of China. In: Toebes B, Ferguson R, Markovic MM et al (eds) The right to health: A multi-country study of law, policy and practice. Springer, T.M.C. Asser Press, The Hague, pp 97–120

Radbruch G (1927) Der Mensch im Recht. Recht und Staat in Geschichte und Gegenwart 46: 5–18. Reprint: Radbruch G (1993) Gesamtausgabe (Collected Works), vol 2 (Kaufmann A ed) (hereafter GRGA 2). Müller, Heidelberg, pp. 467–476. English edition: Radbruch G (2020) Law's image of the human (trans: Jeutner V). Oxford Journal of Legal Studies 40(4): 672–681

Radbruch G (1930) Vom individualistischen zum sozialen Recht. Hanseatische Rechts- und Gerichts-Zeitschrift 13: 458–468. Reprint: GRGA 2: 485–495

Radbruch G (1932) Rechtsphilosophie, 3rd edn. Quelle & Meyer, Leipzig. Reprint: GRGA 2: 206–450. English edition: Radbruch G (1950) Legal philosophy. In: The legal philosophies of Lask, Radbruch, and Dabin (trans: Wilk K). Harvard University Press, Cambridge, Massachusetts, pp. 43–224

Robert Koch-Institut (2022) Corona-Datenspende vom Anfang April 2020. https://corona-datenspende.de/science/. Accessed 28 June 2022

Saul B, Kinley D, Mowbray J (2014) The ICESCR: commentaries, cases and materials. Oxford University Press, Oxford, Articles 4, 12

Schaefer JP (2013) Human dignity: a remedy for the clash of cultures? Human dignity and the mind of Mencius. Archiv für Rechts- und Sozialphilosophie, Beiheft 137:181–191

Scheler M (1916) Der Formalismus in der Ethik und die materiale Wertethik. Neuer Versuch der Grundlegung eines ethischen Personalismus. Niemeyer, Halle

Schmitt C (1967) Die Tyrannei der Werte. In: Buve S (ed) Säkularisation und Utopie. Ebracher Studien. Ernst Forsthoff zum 65. Geburtstag. Kohlhammer, Stuttgart, pp 37–62

She YQ (2020) A 'death squad' that grabs time for pregnant women left behind in Wuhan (in simplified Chinese). Phoenix Public Welfare, Feb 8. https://gongyi.ifeng.com/c/7ttj4lMolBg. Accessed 17 Oct 2025

Somek A (2020a) Necessity; or: the tyranny of goals. CoronaJournal. https://crisis-diary.net/2020/04/14/necessity-or-the-tyranny-of-goals/. Accessed 17 Oct 2025

Somek A (2020b). Die neue Normalität. VerfBlog. https://doi.org/10.17176/20200506-133712-0

Steinsaltz AE-I (ed) (2012) Koren Talmud Bavli, Hebrew/English, vol 2: Shabbat, part 1. Koren Publisher, Jerusalem. Available via Sefaria. https://www.sefaria.org/Shabbat.94b?lang=bi. Accessed 17 Oct 2025

Talukdar S (2022) Right to health in India: Law, policy and practice. SAGE, Los Angeles, London, New Delhi, Singapore, Washington DC, Melbourne

Tobin J (2012) The right to health in international law. Oxford University Press, Oxford

Tonti L (2020) COVID-19: walking the tightrope of vaccination obligations: state compelled vaccinations in the U.S. and Germany. VerfBlog. https://doi.org/10.17176/20200527-013306-0

UNGA 3rd Committee (1962) Draft international covenants on human rights, A/5365 (17 December 1962), para 24

Volkmann U (2020a) Der Ausnahmezustand. VerfBlog. https://doi.org/10.17176/20200320-122803-0

Volkmann U (2020b) Recht und Würde. Das höchste Gut. Frankfurter Allgemeine. April 1. https://www.faz.net/aktuell/feuilleton/debatten/staatsrecht-und-die-wuerde-des-menschen-16705618/bedrueckende-bilder-aus-16705700.html. Accessed 17 Oct 2025

Wagner S (2020) Leben in der Abwägung. VerfBlog. https://doi.org/10.17176/20200515-013618-0

Wang CG, Rao H (2019) The generation, connotation, and implementation mechanism of the right to health in international law (in simplified Chinese). J Comp Law 3:21–36

Wang JS (2020) Guaranteeing the right to health in public health emergency: Focusing on the international covenant on economic, social and cultural rights (in simplified Chinese). J Southwest Univ Polit Sci Law 3:71–82

Weller P (2013) New law and ethics in mental health advance directives: the CRPD and the right to choose. Routledge, London

Wolf S (2020) Von Auserwählten und Systemrelevanten: Zur politischen Theologie der Pandemie. VerfBlog. https://doi.org/10.17176/20200624-003703-0

Wolff J (2020) Maskenpflicht an Schulen und Grundrechte der Kinder. VerfBlog. https://doi.org/10.17176/20200830-183301-0

Wu B, Song CH (2020) 'Besieged' Wuhan's difficult moments: Anxious pregnant women and squeezed medical care (in simplified Chinese). Southern Metropolis Daily, Feb 1. https://xw.qq.com/cmsid/20200201A0KJ0000?pgv_ref=share&ADTAG=share&from=timeline&isappinstalled=0. Accessed 17 Oct 2025

Wuhan Municipal Health Commission (2020) 44 midwifery institutions can carry out maternity health care services (in simplified Chinese), Feb 6. https://wjw.wuhan.gov.cn/ztzl_28/fk/yqtb/202004/t20200430_1197010.shtml. Accessed 17 Oct 2025

Chapter 4
Indigenous Dignity Under Threat in the Brazilian COVID-19 Pandemic

Jairo Lima and Andrei Domingos Fonseca

Abstract The chapter explores the concept of human dignity from both individual and social perspectives, emphasizing the need for a normative, legal, and moral foundation supported by historical, analytical, and systematic arguments. It highlights Indigenous resistance movements' denunciation of an anti-Indigenous agenda in the Brazilian government, particularly during the COVID-19 crisis, due to increased rights violations and exploitation of Indigenous lands. The document discusses the historical impact of colonization on Indigenous populations, including population reduction due to wars, diseases, and social disruption. It also explores the exploitation of Indigenous lands by the Portuguese Crown, the creation of the Indian Protection Service (SPI), and subsequent governmental policies. The text emphasizes the Brazilian government's prioritization of legislative acts based on the exploitation of Indigenous lands, reflecting an "anti-Indigenous" government plan. In addition, the chapter discusses the Indigenous resistance movement's legal actions and the Brazilian State's response to the COVID-19 pandemic's impact on Indigenous communities. References to legal and academic sources, offering a comprehensive exploration of the topic, constitute the seven subsections of this chapter.

4.1 Introduction

The concept of human dignity as an intrinsic value possessed by every person has served as a powerful political rallying point in contemporary societies, as it meets the demand for the continuous creation of new human rights. Thus, the Brazilian Constitution of 1988, which emerged from a democratic process following a dictatorial regime, immediately established human dignity, in its first article, as the foundation of the Republic of Brazil. This political-constitutional commitment serves as

J. Lima (✉) · A. D. Fonseca
State University of Northern Parana (UENP), Jacarezinho, Brazil
e-mail: jaironlima@uenp.edu.br

© The Author(s), under exclusive license to Springer Nature Switzerland AG 2026

J. E. Núñez (ed.), *Perspectives on Crises*,
https://doi.org/10.1007/978-3-032-23836-8_4

the foundation for an extensive list of fundamental rights, particularly in Articles 5 and 6 of the Brazilian Constitution.

However, this recent constitutional norm also needs to be viewed from the perspective of the history of colonization and domination that Brazil experienced for centuries, and the shock that resulted from the European exploitation of local Indigenous life.[1] Here, in the Indigenous world, one day, strange beings appeared—conquering and oppressive Europeans. For the latter, the conquest of these new peoples was a great achievement, but for the natives, it was a rite—a human representation of a cosmic catastrophe. From this process, Indigenous peoples were reduced to the condition of the Other, of non-being, where their concrete lives had no value within a single possible world.[2]

Nevertheless, in this externality where the Other is found, the non-being exists in a concrete form. Despite all the processes in the decimation of Brazilian Indigenous peoples, the surviving communities still resist through their culture, habits, and traditions, crying out for life and respect. Therefore, the constitutional norm of human dignity in Brazil faces the challenge of incorporating Indigenous demands, which extend beyond the limits of Eurocentric philosophical conceptions.[3] Accordingly, in this study, by assessing official documents and, mainly, documents of the Indigenous resistance movement itself, we aim to demonstrate how the COVID-19 pandemic in Brazil has intensified a government policy aimed at the destruction of the Indigenous population, undermining the possibilities for dignified life among the owners of this land. Based on the factual description of the Indigenous situation in Brazil, we will present the actions and omissions of the federal government in protecting Indigenous dignity during the pandemic period. Lastly, we will discuss the judicial intervention carried out by the Brazilian Supreme Court in this matter.

4.2 The Indigenous Framework in Brazil

Indigenous peoples are an inherent part of the process of territorial and political formation in Brazil. The constitutive elements of the country cannot be characterized without considering the populations that have lived and continue to live here; their sociocultural organization and relationship with environmental protection are legacies that need to be constantly remembered.[4]

Several archaeological studies indicate that the occupation of the Brazilian territory by Paleo-Indian populations dates back more than 12,000 years. Studies conducted in the Amazon have revealed records of complex societies, whose

[1] For the Brazilian history of Indigenous peoples, see Almeida (2010) and Grupioni (1992).

[2] Kopenawa and Albert (2013).

[3] For a panorama on Brazilian Indigenous decolonialism, see Gonzaga (2022), and for an Indigenous ontology, see Kopenawa and Albert (2013).

[4] Pacheco de Oliveira and Freire (2006), p. 18.

technological (ceramics) and social (cacicados) development is a fact. Through an ethnic-historical map elaborated by ethnologist Curt Nimuendajú, the presence of Indigenous peoples in Brazil at the arrival of the Portuguese in 1500 comprised approximately 1400 different peoples.[5]

Regarding the population existing at that time,[6] there are disagreements among researchers in the field, as each has adopted a different calculation method. Additionally, the precariousness and incompleteness of colonial sources also play a role. A detailed survey conducted by historian John Hemming estimated that there were likely 2,431,000 Indigenous people in the country in 1500.[7]

Based on this perspective, a specialist in historical demography, Maria Luiza Marcílio, has highlighted critical aspects, such as the population reduction suffered by Indigenous populations due to wars of conquest, massacres, and enslavement, as well as diseases including measles, tuberculosis, and smallpox, which were responsible for the rapid decimation of entire groups.[8] In addition to diseases, hunger accompanied these wars, along with the consequent social disruption and the need to escape to new places where survival resources were unknown.[9]

In this context, contact with different Indigenous peoples triggered in the European colonizer the objective of understanding and shaping these populations together with their "mythical and conceptual universe."[10] Hence, two conceptions of the humanitarian aspect of Indigenous peoples emerged through visions that endowed human and religious significance to the colonial movement. The first conception stated that Indigenous peoples were inferior human beings, savages, and cannibals, but with great potential to become Christians. The second conception, even more extreme, did not recognize the humanity of these people and considered them animals that deserved to be enslaved or killed.[11]

Thus, the inferiority directed as a characteristic of Indigenous peoples justified their "conquest" by Europeans because it was necessary to change their customs and values to integrate them into colonial work. In this scenario, for much of the first century of colonization (the sixteenth century), the natives played a key role in the commercial objectives of the colonizers, who sought to exploit wood, such as Brazilwood, and exotic animals through barter.[12]

[5] Pacheco de Oliveira and Freire (2006), p. 21.

[6] According to the most recent survey by the Brazilian Institute of Geography and Statistics (IBGE), the current number of the Brazilian Indigenous population is 817,963 people. The population is distributed among rural spaces with 502,783 Indigenous people and in urban spaces with 315,180 people. There are 305 distinct groups, who are speakers of 274 different languages. Brazil (2012) Instituto Brasileiro de Geografia e Estatística (IBGE).

[7] Pacheco de Oliveira and Freire (2006), p. 22.

[8] Pacheco de Oliveira and Freire (2006), p. 23.

[9] Cunha (2012), p. 15.

[10] Pacheco de Oliveira and Freire (2006), p. 26.

[11] Pacheco de Oliveira and Freire (2006), pp. 26–28.

[12] Cunha (2012), pp. 18–19.

The colony was the first general government of Brazil, where, over time, relationships changed and became more tense because, on the European side, there were settlers, governments, and missionaries linked by a complex, conflicting, and symbiotic relationship. Eventually, barter was no longer a priority for settlers; instead, Indigenous labor was increasingly directed toward colonial businesses.[13]

In the same context, the interests of the Portuguese Crown were different from those presented by the colony. After all, the Crown sought to guarantee the colony political stability because its fiscal and strategic interests were absolute priorities. In addition to the conflicts of interest among the colonists and the Crown, another sector of great prominence further complicated the situation of Indigenous peoples: the Catholic Church and its religious (Jesuit) order. Ultimately, a significant portion of the conflicts arose from the struggle for control of Indigenous labor in villages, with disputes often centered on the direction of the villages and the authority to oversee Indigenous people's work outside the villages.[14]

Therefore, between the seventeenth and eighteenth centuries, while Portugal was interested in exploiting the Amazon, the Jesuits had already occupied part of this territory for missionary purposes. Due to a series of conflicts, the Jesuits were expelled from the territory, entailing that there would be no other obstacles to enslaving the natives and occupying their land. Thus, starting in the nineteenth century, the interest of the Crown shifted from work to Indigenous lands. A century later, it moved from the soil to the subsoil of these territories.[15]

The twentieth century would be marked by the beginning of the Republican period. It was at this time, in 1910, that the Indian Protection Service (SPI) was created. This was the first governmentalized power mechanism created by the Brazilian State to manage the relationship between Indigenous peoples, different social groups, and other power devices.[16] The SPI was extinguished during the military dictatorship (1964–1985), in 1966, amid accusations of Indigenous genocide, administrative inefficiency, and corruption. Thus, this organ was replaced by the National Indian Foundation (FUNAI)[17] in 1967. Although many years had passed, the policies directed at Indigenous peoples remained related to the government's priorities and not those of the natives. The 1970s were marked by a period of "miracle" investments in infrastructure and mineral exploitation in Brazil. Therefore, in the name of progress, Indigenous peoples were identified as obstacles to be overcome, and forced contact, often violent, for territorial exploitation became frequent.[18]

[13] Cunha (2012), pp. 18–19.

[14] Cunha (2012), pp. 19–20.

[15] Cunha (2012), pp. 20–21.

[16] Lima (1992), p. 155.

[17] FUNAI was created to continue the exercise of state control over Indigenous peoples. In this context, respect for Indigenous culture was dependent on the need for integration and stimulus to change (acculturation). It is therefore possible to observe that FUNAI's objectives (when created) were similar to those of the Indian Protection Service. See Pacheco de Oliveira and Freire (2006), p. 131.

[18] Cunha (2012), p. 21.

In the constant exploitation of Indigenous lands that began in 1980, these original peoples were no longer a hindrance but a military problem, as they were considered dangerous to national security.[19] In this scenario, FUNAI became the subject of intense militarization, and the Brazilian State was able to use this institution as a mechanism for the degradation of Indigenous people.[20] For example, the National Truth Commission (CNV)[21] recognized in 2014 the existence of more than 8,350 deaths of Indigenous people, promoted through the violent actions of the Brazilian State via genocide, ethnocide, contamination by disease, homicide, torture, imprisonment, forced displacement, and other crimes during the military regime.[22]

During the National Constituent Assembly (ANC) of 1987 to 1988, there was a significant increase in nongovernmental organizations supporting traditional peoples, including those that took action in opposition to the dictatorship, whose focus was on organizing an Indigenous movement with a national character.[23] In this context, the group "Union of Indigenous Peoples" emerged to work on the constitutionalization of Indigenous rights, especially in relation to "original rights," which are those rights inherently belonging to the Indigenous, regardless of any government statement.[24]

Meanwhile, the National Security Council (CNS) observed the Indigenous movement and tried to prevent its demands from being constitutionalized. That group sought to maintain an "integrationist" policy[25] directed at these peoples in the name of national security. Thus, the military sought to influence certain constituents so that Indigenous rights would have fewer legal protections than those of colonial times, whose provisions would allow the exploitation and reduction of Indigenous lands as well as cause the continued disappearance of these peoples in Brazil.[26]

In addition, for the most conservative groups in society (FUNAI, the military, large mining companies, landowners, etc.), the only entity that could address the right of possession and permanence of Indigenous people would be FUNAI. These groups were also opposed to the demarcation of traditional lands and the

---

[19] Cunha (2012), p. 21.

[20] Fernandes (2016), pp. 142–175.

[21] The National Truth Commission (CNV) was created through Law 12.528/2011 and was instituted the following year. The objective of the CNV was centered on the clarifications of the serious human rights violations carried out between 1946 and 1988, whose clarifications would affect the right to memory and to historical truth, as well as promoting national reconciliation. President of the Republic, Brazil. Law 12.528, 18 November 2011. https://www.planalto.gov.br/ccivil_03/_ato2011-2014/2011/lei/l12528.htm. Accessed Feb 23, 2026.

[22] CNV (2014).

[23] Cunha (2012), p. 22.

[24] Fernandes (2016), p. 150.

[25] This "integrationist" policy was articulated by the Civil Code, in force at the time, which considered an Indigenous person to be without civil capacity, that is, subject to the tutelary regime. In this type of regime, Indigenous peoples could not fully exercise civil rights and obligations, but the state could assume this role on their behalf.

[26] Fernandes (2016), p. 170.

recognition of Indigenous languages, cultures, and customs, which were defended by the Union of Indigenous Peoples and its supporters.[27]

Despite these clashes, the result of the ANC was positive for Indigenous peoples. Their right to the protection and use of water, energy, and mining resources in Indigenous territories was recognized, in opposition to the homogenizing policy and integrationist approach that had been previously articulated.[28] Furthermore, the recognition of a specific type of education based on each traditional culture challenged national hegemonic knowledge, and the recognition of Indigenous organizations collided with the prior tutelary regime of FUNAI.[29]

In the final text of the 1988 Constitution, there is still recognition of Indigenous ownership and these peoples' right to their territories, where they were the first masters.[30] There is also recognition for the procedural capacity of the Indigenous peoples, their communities, and their organizations to defend their respective individual and collective rights.[31] However, even in the face of these existing rights, there have been and continue to be movements contrary to Indigenous interests, with consolidated roots in the Brazilian State.

Therefore, it is in this context of rights violations that the native peoples of Brazil are included. Among these violations, the constant disrespect for human rights, especially the human dignity of the Indigenous person, can be highlighted. After all, the poorer, the more black, Indigenous, and non-heterosexual, the less human specific subjects are considered by the Brazilian State.[32] Therefore, human dignity cannot be viewed solely from an individual perspective, but also from a social perspective, to ensure that it is grounded in a more robust normative, legal, or moral basis and supported by historical, analytical, and systematic arguments.[33]

Based on this context, numerous Indigenous resistance movements[34] denounced, especially during the COVID-19 crisis, the advance of an anti-Indigenous agenda in the federal government, because such an increase in rights violations could denote the perpetuation of practices based on the exploitation of lands and the extermination of Indigenous peoples. In this case, government interests are centered, once again, on the consolidation of political and economic aspects via constant disrespect of the relationship of belonging between Indigenous people and their traditional

[27] Lopes (2011), p. 132.

[28] Lopes (2011), p. 132.

[29] Lopes (2011), p. 132.

[30] Cunha (2012), p. 22.

[31] Araújo and Leitão (2002), pp. 23–24.

[32] Becker and Oliveira (2016), p. 171.

[33] Feng (2022), pp. 42–44.

[34] Articulation of Indigenous Peoples of Brazil (APIB), Articulation of Indigenous Peoples from Northeast, Minas Gerais and Espírito Santo (APOINME), Terena People's Council, Articulation of Indigenous Peoples of the Southeast (ARPINSUDESTE), Articulation of Indigenous Peoples of the South (ARPINSUL), Great Assembly of Guarani Kaiowá Peoples (ATY GUASU), Coordination of Indigenous Organizations of the Brazilian Amazon (COIAB) and Guarani Yvyrupa Commission (CGY).

land, which remains up to the Brazilian State itself to demarcate. The most emblematic case related to land demarcation in Brazil concerns the temporal landmark thesis that has emerged in the judicial sphere in the demarcation of the Indigenous land called Raposa-Serra do Sol. According to this theory, Indigenous peoples are only entitled to the territories they effectively occupied until the date of the promulgation of the Federal Constitution, that is, October 5, 1998, unless they have proof that until that date, although distant from their claimed territory, they still resisted forced removal.[35] Nevertheless, this time frame was not recognized in the Raposa-Serra do Sol case. However, this subject returned to the fore when the Brazilian Supreme Court (STF) revisited this time frame, bringing it back to the agenda, but this time with broader repercussions as an extraordinary appeal. If this time frame is recognized, there may be an increase in conflicts in the original territories, such as deforestation, land-grabbing, mining, and the cancellation of existing territorial demarcations.

4.3 Anti-Indigenous Health Policies in the Federal Government

The Special Secretariat for Indigenous Health (SESAI)[36] and the FUNAI are responsible for the care of elements related to the health and territory of Indigenous communities in Brazil, respectively. Despite the importance of both organizations, what has been observed over the years is an increased scrapping of public policies directed at Indigenous communities, whose contours have become even more serious in the midst of the pandemic.[37]

From this perspective, the Indigenous resistance has pointed out that the former President, Jair Messias Bolsonaro, was one of the main parties responsible for the perpetuation of an anti-Indigenous agenda in the "bowels of the Brazilian State."[38] The president's speeches have gone beyond having a symbolic meaning, as he has acted through public policies aimed at the destruction of rights and government apparatuses that have been built over decades for native peoples. After all, even before taking office, he stated that in his government there would be no centimeter of demarcated Indigenous land.[39] Since then, this promise has been rigorously fulfilled throughout his term.[40]

[35] Fernandes (2018), p. 170.

[36] SESAI was created by Law no. 12.314/2010 and has a link with the Ministry of Health. In this sense, the agency aims to coordinate and implement the National Indigenous Health Care Policy, as well as the entire management of the Indigenous healthcare subsystem process in the Unified Health System (SUS).

[37] APIB (2021), p. 16.

[38] APIB (2021), p. 16.

[39] Resende (2018).

[40] Instituto Socioambiental (2022).

Given this scenario, the dismantling of public policies directed at Indigenous peoples may be observable in the new direction of FUNAI. In legal terms, this body of the Brazilian State is responsible for the protection and promotion of Indigenous rights. It is also responsible for demarcating Indigenous lands. However, the agency has suffered systematic attacks and structural changes, marked by a lack of human, financial, and technical resources, as well as political interference, with impacts that have negatively affected institutional objectives and the demarcation of Indigenous lands.[41]

According to an Indigenous researcher, Eloy Terena, FUNAI has taken an authoritarian and even colonial approach to the implementation of Indigenous policy. This government body has worked against the rights and interests of Indigenous people because it does not provide legal protection for native territories, while it facilitates exploitation, and persecutes Indigenous leaders. In addition, such practices have gained momentum in recent years, particularly under the administration of Jair Bolsonaro, who has implemented measures favoring agribusiness at the expense of traditional rights. The result of this is that, once again, in the name of economic development, exploratory activities in Indigenous lands have been encouraged, a fact directly linked to the expansion of invasion, deforestation, fire, mining, and land-grabbing on public lands.[42]

Therefore, during the initial months of the pandemic in 2020, even with the growing number of Indigenous people infected and victimized by the coronavirus, the FUNAI spent only 1.18% of its budget to fight the disease among Indigenous peoples.[43] By the end of 2020, only 52% of the estimated budget had been spent by the foundation, according to data collected by the Institute of Socioeconomic Studies (INESC). In addition, according to the same institute, in the period between 2019 and 2021, FUNAI's budget remained stable. However, these numbers, when analyzed in isolation, may mistakenly suggest a possible efficiency of the federal government; however, for nearly a decade, the values made available to the agency were insufficient. Furthermore, the staff levels are thus outdated, and the amount allocated to the foundation's final program remains small.[44]

The scrapping of the agency and public policies aimed at Indigenous peoples becomes even clearer when analyzing two important surveys by the INESC.[45] The first concerns the resources allocated to the regularization, demarcation, and inspection of Indigenous Lands (TIs) and the protection of isolated Indigenous peoples. In 2021, the resources allocated to this agenda received their largest budget in three years. Although apparently positive information, FUNAI itself, in its management reports of 2019 and 2020, announced the establishment of a "land harmonization" policy based on the investment of resources in compensation for "good faith

[41] APIB (2021), p. 16.

[42] Terena (2022).

[43] APIB (2020), p. 14.

[44] INESC (2022), p. 67.

[45] INESC (2022), p. 67.

improvements" on Indigenous lands. This means that between 2019 and 2021, approximately 45% of the budget, which was allocated to all stages of the land demarcation process, ended up in the hands of non-Indigenous landowners, thus inverting the logic of the existence of these resources. The second INESC survey refers to the budget allocated to Indigenous health. The number of resources allocated to this sector fell between 2019 and 2021. In the pandemic period, there was a 7% cut in authorized resources, and the execution in 2021 was the lowest in three years.[46]

Thus, it is possible to note some points for analysis. The first point relates to the government agencies responsible for protecting Indigenous interests, which continue to conduct studies with objectives that are contrary to these groups. The second is related to the lack of demarcation of Indigenous lands in recent years and to the decrease in the budget related to Indigenous health during the COVID-19 pandemic. Accordingly, several dilemmas with impacts on the survival of Brazilian Indigenous communities are evident. The following section thus presents some of these problems that have gained prominence in the complaints presented by Indigenous resistance movements, especially during the coronavirus pandemic.

4.4 Hiding the Number of Indigenous Deaths

The first confirmed case of COVID-19 among Indigenous peoples in Brazil was that of an Indigenous Health Agent (AIS) of the Kokama people in the Special Indigenous Health District (DSEI)[47] near the Alto Solimões River in the municipality of Santo Antônio do Içá in the State of Amazonas.[48] This young woman was with a doctor of the SESAI on March 25, 2020, after the professional had returned from vacation in the city of São Paulo. The doctor was diagnosed with coronavirus; however, he had also performed several medical visits in that region, contaminating several Indigenous people.

It is a curious incident given that, on March 11, 2020, the World Health Organization had already characterized the COVID-19 crisis as a pandemic. Similarly, the Ministry of Health declared community transmission of COVID-19 in

[46] INESC (2022), p. 67.

[47] The Special Indigenous Health District (DSEI) is the decentralized management unit of the Subsystem of Indigenous Health Care (SasiSUS). It is a model of service organization that includes a set of technical activities that are based on rationalized and qualified measures of healthcare. In addition, it promotes the reordering of the health networks and health practices through the administrative-managerial activities that are necessary to provide care, based on social control.

[48] It is noteworthy that Brazilian scientific institutions, such as the Oswaldo Cruz Foundation, have already announced, since the beginning of the pandemic, the high geographical and sociodemographic vulnerability of Indigenous peoples to COVID-19. See FIOCRUZ (2020), p. 4.

the country on March 20, 2020, through Ordinance no. 454.[49] This administrative act also announced the need for home isolation in cases such as the one listed above.

According to data provided by SESAI[50] on the official website of the institution, through an epidemiological bulletin, updated on May 2, 2022, the number of Indigenous people who have died due to COVID-19 is 908. The most significant number of deaths is located in the following DSEIs: east of Roraima (114 deaths), Mato Grosso do Sul (112 deaths), and Alto Solimões River (54 deaths). Furthermore, regarding updates on cases, this information is initially provided by the 34 DSEIs of the country, subsequently validated by the Department of Indigenous Health Care (DASI), and then made available on the institution's website.

Meanwhile, given the high number of infections in their community, other difficulties also began to be denounced by the Kokama people. One of these difficulties referred to the hospitals in Amazonas that registered Indigenous people who died as a result of COVID-19 based on their "Brown skin,"[51] which is an entirely different form of racial identification in Brazil, thus enabling a mismeasuring of Indigenous deaths. Due to this underreporting and difficult access to SESAI data, the Articulation of Indigenous Peoples of Brazil (APIB)[52] created the "National Committee for Indigenous Life and Memory" to enable the dissemination of data that are closer to reality. Contrary to the data provided by SESAI, the National Committee for Indigenous Life and Memory, through its own methodology, has argued that the number of Indigenous people that became victims of COVID-19 is actually 1304. The creation of this parallel committee began when differences were found in the local identifications within the official information presented by SESAI on the number of cases of Indigenous people infected and killed by COVID-19.[53]

According to the APIB, the situation illustrated above occurred for several reasons. One of them was the refusal of SESAI to acknowledge or recognize the identities of Indigenous residents in urban regions or territories with non-approved demarcations. In addition, the registration of deceased or contaminated Indigenous people as "Browns" and the absence of information on race, color, and peoples in the information systems of the Unified Health System (SUS) demonstrated the non-recognition and invisibility of Indigenous lives. Consequently, these problems in official institutions have prevented more rigorous analyses of the impact of the disease on Indigenous villagers and residents in urban contexts[54] and also impaired the burial of deceased Indigenous people according to their traditional and cultural

[49] Ministry of Health, Brazil. Ordinance no. 454, March 20, 2020. https://www.in.gov.br/en/web/dou/-/portaria-n-454-de-20-de-marco-de-2020-249091587. Accessed Feb 23, 2026.

[50] SESAI (2022).

[51] APIB (2020), pp. 12–13.

[52] The Brazilian Indigenous resistance movement has, as part of its structuring, local, regional and national organizations, whose highest level of grouping takes place through the APIB. The objective of the APIB is to promote the defense of rights, the union, and the organization of different Indigenous movements.

[53] APIB (2020), p. 96.

[54] APIB (2020), pp. 96–97.

rites, since many killed by COVID-19 had been buried together with non-Indigenous people.[55]

In this context, the Ordinance no. 344 of 2017 of the Ministry of Health had already made it mandatory to record racial information in their systems.[56] However, organizations within the Unified Health System ignored this regulation in their service forms. The result was that more than half of the records related to color and race were classified as unknown.[57] Hence, mandatory registration in the fields of race, ethnicity, and Indigenous ethnicities occurred only through judicial decision, after the performance of agencies such as the Public Defender's Office (DPU) and the Public Prosecutor's Office of the State of Amazonas (MPF/AM) via legal recommendations 07/2020.[58] Furthermore, Law no. 14.021 of July 7, 2020, made it mandatory to register and declare race and color when related to Indigenous people in public health systems, as well as enabling the identification of any individuals served.[59] According to the APIB, information such as this, if available in the official database, could assist in the development of public policies related to health, budgets, and decision-making in the State, whose aid could then reach Indigenous leaders committed to managing actions for isolation and hygiene in their villages.[60]

4.5 Coronavirus Proliferation Inside Indigenous Communities

Given this scenario of underreporting, the APIB conducted a survey outlining the onset of contagion in some TIs in the country during the first months of the pandemic. According to the movement, government agents actively contributed to the spread of the coronavirus in Brazilian Indigenous communities via the negligence of SESAI health teams and army professionals in isolated territories, as well as the significant processes of institutional racism practiced by public hospitals, which engaged in the registration of deceased and contaminated Indigenous people as Brown people.[61] In addition, agribusiness and large slaughterhouses were other means for this contamination process due to the high rate of confinement of Indigenous and non-Indigenous people in these closed environments during the pandemic. After all, if there is no territory for natives to carry out their subsistence

[55] CIMI (2020).

[56] Ministry of Health, Brazil. Ordinance no. 344, February 1, 2017. https://bvsms.saude.gov.br/bvs/saudelegis/gm/2017/prt0344_01_02_2017.html. Accessed Feb 23, 2026.

[57] CIMI (2020), p. 97.

[58] MPF/AM, Legal Recommendation no. 07/2020. https://www.ok.org.br/wp-content/uploads/2020/09/recomendacao_MPF_MS_racacor.pdf. Accessed Feb 23, 2026.

[59] President of the Republic, Brazil. Law no. 14.021, July 7, 2020. https://www.in.gov.br/en/web/dou/-/lei-n-14.021-de-7-de-julho-de-2020-265632745. Accessed Feb 23, 2026.

[60] APIB (2020), p. 97.

[61] APIB (2020), p. 12.

activities, these people can only work for their exploiters. In the State of Mato Grosso do Sul, for example, the first cases of COVID-19 contamination among the Guarani and Kaiowá people occurred through large agribusiness companies, a sector responsible for the destruction of traditional territories.[62]

Another dilemma involving original territories that has been widely denounced by Indigenous resistance is related to the possible presence of missionaries in Indigenous lands, particularly in areas of voluntary isolation and recent contact. This practice was also legitimized by Law no. 14.021 of 2020, in Article 13, which enabled the existence of religious missions in territories of isolated Indigenous peoples and those of recent contact.[63] Voluntary isolation was a strategy adopted long ago by Indigenous peoples to protect against diseases caused by non-Indigenous peoples. The practice is very similar to the "social distancing" applied during the pandemic. Conversely, the Indigenous of recent contact are those who have permanent and/or intermittent contact with various sectors of national society; however, these peoples have peculiarities in relation to other social groups because they maintain their forms of social organization, and their own collective dynamics are solidified. These mechanisms characterize the autonomy of Indigenous peoples in relation to the government and society in general.

An example of this presence is the invasions carried out by members of the New Tribes Mission group, who aimed at changing the policy of noncontact and promoting the Christian conversion of Indigenous peoples. During the pandemic, this situation has had several consequences, represented by the judicialization of a case against the religious group in the Vale do Javari.[64] The denounced missionary practice violates international recommendations, of which Brazil is a signatory. The Inter-American Commission on Human Rights (IACHR), in Resolution no. 01/2020, Pandemic and Human Rights in the Americas, paragraph 55, has announced the indispensable character of respect for noncontact with Indigenous peoples;[65] after all, throughout history, diseases have been responsible for exterminating entire Indigenous communities.

On the other hand, former President Jair Bolsonaro refused to sanction provisions of Law no. 14.021/2020 that would have made it mandatory for the government to guarantee villages access to drinking water, emergency hospital beds, ventilators, oxygenation machines, the internet, and food baskets.[66] These vetoes were justified by the creation of expenses for the Federal Executive without a corresponding budget that would illustrate their potential financial impacts. However,

---

[62] Johnson and Faria (2020), p. 42.

[63] President of the Republic, Brazil. Law no. 14.021, July 7, 2020. https://www.in.gov.br/en/web/dou/-/lei-n-14.021-de-7-de-julho-de-2020-265632745. Accessed Feb 23, 2026.

[64] APIB (2020), p. 21.

[65] Inter-American Commission on Human Rights. Pandemic and Human Rights in the Americas: Resolution 01/2020. https://www.oas.org/pt/cidh/decisiones/pdf/Resolucao-1-20-pt.pdf. Accessed Feb 23, 2026.

[66] DIP (2021), p. 8.

after a month, a large portion of the vetoes made by Bolsonaro were overthrown by the National Parliament.[67]

In this same context, there was also a failure by the government to comply with international recommendations of the United Nations High Commissioner for Human Rights and with guidelines of the IACHR. The first, through the document "Guidelines relative to COVID-19," recommended to the relevant states certain actions, such as respecting traditional Indigenous medicine, regulating access to territories, and installing sanitary barriers.[68] Conventional medicine has been highlighted in the agenda of Indigenous resistance due to a series of criminal attacks to the Kaiowá and Guarani Indigenous communities in the State of Mato Grosso do Sul directed at prayer houses.[69]

In a recent report on this agenda, the female Indigenous movement Kuñangue Aty Guasu and its observatory have identified that the number of prayer houses burned during the pandemic crisis is practically twice as many as those burned between 2014 and 2019.[70] In addition, Indigenous female spiritual healers, defenders of traditional rites for the maintenance of life in their communities, were "judged in public and their houses were burned; they were expelled from their community, humiliated, condemned as 'witches' and 'sorceresses.'"[71]

Furthermore, regarding the recommendations of the IACHR, in its document Pandemic and Human Rights in the Americas, the need to inform Indigenous communities about the pandemic in their traditional languages is also exposed, in addition to the need to stop the advance of legislative projects structured by extractive agendas for Indigenous lands during the advance of the coronavirus. These recommendations, however, were not fulfilled because at the beginning of 2021, due to the election of new presidents of the Chamber of Deputies and the Federal Senate, Bolsonaro presented an unprecedented package of priorities to be approved. Among the priority agendas was Bill no. 191/2020, which aimed, during the pandemic, to prioritize the opening of Indigenous lands to mining.[72]

To illustrate the development of these conflicts, the Yanomami's Indigenous land has been invaded by prospectors with much violence during the pandemic.[73] Actions such as this demonstrate the ineffectiveness of the government in protecting Indigenous peoples, defending traditional territories, and promoting health. A precautionary measure was already in place—Recommendation no. 563/2020, granted by the IACHR through Resolution no. 35 of July 17, 2020, in favor of the Yanomami

---

[67] DIP (2021), pp. 8–9.

[68] DIP (2021), p. 5.

[69] Prayer houses are places where Indigenous peoples develop aspects related to traditional medicine, spirituality, and ancestry.

[70] Kuñangue Aty Guasu (2022), pp. 20–21.

[71] Kuñangue Aty Guasu (2022), p. 19.

[72] Terena (2022), pp. 6–7.

[73] Yanomami and Ye'Kwana (2022).

and Yye'Kwana[74]—which sought to protect the right to life and personal integrity of these communities.

Thus, given their high sociodemographic vulnerability, the lack of data transparency, or an effective plan to confront the pandemic by the government, and the increase in violence and conflicts involving Indigenous people during the pandemic, the APIB and its organizations created an emergency coping plan, specific to these people. One of the results of this articulation was the filing of a lawsuit (ADPF n. 709[75]) at the Brazilian Supreme Court (STF) in which, for the first time in history, Indigenous lawyers went to the STF to demand the protection of Indigenous human dignity.

4.6 Indigenous Dignity in the Court

The APIB filed a case, together with the Fundamental Rights Clinic of the Law School at the State University of Rio de Janeiro (UERJ) and six Brazilian political parties, in the STF on June 29, 2020. One of the initial concerns of the organization was centered on the acceptance of the case, because for the first time in the history of the country, an Indigenous organization was using the STF in judicial review competence.[76]

Incidentally, this activity, in addition to having an innovative character, was also quite difficult due to the tutelary regime directed at Indigenous peoples, which had prevented them from having a postulatory capacity until 1988. Moreover, on a previous occasion (2014), the STF had refused a criminal complaint filed by another Indigenous organization to the detriment of federal deputies, who were accused of committing a crime of racism. Justice Luís Roberto Barroso decided to close the procedure due to a lack of standing to sue, as he believed it was up to FUNAI to represent Indigenous peoples, rather than their own articulations.[77] Hence, inviting political parties legitimized by the Constitution to sue before the STF was part of a precautionary strategy of the APIB in case its lack of standing to sue was recognized.[78]

Contrary to expectations, on July 8, 2020, Justice Barroso recognized the APIB's legitimacy to sue as a class representative entity and thus partially granted the

---

[74] Inter-American Commission on Human Rights. Resolution 35/2020 (precautionary measure no. 563-20). Members of the Yanomami and Ye'kwana Indigenous Peoples in relation to Brazil. https://www.oas.org/es/cidh/decisiones/pdf/2020/35-20MC563-20-BR-PT.pdf. Accessed Feb 23, 2026.

[75] Brazil, 2020. Supremo Tribunal Federal (STF). Arguição de Descumprimento de Preceito Fundamental 709. Ministro relator Luís Roberto Barroso. Brasília, DF. https://portal.stf.jus.br/processos/detalhe.asp?incidente=5952986. Accessed Feb 23, 2026.

[76] For other cases of the STF in the pandemic, see Lima and Safta (2021).

[77] Godoy et al. (2021), pp. 2177–2178.

[78] Terena (2021).

injunction. The monocratic decision of the rapporteur granted all the requests presented by the APIB, except the request related to the removal of invaders from Indigenous lands, due to the high complexity of the subject.[79] In the decision, requests regarding Indigenous people in isolation and those in recent contact, as well as requests for Indigenous people in general, were granted. Regarding the first group, the creation of sanitary barriers to prevent unauthorized entry into these spaces and the establishment of a situation room were determined[80] to manage actions to combat the pandemic. For the Indigenous population in general, it was determined that the services of the Subsystem of Indigenous Health Care (SasiSUS) should be accessible to all Indigenous villagers, regardless of the homologation status of their lands, and to non-villager Indigenous people when the general Unified Health System was unavailable. Additionally, the creation and monitoring of a COVID-19 coping plan for Brazilian Indigenous peoples, in collaboration with the government and Indigenous communities, was determined.

Despite this outstanding achievement of the Indigenous resistance movement amid one of the greatest global health crises, what was perceived was a constant omission by the Brazilian State prior to this decision of the Supreme Court, as most of the sanitary barriers had been installed by the Indigenous movements themselves.[81] On the other hand, those installed by the government have been implemented without respect for sanitary procedures and without permanence in the Indigenous territories. In addition, there are already findings of the failure of the situation room, which aimed to create an "intercultural dialogue" on isolated Indigenous peoples and those of recent contact.

Despite the imposing character of the ADPF 709 decision for the internal legal system, it was insufficient to ensure the effectiveness and compliance with the decisions deferred in favor of Indigenous peoples by the Brazilian federal government. Only after eight months, the plan to confront COVID-19 was presented by the government, which was not enough to stop the alarming number of Indigenous people who fell victim to the coronavirus.[82] Given that situation, the APIB denounced former President Jair Bolsonaro at the International Criminal Court for the crime of genocide due to his continuous attacks on Indigenous dignity that resulted in actions and omissions.[83]

According to the Rome Statute, the crime of genocide is characterized by any act committed with the intention of destroying, in whole or in part, a national, ethnic,

---

[79] Godoy et al. (2021), p. 2183.

[80] The situation room is provided for in Ordinance no. 4094/18. It is an administrative act of a technical nature, responsible for supporting "the decision-making of managers and the action of local teams in the establishment of contact situations, outbreaks, or epidemics involving isolated Indigenous peoples and recent contact." Joint Ordinance no. 4094, December 20, 2018. Brazil, Ministry of Health; President of Funai. https://www.in.gov.br/materia/-/asset_publisher/Kujrw0TZC2Mb/content/id/57220459. Accessed Feb 23, 2026.

[81] Terena (2022), p. 18.

[82] Terena (2021), p. 153.

[83] APIB (2021).

racial, or religious group. Among these acts are the following: killings of members of groups, serious harm to the mental or physical integrity of members of groups, intentional subjection of the group to conditions of life to cause its total or partial physical destruction, imposition of measures that prevent births in the group, and forced transfers of children from one group to another.

However, the genocide carried out in Brazil against Indigenous peoples materialized differently, as it had a relatively small number of deaths, eventually without the direct involvement of the government and without mass deaths. Furthermore, proving the specific intention to destroy is considerably difficult when faced with government omissions. In the Brazilian case, there is also a cultural aspect in the deaths during the pandemic, which is not captured by the genocide crime in the Rome Statute and therefore may not lead to criminal responsibility. This cultural aspect corresponds to the extermination of the ethnic difference (ethnocide) carried out by the permanence of a conquering Eurocentric ideal in Brazilian politics, where there is no room for Indigenous dignity.

4.7 Concluding Remarks

As observed throughout the present study, human dignity among Brazilian Indigenous peoples has been constantly violated to the detriment of the political and economic interests of governments. This situation was no different in one of the major health crises that has permeated humanity in recent years. The financial, geographic, and demographic vulnerability of Indigenous peoples in relation to the coronavirus has been highlighted by several Brazilian scientific institutions since the beginning of the pandemic. However, this was not enough for the Brazilian government to carry out effective plans to combat the pandemic in Indigenous communities.

In this period, there was a constant scrapping of the institutions for the protection of Indigenous peoples, such as FUNAI and SESAI, which began to carry out policies contrary to Indigenous interests. Among these policies were the reduction in the budget allocated to Indigenous health in the middle of the pandemic and the use of the budget related to the demarcation of Indigenous lands for the compensation of "good faith improvements" made by invaders in traditional territories.

Thus, the existence of an "anti-Indigenous" policy, led by the Brazilian Federal Executive branch, was confirmed and denounced by Indigenous institutions. In this context, it was possible to verify that, throughout the pandemic period, several violations of the dignity of these individuals were committed. Among them, the following stand out: (1) involvement of government agents in the proliferation of the virus; (2) underreporting in the disclosure of the number of Indigenous people killed or contaminated by COVID-19; (3) disrespect for traditional rites and original cultural aspects through institutional racism; (4) the role of agribusiness and slaughterhouses (destroyers of traditional habitats) as conductors of contamination; (5) religious missions in isolated and recently contacted Indigenous communities; (6)

noncompliance with international recommendations for the protection of Indigenous peoples; (7) attempts by the Brazilian government to veto essential provisions for confronting COVID-19; (8) arson in prayer houses; and (9) violent conflicts in traditional territories.

Such violations, as revealed in this study, demonstrate that the Brazilian government has also sought to prioritize the advancement of legislative acts based on the exploitation of Indigenous lands. Government support for the time frame theory reflects how this thesis is directly linked to developmentalist policies that, if approved, can be implemented more quickly and easily because of the possible recognition of the time frame. Therefore, all these actions are part of something that is very well-structured: the "anti-Indigenous" government plan of the former President Jair Messias Bolsonaro. For this chief of the Federal Executive branch, it does not matter that traditional territories are the spaces for the survival of the Indigenous person and culture. The government has thus fulfilled its campaign promise by not demarcating an inch of Indigenous land and by preventing the promotion of effective public policies for this minority group.

Accordingly, it was left to the Indigenous movement, as pointed out in this research, to resist. One of the most notable examples of this occurred in the case of ADPF 709. It was on this occasion that, for the first time in the history of Brazil, its Indigenous peoples addressed the Supreme Court of the country in their own name and had their demands met. Although the government has not met the requirements of the STF, this action reinforced the rupture of these original peoples with a colonial and stereotyped idea of Indigenous identity.

The Brazilian Indigenous population is also composed of lawyers, teachers, politicians, and members of several other professions who are members of society. Former President Jair Bolsonaro even declared in 2020 that "more and more, the native is a human being like us."[84] It is through this conception that the government has carried out its actions directed at Indigenous peoples. If the former president of the country does not recognize the humanity of these people, how can there be respect for the human dignity of the Indigenous person in his administration?

This rhetorical question has also been accompanied by fires in the traditional houses of Indigenous prayers and by the advance of religious missions aimed at achieving the Christian conversion of Indigenous peoples during the pandemic. Several colonial practices still take shape in the Brazilian Democratic State. However, the Federal Constitution of 1988 presents provisions that establish the recognition of the human dignity of Indigenous persons and provide this population, for example, mechanisms that enable them to access the STF to claim their constitutional rights.

Consequently, Indigenous organizations have played a crucial leading role in the claims for the protection of their territory, health, and lives throughout Brazil during the pandemic. The Federal Executive branch was inert during this period, but Indigenous articulations were organized and occupied essential spaces,

---

[84] G1 News (2020).

providing them with subsidies in their fight against the possible genocides underway in the country. All this activism confronts the racist logic imposed on Indigenous peoples, but it does not eliminate it because natives are daily penetrated by this device of power, which is rooted in the most distinguished sectors of Brazilian society.

References

Almeida M (2010) Os índios na história do Brasil. FGV, Rio de Janeiro

APIB (2020) Articulação dos Povos Indígenas do Brasil. Nossa luta é pela vida: COVID-19 e povos indígenas. https://emergenciaindigena.apiboficial.org/files/2020/12/APIB_nossalutaepelavida_v7PT.pdf. Accessed 23 Feb 2026

APIB (2021) Articulação dos Povos Indígenas do Brasil. Dossiê internacional de denúncias dos povos indígenas do Brasil. https://apiboficial.org/files/2021/08/DOSSIE_pt_v3web.pdf. Accessed 23 Feb 2026

Araújo A, Leitão S (2002) Direitos indígenas: avanços e impasses pós-1988. In: Souza Lima A, Barroso-Hoffmann M (eds) Além da tutela: bases para uma nova política indigenista. Contra Capa Livraria, Rio de Janeiro, pp 23–33

Becker S, Oliveira E (2016) Educação e direitos para (in) humanos? Desafios e reflexões sobre os dilemas de LGBT's perante o discurso jurídico Brasileiro. Revista Tempos e Espaços em Educação 9(19):163–180

Brazil (2012) Instituto Brasileiro de Geografia e Estatística (IBGE). Os indígenas no Censo Demográfico 2010: Primeiras considerações com base no quesito cor ou raça. Ministério do Planejamento, Orçamento e Gestão. IBGE. https://indigenas.ibge.gov.br/images/indigenas/estudos/indigena_censo2010.pdf. Accessed 23 Feb 2026

CIMI (2020) Conselho Missionário Indígena. Ignorados pelo Estado, povos indígenas no Amazonas e Roraima contam com solidariedade para enfrentar covid-19. CIMI. Available at: https://cimi.org.br/2020/09/ignorados-pelo-estado-povos-indigenas-no-amazonas-e-roraima-contam-com-solidariedade-para-enfrentar-covid-19/. Accessed 23 Feb 2026

CNV (2014) Comissão Nacional da Verdade. Relatório da Comissão Nacional da Verdade. Volume 2, Text 5: Violações de direitos humanos dos povos indígenas. https://www.gov.br/memorias-reveladas/pt-br/assuntos/comissoes-da-verdade/volume_2_digital.pdf. Accessed 23 Feb 2026

Cunha M (2012) Índios no Brasil: história, direitos e cidadania, 1st edn. Claro Enigma, São Paulo

DIP (2021) Desenvolvimento e Direito dos Povos Indígenas. Research Report: Development and Indigenous Peoples' Law Research Group. https://papers.ssrn.com/sol3/papers.cfm?abstract_id=3833644. Accessed 23 Feb 2026

Feng W (2022) Dignidad humana, personalidad y control de constitucionalidad: ¿normatividad fuerte sin metafísica? UNIVERSITAS. Revista de Filosofía, Derecho y Política 37:2–50

Fernandes P (2016) Povos indígenas, segurança nacional e a Assembleia Nacional Constituinte: as Forças Armadas e o capítulo dos índios da Constituição brasileira de 1988. InSURgência: revista de direitos e movimentos sociais, Brasília 1(2):142–175

Fernandes P (2018) A proteção das terras indígenas no direito internacional: marco temporal, provincianismo, constitucional e produção legal da ilegalidade. In: Carneiro da Cunha M, Barbosa S (eds). Direito dos povos indígenas em disputa. Editora Unesp, São Paulo, pp 139–174

FIOCRUZ (2020) Fundação Oswaldo Cruz. Risco de espalhamento da COVID-19 em populações indígenas: considerações preliminares sobre vulnerabilidade geográfica e sociodemográfica. Rio de Janeiro: Fiocruz/ENSP/PROCC; FGV. https://www.arca.fiocruz.br/handle/icict/40980. Accessed 23 Feb 2026

G1 News (2020). "Cada vez mais, o índio é um ser humano igual a nós," diz Bolsonaro em transmissão nas redes sociais. https://g1.globo.com/politica/noticia/2020/01/24/cada-vez-mais-oindio-e-um-ser-humano-igual-a-nos-diz-bolsonaro-em-transmissao-nas-redes-sociais.ghtml. Accessed 23 Feb 2026

Godoy M, Santana C, Oliveira L (2021) STF, povos indígenas e Sala de Situação: diálogo ilusório. Revista Direito e Práxis 12(3):2174–2205

Gonzaga A (2022) Decolonialismo indígena, 2n edn. Matrioska, São Paulo

Grupioni L (1992) Índios no Brasil. Secretaria da Cultura, São Paulo

INESC (2022) Instituto de Estudos Socioeconômicos. A conta do desmonte: Balanço do orçamento geral da União 2021. https://www.inesc.org.br/wp-content/uploads/2022/04/BalancoOrcamento2021-Inesc-1.pdf. Accessed 23 Feb 2026

Instituto Socioambiental (2022) Situação jurídica das TIs no Brasil hoje. https://pib.socioambiental.org/pt/Situação_jurídica_das_TIs_no_Brasil_hoje. Accessed 23 Feb 2026

Johnson F, Faria L (2020) Pandemias, profecias e autonomias: os Guarani e Kaiowá contra a COVID-19. Cadernos de Campo 29(SUPL):42–52

Kopenawa D, Albert B (2013) The falling sky: Words of a yanomami shaman. Harvard University Press, Cambridge, MA

Kuñangue Aty Guasu; O.K.A. Obervatório Kuñangue Aty Guasu (2022) Intolerância religiosa, racismo religioso e casa Kaiowá e Guarani queimadas. Dourados. https://apiboficial.org/files/2022/03/Relatório_Intolerância-religiosa-racismo-religioso-e-casa-de-rezas-queimadas-em-comunidades-Kaiowá-e-Guarani.pdf. Accessed 23 Feb 2026

Lima A (1992) O Governo dos Índios sob a gestão do SPI. In: Carneiro da Cunha M (ed) História dos Índios no Brasil. Companhia das Letras. Secretaria Municipal da Cultura, FAPESP, São Paulo

Lima J, Safta M (2021) Responses to the COVID-19 pandemic from the Brazilian Supreme Court and Romanian Constitutional Court. Revista de Drept Constitutional 2:29–49

Lopes D (2011) O Movimento Indígena na Assembléia Nacional Constituinte (1984–1988). Dissertation, (Mestrado em História Social do Território), Universidade do Estado do Rio de Janeiro, São Gonçalo

Pacheco de Oliveira J, Freire C (2006) Introdução; Regime dos aldeamentos missionários [1549–1755]. In: A presença indígena na formação do Brasil. DF, Ministério da Educação, Secretaria de Educação Continauda, Alfabetização e Diversidade/Laced, Brasília, pp. 17–68

Resende S (2018) "No que depende de mim, não tem mais demarcação de terras indígena," diz Bolsonaro a TV. Folha de S. Paulo. https://www1.folha.uol.com.br/poder/2018/11/no-que-depender-de-mim-nao-tem-mais-demarcacao-de-terra-indigena-diz-bolsonaro-a-tv.shtml. Accessed 23 Feb 2026

SESAI (2022) Secretaria Especial de Saúde Indígena. Boletim Epidemiológico da SESAI n. 548. https://api.saudeindigena.icict.fiocruz.br/api/core/bitstreams/d48dc4e7-1dd8-4bbb-91e7-607cb36aa3e5/content Accessed 23 Feb 2026

Terena L (2021) Violência contra os povos indígenas no Brasil: aspectos atuais de um genocídio em trâmite. In: Conflitos no Campo Brasil 2020. https://www.cptnacional.org.br/publicacoes-2/destaque/5664-conflitos-no-campo-brasil-2020. Accessed 23 Feb 2026

Terena L (2022) Movimento e resistência indígena no contexto pandêmico brasileiro. Revista Trabalho Necessário 20(41)

Yanomami H, Ye'Kwana A (2022) Yanomami sob ataque: garimpo ilegal na Terra indígena Yanomami e propostas para combatê-lo. https://acervo.socioambiental.org/acervo/documentos/yanomami-sob-ataque-garimpo-ilegal-na-terra-indigena-yanomami-e-propostas-para. Accessed 23 Feb 2026

Chapter 5
Response to Part I: Human Dignity in Times of Crisis: A Contested Concept

Natalina Stamile and Kay Lalor

Abstract This response to the human dignity section explores the intricate relationship between crisis, emergency, and human dignity, particularly in the context of the COVID-19 pandemic. It highlights the contested and complex nature of human dignity, and its foundational status in human rights law, while acknowledging its shifting and difficult-to-define character. The authors emphasize the role of dignity as a tool for negotiating tensions within the legal system, underscoring its institutional function and the multiplicity of interpretations it engenders. The COVID-19 pandemic is portrayed as a magnifying glass that exposes and exacerbates existing societal inequalities, thereby impacting human dignity in various dimensions. The chapters in this section shed light on the implications of the pandemic for human dignity, especially within healthcare settings, and reveal the extent to which the fluidity of dignity becomes most apparent in times of crisis. They also address the transformation of government mechanisms and the subordination of the political by the economic in response to the pandemic, offering critical reflections on the state of exception and the implications for political decisions. Overall, the texts provide a comprehensive examination of the multifaceted nature of human dignity in the face of crisis and emergency.

N. Stamile
Department of Law, University of Brescia, Brescia, Italy
e-mail: natalina.stamile@unibs.it

K. Lalor (✉)
Manchester Law School, Manchester Metropolitan University, Manchester, UK
e-mail: k.lalor@mmu.ac.uk

© The Author(s), under exclusive license to Springer Nature Switzerland AG 2026
J. E. Núñez (ed.), *Perspectives on Crises*,
https://doi.org/10.1007/978-3-032-23836-8_5

5.1 Introduction

The term "crisis" is almost always related to the term "emergency," and further, with the idea of a state of emergency.[1] Thus, the binomial that "spaces of crisis" always require "emergency responses" seems to have become an automatic operation. And if the crisis–emergency binomial refers to phenomena that are difficult to enclose within the tight "mesh" of law, the continuous reference that is made to crisis tells us a lot about the profound transformation of governmental mechanisms and the principles of legitimation of political decisions in the contemporary age. Furthermore, talking about crisis and emergency seems to necessarily involve reflections related to the state of exception without always distinguishing between the two.

Crisis, emergency, exceptionality, in some way announce what has today, in times of pandemic and post-pandemic, become clear: the state of exception has become the rule and the political is subordinated by the economic.[2] In this way, in exploring responses to the COVID-19 pandemic through the lens of healthcare, the chapters in this section acknowledge, reflect, and explore the complex and contested nature of human dignity. They take seriously the way that dignity is challenged with and by moments of crisis.

There is a long legal and academic literature of the complex and contested nature of dignity. The term is fundamental and foundational to the major human rights documents of the post-World War II period. Dignity features in Article 1 of the Universal Declaration of Human Rights:

> All human beings are born free and equal in dignity and rights. They are endowed with reason and conscience and should act towards one another in a spirit of brotherhood.[3]

Dignity and human dignity are also referenced in numerous regional human rights charters, often in relation to protections against the most inhuman forms of treatment. For example, Article 5 of the African Charter on Human and People's Rights holds:

> Every individual shall have the right to the respect of the dignity inherent in a human being and to the recognition of his legal status. All forms of exploitation and degradation of man particularly slavery, slave trade, torture, cruel, inhuman or degrading punishment and treatment shall be prohibited.[4]

The Inter-American Convention on Human Rights references dignity in its protections of the right to humane treatment, freedom from slavery, and the protection of privacy. Similarly, within European Court of Human Rights case law, grave

[1] For more details see Cuono and Gargiulo (2017).

[2] Cossio-Sepúlveda and Giraldo-Urrego (2020).

[3] Universal Declaration of Human Rights (adopted 10 December 1948) UNGA Res 217 A(III) (UDHR) art 1.

[4] African Charter on Human and Peoples' Rights (adopted 27 June 1981, entered into force 21 October 1986) (1982) 21 ILM 58 (African Charter) art 5.

violations of a person's dignity can amount to a breach of Article 3 of the European Convention on Human Rights.[5]

Beyond the Conventions and decisions of national and international courts, it is important to stress that after the Second World War, and especially after the horrors committed by Nazism, the dignity of the person assumed a central role in constitutionalism. For example, the Basic Law for the Federal Republic of Germany (Grundgesetz für die Bundesrepublik Deutschland) of 1949, the Italian Constitution of 1948, and the Constitution of the French Republic of 1946 share the claim to the value of the person as an absolute priority and the firm reaction against totalitarianism. In this context, the marked underlining of the centrality of fundamental rights in the overall constitutional framework is placed above all: fundamental rights referring not to the abstract individual, considered as a mere center of imputation of active and passive legal situations. Thus, as many constitutionalist scholars highlight, these Constitutions express clearly the nexus between person, dignity, and fundamental rights. The dignity of person is recognized to all persons as such, and it is realized because all fundamental rights are attributed and guaranteed. The concept is perceived to be absolute and inviolable, not comparable with other principles or values[6] or as "ideal synthesis of the fundamental values of the constitutional system."[7] Therefore, dignity is identified not only as a supreme, absolute value but also as inviolable, that cannot even be compared with other principles or values.

Yet this foundational status within human rights law often obscures the contested meaning of dignity. It has been referred to as a "loose cannon, open to misinterpretation"[8] or even a "jurisprudential Legoland – to be used in whatever form or shape is required by the demands of the judicial designer."[9] Dignity here takes on a paradoxical character, where it underpins foundational legal values and findings, but itself remains shifting, difficult to define or multiplicitous. For some, this shifting nature amounts to a potential for incoherence. For example, Christopher McCrudden argues that "there are several conceptions of dignity that one can choose from, but one cannot coherently hold all of these conceptions at the same time."[10] This does not, however, lead McCrudden to entirely dismiss dignity, but to emphasize its institutional function, as a concept that allows for local and contextual judicial interpretation and incorporation of human rights: "Dignity appears to become other than impossibly vague only when it is tethered to a coherent community of interpretation."[11] Reva Siegal suggests that McCrudden's account of dignity might be understood as a "court-centered institutional and professional account of digni-

[5] See e.g., MC and another v Romania [2016] ECHR 12060/12; Balazs v Hungary [2015] ECHR 15529/12.

[6] Ferrajoli (2019).

[7] See Silvestri (2009), esp. p. 85.

[8] Gearty (2004), see also Steinmann (2017).

[9] See Steinmann (2017), p. 3.

[10] McCrudden (2008), p. 723.

[11] McCrudden (2008), p. 723.

ty's authority: dignity meets needs of judiciary negotiating tensions of globalization."[12] Dignity here becomes a kind of tool for negotiating the tensions of law. It is foundational to legal texts, but ultimately serves the operation of law, and does not have a singular meaning independent of this legal function.

At this point, it is evident that the concept of human dignity is complex and that talking about it is not an easy task, especially considering that there are numerous (re)definitions sometimes in conflict with each other. Thus, the debate often presents opposing possible views.[13] Some scholars argue that human dignity could be thought of as a useless concept,[14] or a vacuous concept,[15] or a mere rhetorical expression[16] that covers a lack of rationale behind an argument. Human dignity is considered by many to be a thick concept because it seems to be characterized by an invariable semantic content. In this way, it could be possible to define human dignity in relations to other specific fundamental rights or principles. For instance, Ruth Macklin suggests that "it means no more than respect for persons and their autonomy,"[17] while others argue that equality and non-discrimination are the foundation of human dignity;[18] or more generally that human dignity applies particularly to the prohibition of torture.[19]

It is clear, therefore, that the semantic content of the expression of human dignity is varied because of its own dual dimension as a normative concept and as a legal concept.[20] If we assume this distinction, it would be possible to (re)read it through the relationship between liberty and dignity. In this way, we could distinguish at least two different meanings of dignity—these two meanings echo definitions of positive and negative liberty in the form of legal and moral dignity. On the one hand, moral dignity is independent of law. On the other, legal dignity consists of the legal liberty, that is, it implies and it is implied by the legal liberty. In the first case, we have the dignity in the subjective sense which is equivalent to a form of heroism, in the second case we have dignity in the objective sense, as it is what is recognizable within a legal liberal order.[21] In these few short passages, therefore, we can understand how dignity could be characterized as an essentially contested idea[22] and, as a result, comprehend the questions and challenges that addressing human dignity in the context of COVID-19 presented for the authors in this section. From the vantage point of several years after the pandemic, in a world that appears inevitably and

[12] Siegel (2012).

[13] On this respect see for example, d'Avack (2019), pp. 11–22, esp. p. 13.

[14] See Macklin (2003), pp. 1419–1420.

[15] See Bargarić and James (2006).

[16] See Reichlin (2017).

[17] Macklin (2003).

[18] See for example Ferrajoli (2018, 2019).

[19] On this respect see for example Webster (2016); Stamile (2018, 2024).

[20] See Schachter (1983), and also Ferrajoli (2019).

[21] Ferrajoli (2019) esp. pp. 30–31.

[22] Rodriguez (2015).

irreversibly changed, and seemingly trapped in a constant state of crisis and emergency, we might even ask whether dignity remains a useful or meaningful concept. However, as the chapters in this section demonstrate, dignity retains a resonance that is not easily dismissed, despite conflict, contestation, and persistent challenges.

In this sense, the COVID-19 pandemic becomes not only an empirical test of the concept of dignity but also a critical space through which its multiple meanings have been rearticulated, negotiated, and, at times, destabilized. The experience of global crisis revealed that dignity operates simultaneously as a moral ideal, a legal principle, and a social practice—each dimension being exposed, stretched, and sometimes contradicted under the pressures of emergency governance and structural inequality. Far from rendering the concept obsolete, these tensions reaffirm its analytical and normative relevance, precisely because they compel us to confront the disjunctions between theory and lived experience. The chapters in this section engage directly with this dynamic, examining how dignity was invoked, constrained, and transformed across diverse contexts—from healthcare systems and Indigenous rights to ethical and philosophical reflections on vulnerability and responsibility.

5.2 The Chapters

The chapters in this section sit at the tensions inherent to questions of dignity and law. Their focus on the COVID-19 pandemic and human dignity reveals the extent to which the fluidity of dignity, and the nebulous, multiplicitous nature of the concept, is revealed most starkly in times of crisis. Without doubt, the pandemic marks a before and an after. For many, the pandemic exacerbated existing issues just as much as it created new forms of crisis. For this reason, the pandemic has been compared to a "magnifying glass" on our societies.[23] It arose in a situation where injustice was already normal: although we live in constitutionalized contexts, inequality has not stopped growing in recent years, which in turn produces vulnerable people and especially people who are made vulnerable. Thus, dramatically, the panorama that the pandemic offers us is that of a situation of general, structural, and systemic inequality but it also manifests itself in a vertical, horizontal, and intersectional way which also (but not only) involves dignity. For example, the virus starkly exposed existing vectors of inequality and exclusion, existing limitations of decision-making by states and institutions, and existing fractures within frameworks for recognizing and valuing human life. Through the lens of dignity, and with particular reference to healthcare settings, the chapters demonstrate this exacerbation of existing issues clearly. The topics of each chapter differ: Wei Feng and Jingshu Wang explore the different dimensions of dignity that inhere in the right to health, Jairo Lima and Andrei Domingos Fonseca address threats to Indigenous dignity during the COVID-19 pandemic, and José-Antonio Santos writes about the temporalities of

[23] Pozzolo et al. (2021).

dignity and responsibility as an ethical tool of dignity. However, all three chapters are able to use these topics to excavate debates around questions of human dignity that pre-date but were tragically illuminated by the pandemic and to show how the pandemic exposed the inequalities of who is afforded respect for their dignity, particularly in times of crisis. In particular, crosscutting themes of dignity and responsibility, and dignity and inequality, underpin the analysis in the chapters.

5.2.1 Dignity and Responsibility in Times of Crisis

Even in periods not necessarily denoted as crisis, the importance of dignity in healthcare settings is a key concern as a measure of patient care and healthcare ethics.[24] The severe crisis of healthcare resources caused by the pandemic, coupled initially with a lack of methods for properly preventing or treating the virus, recalibrated the question of patient dignity. In their paper, Feng and Wang offer a systematic account of some of the tensions that emerged:

> Here, we could single out at least four groups of tension or collision of rights and values: 1) One can easily encounter the question of whether the right to life as such, and the right to health, enjoy an unconditional preference to any other rights, such as the freedom of travel, religion, and communication. This issue can be called the hierarchy doubt. 2) Can one still claim to experience life and living with dignity, when life involves all kinds of limitations or even living in a persistent vegetative state? This difficulty reveals the naturalistic fallacy between human life and human dignity. 3) How can patients be equally treated when the capacity problem faced by hospitals and medical personnel is alarming? There is also the problem of triage with insufficient life-saving equipment for a rising number of patients. Or, to put the question simply, which patient can be equipped with the ventilator first to keep him- or herself alive? This challenge could be symbolized as the triage dilemma. 4) Finally, given the fast-developing pace of digital technology, can the once negative function of the right to self-determination of information cope with the pandemic, by simply ignoring the significant positive function of data for social reliance, donation, participation, and, finally, solidarity?[25]

Dignity is woven through with questions of *balancing*: of weighing rights and different sets of circumstances against each other to try to reach ethical forms of treatment and practice. These questions of balance are not necessarily new—either to literatures of dignity or to broader questions of human rights. However, by taking their four collisions of rights and values in the context of dignity and healthcare in the COVID-19 pandemic seriously, Feng and Wang are able to engage profoundly and deeply with the different dimensions of human dignity in both a philosophical and practical register.

All three chapters in the section share Feng and Wang's commitment to engaging deeply with the philosophical and practical aspects of dignity in healthcare crises, albeit with different orientations and focuses. Interestingly, within all three papers,

---

[24] Jacobson (2007); Jones (2015); Matiti et al. (2007).

[25] Feng and Wang, Chap. 3, Sect. 3.3, in this volume.

the theme of responsibility and its relationship to dignity also emerges. Questions of responsibility are most clearly theorized in the chapter by Santos, who explores dignity, ethics, and responsibility in healthcare, and in the face of suffering. However, in all three papers, different vectors of the consideration of responsibility emerge. Within the "ethics of *emergency*"[26] of the pandemic, the chapters show the way in which responsibilities are categorized, upheld, and ignored, at a global scale, through the codification of the right to health; at a national scale, in the responsibility of different state bodies for providing healthcare and for protecting a population from pandemics; at an interpersonal scale, in the interactions of healthcare providers and patients; and at the level of the individual, with the theorization of an ethics of responsibility that can underpin individual dignity.

One notable aspect of the intertwinement of responsibility and dignity is the way in which it highlights the relational nature of dignity. Dignity is maintained, understood, and manifested through interactions and through relations with others.[27] In this sense, the malleability of dignity discussed above becomes something very different: dignity is something that is created with and through the other, and through others, and thus its multiplicity is not an indication of conceptual emptiness but of the contextual and relational nature of how dignity is given form.

And this is precisely what we should remember. Life is fragile and the planet is fragile too. In our lives accelerated by rapidly spreading consumerism and capitalism, we had forgotten this fragility and the condition of being human. With COVID-19 and because of COVID-19 we have isolated ourselves to the point of perhaps even feeling afraid of ourselves. But, isolating oneself could also mean thinking about the good of others. That is an expression of the responsibility that gives rise to solidarity toward the other as a mirror of ourselves and not as an enemy to destroy.

5.2.2 *Inequality and Dignity and Vulnerability*

In Chap. 2, Santos writes: "The crisis of the COVID-19 pandemic shows that weakness must be met with responsibility toward the human being in a situation of fragility"[28] and notes the "impossibility of a world without vulnerable subjects in times of pandemic"[29] and that all might be vulnerable or weak at different points in their lives. Although not directly cited in the paper, Santos' exploration of fragility recalls Martha Fineman's vulnerability theory, and her exploration of the "vulnerable legal subject": "a political vision of how the human condition is profoundly shaped by an inherent and constant state of vulnerability across the life-course from

[26] Santos, Chap. 2, Sect. 2.5, in this volume.

[27] See Baer (2009) for further elaboration of dignity as a relational concept with liberty and equality.

[28] Santos, Chap. 2, Sect. 2.1, in this volume.

[29] Santos, Chap. 2, Sect. 2.1, in this volume.

birth until death."[30] This subject sits as a challenge to the traditional legal subject, the "autonomous, independent and fully-functioning adult, who inhabits a world defined by individual, not societal responsibility, where state intervention or regulation is perceived as a violation of his liberty."[31]

The emergency of the COVID-19 pandemic exposes our shared vulnerability, and our vulnerability to grave violations of dignity within healthcare settings. But just because vulnerability is shared, this does not mean that it is shared equally. The resources and relationships through which we are able to navigate situations of vulnerability or seek to secure our human dignity are not equally distributed.[32]

The impact of this inequality within the pandemic has been well documented. For example, writing within the UK context, Sabrina Germain and Adrienne Yong note that,

> it only took six months of a global pandemic to bring to light structural inequalities that have existed for decades. The focus on the higher mortality rate from the virus for men worldwide somewhat eclipses the widening inequalities of gender and race (Flood et al. 2020, 6). Research has shown that ethnic minority and migrant women are disproportionately affected by existing barriers to access to healthcare (Mirza and Sheridan 2003; Jayaweera 2018). These barriers have been generated and embedded by a system that overlooks the intersectional barriers raised by being an ethnic minority and/or a migrant woman (Mirza 1997).[33]

These barriers are discussed at length in the chapter by Lima and Domingos Fonseca where the threat to Indigenous dignity—and the indignity experienced as a result—is discussed at length. For Indigenous people in Brazil (but not only in Brazil), the threat of the COVID-19 pandemic was structural, found within the failure to act of government institutions and the failure to fully acknowledge the extent of the harm caused by the pandemic to Indigenous peoples. But the indignity suffered was also existential—it resulted from ongoing practices of coloniality and othering of Indigenous people, which contribute to their exclusion from the realm of those who can be afforded dignity. The chapter documents the forms of resistance and actions to fight back against "the racist logic imposed on Indigenous peoples,"[34] even in the face of institutional discrimination, silencing, and othering.

In their exploration of Indigenous dignity and resistance to indignity, Lima and Domingos Fonseca excavate a key theme present in all three chapters: that dignity in times of crisis emerges from relational practice and has a strong social dimension. Just as crises exacerbate existing questions of dignity, they also expose new forms of resistance, protection, theorization, and assertion of dignity. As such, the chapters show that crises expose the faultlines and structural weaknesses of our social and

---

[30] Fineman (2015).

[31] Fineman (2015).

[32] See Judith Butler's (2010) writing on precarious and grievable life.

[33] Germain and Yong (2020). See also Keys et al. (2021). For more details about the structural inequalities and the pandemic see also Ribotta (2021); Guaglianone and Stamile (2021).

[34] See Lima and Domingos Fonseca, Chap. 4, Sect. 4.7, in this volume.

political lives but, from these faultlines, new ways of thinking about, and working toward, the protection of dignity emerge.

Despite this, it seems that the question formulated by Judith Butler remains open: they ask "what consequences this pandemic will have for thinking about equality, global interdependence and our obligations toward one another?"[35] Without doubt, on the one hand, we are all similarly exposed to contagion, yet on the other hand, there are several factors that affect some people more than others. So, and after all, the virus *alone* does not discriminate but

> social and economic inequality will make sure that the virus discriminates [...] we humans surely do, formed and animated as we are by the interlocking powers of nationalism, racism, xenophobia, and capitalism. It seems likely that we will come to see in the next year a painful scenario in which some human creatures assert their rights to live at the expense of others, re-inscribing the spurious distinction between grievable and ungrievable lives, that is, those who should be protected against death at all costs and those whose lives are considered not worth safeguarding against illness and death.[36]

References

Baer S (2009) Lecture: dignity, liberty, equality: a fundamental rights triangle of constitutionalism. Univ Toronto Law J 59:417–468

Bargarić M, James A (2006) The vacuous concept of dignity. J Human Rights 5(2):257–270

Butler J (2010) Frames of war: when is life grievable? Verso, New York

Butler J (2020) Capitalism has its limits. https://www.versobooks.com/en-gb/blogs/news/4603-capitalism-has-its-limits. Accessed 17 Dec 2025

Cossio-Sepúlveda DL, Giraldo-Urrego LM (2020) El estado de excepción como norma. Una mirada crítica a propósito de la emergencia generada por la COVID-19. Opinión Jurídica 19(40):277–294

Cuono M, Gargiulo E (2017) Emergenza, crisi, sicurezza. Decisioni extra-ordinarie tra governo centrale e amministrazioni locali. Diritto & Questioni Pubbliche 2:15–36

d'Avack L (2019) Il paradigma dignità: usi etici e giuridici. Rivista di filosofia del diritto 1:11–22

Ferrajoli L (2018) Manifesto per l'uguaglianza. Laterza, Roma-Bari

Ferrajoli L (2019) Dignità e libertà. Rivista di filosofia del diritto 1:23–32

Fineman M (2015) Fineman on vulnerability and law. New Legal Realism: Empirical Law and Society. http://newlegalrealism.org/2015/11/30/fineman-on-vulnerability-and-law/. Accessed 17 Dec 2025

Gearty C (2004) Principles of human rights adjudication. Oxford University Press, Oxford

Germain S, Yong A (2020) COVID-19 highlighting inequalities in access to healthcare in England: a case study of ethnic minority and migrant women. Fem Leg Stud 28:301–310

Guaglianone L, Stamile N (2021) Algunas reflexiones a partir del contexto italiano: Diferencia de género y relaciones de trabajo en épocas de pandemia. In: Pozzolo S, Moreso JJ, Grández PP (eds) Derecho, derechos y pandemia. Palestra editores, Lima, pp 227–273

Jacobson N (2007) Dignity and health: a review. Soc Sci Med 64:292–302

Jones DA (2015) Human dignity in healthcare: a virtue ethics approach. New Bioeth 21:87–97

[35] Butler (2020).

[36] Butler (2020).

Keys C, Nanayakkara G, Onyejekwe C et al (2021) Health inequalities and ethnic vulnerabilities during COVID-19 in the UK: a reflection on the PHE reports. Fem Leg Stud 29:107–118
Macklin R (2003) Dignity is a useless concept (it means no more than respect for persons or their autonomy). Br Med J 327:1419–1420
Matiti M, Cotrel-Gibbons E, Teasdale K (2007) Promoting patient dignity in healthcare settings. Nurs Stand 21(45):46+
McCrudden C (2008) Human dignity and judicial interpretation of human rights. Eur J Int Law 19:655–724
Pozzolo S, Moreso JJ, Grández PP (eds) (2021) Derecho, derechos y pandemia. Palestra editores, Lima
Reichlin M (2017) La discussione sulla dignità nella bioetica contemporanea. BioLaw J 4(2):93–101
Ribotta S (2021) Desigualdad y pobreza en la vida de las mujeres atravesando la pandemia. In: Pozzolo S, Moreso JJ, Grández PP (eds) Derecho, Derechos y Pandemia. Palestra editores, Lima, pp 181–226
Rodriguez P-A (2015) Human dignity as an essentially contested concept. Cambridge Rev Int Aff 28(4):743–756
Schachter O (1983) Human dignity as a normative concept. Am J Int Law 77(4):848–854
Siegel RB (2012) Dignity and sexuality: claims on dignity in transnational debates over abortion and same-sex marriage. Int J Const Law 10:355–379
Silvestri G (2009) Dal potere ai principi. Libertà ed eguaglianza nel costituzionalismo contemporaneo. Laterza, Roma-Bari
Stamile N (2018) La tortura, Ieri, Oggi, Domani (?) In: Santano AC, Meneses Lorenzetto B, Gabardo E (eds) Direitos fundamentais na Nova Ordem Mundial. Íthala, Curitiba, pp 153–176
Stamile N (2024) Into the abyss of evil: Some reflections on torture and human rights. Revista Direitos Fundamentais & Democracia 29(2):221–251
Steinmann A (2017) The core meaning of human dignity. Potchef Electr Law J 19:1–32
Webster E (2016) Interpretation of the prohibition of torture: making sense of 'dignity talk'. Human Rights Rev 17(3):371–390

Part II
Climate Change

Chapter 6
Regulating Greenhouse Gases as Criteria Pollutants in the United States and Brazil

Oswaldo Lucon

Abstract In recent years the world has witnessed pandemics, conflicts, and economic downfalls. Climate change is to a considerable extent behind all these crises, and their increasing frequency and magnitude requires nations to act collaboratively and with greater ambition. Curbing greenhouse gas emissions is a necessity, requiring full implementation of commitments pledged by countries to the UN Convention on Climate Change under the Paris Agreement. Trickling down agreements into local regulations, it will be necessary to consider such gases as pollutants and control them—as with conventional air pollution enforcement. Through a half-century comparison with Brazil, this article describes how the United States is still a global benchmark for climate policies, despite the Supreme Court decision repealing the Clean Air Act. It shows expectations that greenhouse gases should become considered as criteria pollutants by the US Environmental Protection Agency. In particular, the Brazilian attempts to establish such provisions in its own territory can be considered as a means to gauge the effectiveness of the Paris Agreement from grassroots implementation. This study's focus on regulating greenhouse gases certainly applies to many other democratic jurisdictions and opens a reflection on how to ensure that the global mean temperature goals can be achieved.

O. Lucon (✉)
Institute of Energy and Environment (USP-IEE), University of São Paulo, São Paulo, Brazil

Forestry Foundation, São Paulo State Government, São Paulo, Brazil

Mauá Institute of Technology, São Paulo, Brazil
e-mail: olucon@sp.gov.br

© The Author(s), under exclusive license to Springer Nature Switzerland AG 2026
J. E. Núñez (ed.), *Perspectives on Crises*,
https://doi.org/10.1007/978-3-032-23836-8_6

6.1 Introduction

Human-induced climate change has considerable potential to be far-reaching and multidimensional. Literature shows how it is one of the main drivers of pandemics, conflicts, and economic crises.[1] The negotiated and approved Summary for Policymakers of the most recent Intergovernmental Panel on Climate Change (IPCC) report recognizes that net anthropogenic greenhouse gas (GHG) emissions have continued to rise, as have cumulative net CO_2 emissions since 1850, with the average annual GHG emissions during 2010–2019 being higher than in any previous decade.[2] Furthermore, predicted global GHG emissions in 2030 associated with the implementation of Nationally Determined Contributions (NDCs), announced prior to COP26, would make it likely that warming will exceed 1.5 °C during the twenty-first century, and that limiting warming to below 2 °C would then rely on a rapid acceleration of mitigation efforts after 2030. In that sense, climate governance that enables mitigation requires, among other measures, the setting of targets and enhancing regulatory certainty, functions that can be promoted by climate relevant laws.

This chapter will explore the lost track of pollution control applied to GHG emissions by once empowered environmental agencies, emphasizing the cases of the United States and Brazil, two large emitters where climate policies are not consolidated and where there are many parallels, taking as a basis the benchmarks from the US 1970 Clean Air Act,[3] a law that since its beginnings has been adapted to many other jurisdictions worldwide for air pollution command and control. In the early 2010s the North American Environmental Protection Agency (EPA) made efforts to include GHGs as criteria pollutants,[4] creating expectations that countries and subnational governments could soon follow a similar regulatory path and address the threats posed by anthropogenic sources of such gases in a timeframe compatible with the global state of climate emergency.

There were great expectations that the United States, a signatory of the 1992 Climate Change Convention, the 1997 Kyoto Protocol, and the 2015 Paris Agreement, would pave the way for other countries to achieve a well-established global regime. However, this objective was seriously hampered by the failure of the US Congress to ratify the Protocol in 2005[5] and the announcement of the country's withdrawal from the Agreement in 2017.[6] Such facts have induced many political stalemates around the world, affecting the credibility of the United Nations system as a whole. In a populist move mimicking the US, the recently elected Brazilian President Jair Bolsonaro announced that the country would also leave the Paris

---

[1] Birkmann et al. (2022); Cissé et al. (2022); O'Neill et al. (2022).

[2] Shukla et al. (2022a).

[3] US EPA (2015c).

[4] US EPA (2015a).

[5] Bang et al. (2012); Hovi et al. (2012).

[6] Pompeo (2019).

Agreement;[7] while this did not happen, the announcement demonstrates the influence of US politics.

Similarly, many of the creative strategies trying to fill in the gaps in legislation and action were mirrored across the world. The US subnational "We Are Still In" campaign was boosted by regional networks such as the Under2 Coalition.[8] In Brazil, the "We Are Still In" effect held substantial political appeal, but the experience has shown that in this case mimicking the example from the North has brought about limited practical results.[9] The North American Confederation and the South American Federation have very different constitutional aspects, with a far more limited jurisdiction in the latter regarding energy, production and consumption, and financing.

In both countries, emphasis has been given to the promoted voluntary initiatives of federal governments. In the US, these include approaches for gases with high global warming potential (GWP), coalbed methane, methane for oil and gas industry, landfill gas, and other climate protection programs;[10] in Brazil, there have been initiatives for forests[11] and the basic foundations of a carbon market.[12]

6.1.1 Rationale: Urgency

There is little controversy about the urgency of reducing GHG emissions to address the threats posed by global warming. There is already robust scientific evidence, especially from the reports of the IPCC, that the main greenhouse gases (GHGs) released into the atmosphere contribute to the problem of climate change, threatening public health and the well-being of current and future generations.[13] In light of current scientific knowledge, not all risks and potential impacts can be quantified or characterized with uniform metrics; however, existing science quite robustly supports the evident threats of global warming to public health and the well-being of populations. The systematic increase in greenhouse gas concentrations is associated with climate change, with the risks linked with changes in air quality, increases in temperatures, changes in patterns of intensity and frequency of extreme weather events, losses in agriculture affecting the supply of food, dangerous alterations in existing water resources, spread of epidemics, heat islands and phenomena of concentration of local pollutants, and other episodes with serious adverse effects on the

---

[7] Agencia Brasil (2018).

[8] America Is All In (2025); We Are Still In (2025); The Climate Group (2025).

[9] Centro Brasil no Clima (2022).

[10] The respective regulations and standards are as follows: US EPA (2015b, 2015e, 2016a, 2016b, 2016c.

[11] MMA (2022).

[12] Politica por Inteiro (2022); Reis et al. (2022); Philodemos and Scopel (2022).

[13] Masson-Delmotte et al. (2021).

health of large population areas.[14] The negative effects on the economy, society, and ecosystems caused by extreme weather events tend to intensify and become more frequent if effective measures to mitigate greenhouse gas emissions are not taken in the short term.[15] There is thus a pressing need to discipline national production and consumption in relation to an economy that is both competitive and low-carbon.

International law has incorporated such evidence. The provisions adopted by the 2015 Paris Agreement of the United Nations Framework Convention on Climate Change (UNFCCC) consider in particular the national contributions determined by the member countries to reduce their GHG emissions toward the so-called climate neutrality, or "net-zero." Signatory countries must, by the text of the agreement, detail their pledges for achieving the common objective of keeping global mean temperature "well below" 2 °C compared to preindustrial levels. This bottom-up architecture allows each party nation to propose their own strategies, which need to be measurable, reportable, and verifiable (MRV), and submitted to a ratcheting process, taking stock of implementation.[16]

6.1.2 Addressing the Implementation Gap

The NDCs communicated by party countries are recorded in a public registry maintained by the Climate Change Convention Secretariat[17] and tracked by several external sources.[18] Implementation has not been following paths compatible with what was pledged, showing that there might be gaps in terms of appropriate regulation internalizing these commitments.

Mechanisms to reduce GHGs include carbon taxes and/or cap-and-trade systems,[19] but in any case, regulation is a key factor to induce the necessary changes. To enforce targets and timeframes for GHG emission reductions, such gases should exist in the legal systems in a clear and explicit way, with appropriate metrics that both enable a measurable, reportable, and verifiable (MRV) framework at a global level and effective control at the local level. The latter has a crucial element: the recognition of GHGs as pollutants, regulating their emissions.

[14] Pörtner et al. (2022).

[15] Shukla et al. (2022b).

[16] UNFCCC (2022a).

[17] UNFCCC (2022b).

[18] UNEP (2021a); CAT (2022a, 2022b); WRI (2022).

[19] Kosnik (2018); Wood (2018); Stavins, (2019), p. 62.

6.1.3 The Importance of the US Clean Air Act

Undoubtedly one of the most relevant global benchmarks for air pollution control is the US 1970 Clean Air Act.[20] Since its first implementation it has been followed by many countries, improving air quality dramatically around the world.[21] Taking Brazil as an example, legislation in this country started controlling emissions from stationary and mobile sources in 1973, adopting as a basis the EPA's guidelines, particularly the so-called AP-42, Compilation of air emission factors.[22]

As in many other places around the world,[23] Brazil[24] and the US[25] struggle to enforce legislation to control anthropogenic GHG emissions to prevent global warming. Despite their obligations under the UNFCCC's Common but Differentiated Responsibilities and Respective Capabilities (CBDR) Principle, also called differentiation,[26] many barriers persist in both cases, preventing consistent legal countrywide frameworks that could establish sectoral emission reduction targets and timetables.

6.2 United States: From Local Pollutants to Global Warming Precursors

Since the 2014 US Supreme Court decision, several regulatory initiatives have been trying to circumvent direct enforcements of GHG reduction—standards, investments, tax incentives, programs, and support for technology innovation—implemented under various legal authorities.[27] Despite all fragmented efforts, it is difficult to see changes in the regulatory horizon, inducing stalemates in many climate policies throughout the world.

[20] US EPA (2013, 2025a, 2025b).

[21] Gardiner and Theobald (2011), p. 20; UNEP (2021b).

[22] US EPA (2025c).

[23] Eskander et al. (2021).

[24] Rajão et al. (2021), p. 4; Angelo (2022); CAT (2022a); Marengo et al. (2022); Unterstell and Martins (2022), p. 17.

[25] US EPA (2015a); Setzer and Vanhala (2019); CAT (2022b); Franta (2022).

[26] UNFCCC (1992).

[27] US EPA (2015d).

6.2.1 Background: Local Pollutants

The 1970 Clean Air Act is a comprehensive federal law that regulates air emissions from stationary and mobile sources, authorizing the EPA to establish National Ambient Air Quality Standards (NAAQS) to protect public health and public welfare and to regulate emissions of hazardous air pollutants. In December of that year, the United States EPA was created,[28] and since 1972 it has been publishing AP-42, the world's most adopted Compilation of Air Pollutant Emissions Factors.[29] These guidelines are adopted in many places around the world, including the European Community and Brazil.[30]

6.2.2 GHG Emissions Control

The widespread use of AP-42 as a regulatory benchmark has long been expected to evolve to greenhouse gas emissions. In April 2007 the US Supreme Court ruled that GHGs are air pollutants covered by the Clean Air Act and that the EPA may regulate GHGs if they are determined to be a danger to human health.[31] A month later, Presidential Executive Order 13432 required the EPA to use its authority under the Clean Air Act to regulate GHGs from mobile sources, working in coordination with several other federal agencies.[32]

Two years later the EPA issued a report concluding that current and projected levels of six GHGs threaten the health and human welfare of current and future generations.[33] Within the next year, in 2010, the Tailoring Rule limited air permitting guidelines to the largest stationary sources of GHGs.[34] Sources emitting or having the potential to emit GHGs at or above 0.1 million tons per year of carbon dioxide (CO_2) were subject to a 5-stage phase-in of GHG permitting requirements. Such a universe was responsible for nearly 70% of total national stationary source GHG emissions.[35] Standards for mobile sources were also established, pursuant to Section 202 of the Act, while GHGs from stationary sources were controlled under the authority of Part C of Title I of the Act.

---

[28] US EPA (2025a, 2025d).

[29] US EPA (2025c).

[30] EEA (2019); CETESB (2009).

[31] US Department of Justice, 2015. Massachusetts v. EPA, 549 U.S. 497 (2007). https://supreme.justia.com/cases/federal/us/549/497/. Accessed Dec 20, 2025.

[32] Office of the Federal Register (2007).

[33] US EPA (2009).

[34] US EPA, 2011. PSD and Title V permitting guidance for greenhouse gases. Office of Air Quality Planning and Standards, US Environmental Protection Agency. https://www.epa.gov/sites/default/files/2015-07/documents/ghgguid.pdf. Accessed Dec 18, 2025.

[35] Mangino (2010).

A comprehensive authority to address climate change does not exist. The US Congress is still reluctant in terms of adopting GHG targets, policy approaches, and funding. Participation in the Paris Agreement raises many issues concerning the ambition, relative level of effort, and performance of other parties for GHG mitigation, adaptation, technology, financing, and related implications for trade. In 2009, the American Clean Energy and Security Act ("Waxman-Markey") tried to establish an economy-wide cap-and-trade system to reduce GHG emissions, but the Senate did not authorize it. Later, the Obama Administration pursued GHG emissions abatement under existing authorities,[36] an initiative dropped by Obama's successor.

6.2.3 *The Legal Setback*

Many legal actions followed[37] and in 2014 the Utility Air Regulatory Group, a coalition of power companies, argued that the science used by the EPA in deciding the regulations was inaccurate, challenging the legality of the Act in tribunals. A Supreme Court decision ruled that the EPA can regulate greenhouse emissions on large stationary sources of pollution, such as power plants and other large emitters, but cannot overstep its authority on smaller stationary sources.[38] Permits had to return to conventional pollutants and only limit GHG emissions based on the application of Best Available Control Technologies.[39] The problem was both with the threshold (the Clean Air Act imposes specific requirements on stationary sources that potentially emit 250 tons per year of "any air pollutant" or 100 tons per year for certain types of sources) and the substance (the "any air pollutant" language in that section of the law specifically refers to regulated air pollutants, i.e., the conventional ones, not greenhouse emissions, in a discretionary way). GHG control-related information was also limited in 2017, when President Donald Trump restricted the GHG information on the EPA's website,[40] until the restoration in 2021 under President John Biden's administration.[41]

[36] The White House (2013).

[37] Wold et al. (2013).

[38] Utility Air Regulatory Group v. EPA, 573 U.S. 302 (2014). Justia Law. https://supreme.justia.com/cases/federal/us/573/302/. Accessed Aug 9, 2025.

[39] US EPA (2015d).

[40] Mooney and Eilperin (2017).

[41] US EPA (2021d).

6.2.4 Circumventing Strategies

Since the Supreme Court restriction, the EPA has tried to restore the previous command and control approaches in a more fragmented way. Under Executive Order 13990, the EPA is considering rulemaking proposals to address large sources such as transportation, oil and natural gas, and power sectors.[42]

By far the largest category of stationary sources of GHGs in the country, the existing power plants, are still not covered by GHG regulations. The 2015 Clean Power Plan (CPP) was repealed by the Supreme Court in 2016 and by the EPA itself in 2019, being replaced by the Affordable Clean Energy rule (ACE) aiming to restore rule of law through emission guidelines for states to use when developing plans to limit CO_2 at their coal-fired electric generating units.[43] The ACE rule narrowed the interpretation of the CPP to the best systems of emission reduction, based solely on efficiency improvements. In 2021, a federal appellate court vacated and remanded the ACE rule to the EPA, leaving it unclear how it will be applied.[44]

Since 2015, and still in effect, Section 111(b) of the Clean Air Act covers New, Modified, and Reconstructed Electric Utility Generating Units, where the EPA sets New Source Performance Standards (NSPS) for GHG emissions from new fossil fuel-fired utility boilers and natural gas-fired stationary combustion turbines.[45] In 2022, through a draft white paper on controlling GHG emissions from new stationary combustion turbines, the EPA aimed to inform future rulemaking efforts, with a particular focus on natural gas-fired power generating sources.[46] For the oil and gas sector, a proposed rule aims to significantly reduce methane emissions from new sources, while also requiring states to reduce such emissions in their existing sources nationwide.[47] In 2021 the EPA issued a federal plan to control methane in existing municipal solid waste landfill sites, updating old guidelines.[48] The American Innovation and Manufacturing Act 2020 directs the EPA to address hydrofluorocarbons (HFCs), gases with high global warming potentials, by providing new authorities to phase down the production and consumption of listed substances, manage these gases and their substitutes, and facilitate the transition to next-generation

---

[42] US EPA (2021a).

[43] US EPA, 2019. Affordable Clean Energy Rule. https://www.epa.gov/stationary-sources-air-pollution/affordable-clean-energy-rule. Accessed Aug 9, 2025.

[44] Congressional Research Service (2021).

[45] US EPA, 2018. NSPS for GHG emissions from new, modified, and reconstructed electric utility generating units. https://www.epa.gov/stationary-sources-air-pollution/nsps-ghg-emissions-new-modified-and-reconstructed-electric-utility. Accessed Aug 9, 2025.

[46] US EPA (2022).

[47] US EPA (2021b).

[48] Office of the Federal Register, National Archives and Records Administration, 2021. 86 FR 27756 - Federal Plan requirements for municipal solid waste landfills that commenced construction on or before July 17, 2014, and have not been modified or reconstructed since July 17, 2014. https://www.govinfo.gov/app/details/FR-2021-05-21/2021-10109. Accessed Aug 9, 2025.

technologies not relying on HFCs.[49] In 2021 the EPA issued a final rule to phase down production and consumption of HFCs by 85% over the next 15 years.[50]

For mobile sources, the EPA issued federal GHG emissions standards for passenger cars and light trucks for model years (MY) 2023 through 2026—a launch point for the next phase of standards for MY 2027 and beyond.[51] The EPA is planning to initiate a separate rulemaking to establish multi-pollutant emission standards under the Clean Air Act for MY 2027, accelerating the transition toward zero emissions. The EPA also has plans to reduce GHGs from heavy-duty vehicles through new standards in MY 2027 and beyond,[52] including standards to capture market shifts to zero-emission technologies in certain segments of this sector. GHG standards for aircrafts cover airplanes used in commercial aviation and large business jets.[53]

Transportation is the largest source of GHG in the country. In 2010 the EPA promulgated emission standards for automobiles and light trucks. These standards were aligned with other national programs for fuel efficiency, as well as a Californian rule. From 2011, fuel efficiency and GHG standards covered newly manufactured heavy-duty vehicles and engines. In 2020, however, a rule relaxed GHG and fuel economy standards for light-duty vehicles—under protests and court appeals from various states, local governments, and environmental and consumer organizations. The EPA also withdrew a waiver allowing California to set GHG emission standards that were stronger than the national ones.[54]

Supported by the 2005 Energy Policy Act and under the EPA's jurisdiction, the Renewable Fuel Standard Program is a national quota-based policy requiring volumes in order to replace petroleum-based transportation fuels.[55] The Clean Air Act (40 CFR Part 98) provides a rule on data transparency, through which facilities that meet reporting thresholds must report emissions to the program annually. The Greenhouse Gas Reporting Program presents collected data from large GHG

[49] The White House, 2020. 42 USC 7675: American innovation and manufacturing. https://uscode.house.gov/view.xhtml?req=granuleid:USC-prelim-title42-section7675(a)&num=0&edition=prelim. Accessed Aug 9, 2025.

[50] US EPA (2021c).

[51] US EPA, 2021. Final rule to revise existing national GHG emissions standards for passenger cars and light trucks through model year 2026. https://www.epa.gov/regulations-emissions-vehicles-and-engines/final-rule-revise-existing-national-ghg-emissions. Accessed Aug 9, 2025.

[52] US EPA, 2021. Clean Trucks Plan. https://www.epa.gov/regulations-emissions-vehicles-and-engines/clean-trucks-plan. Accessed Aug 9, 2025.

[53] US EPA, 2016. Regulations for Greenhouse Gas Emissions from Aircraft. https://www.epa.gov/regulations-emissions-vehicles-and-engines/regulations-greenhouse-gas-emissions-aircraft. Accessed Aug 9, 2025.

[54] Congressional Research Service (2021).

[55] US EPA, 2015. Regulations and Volume Standards for Renewable Fuel Standards. https://www.epa.gov/renewable-fuel-standard-program/regulations-and-volume-standards-renewable-fuel-standards. Accessed Aug 9, 2025.

emission sources across a range of sectors, and potential emissions from product suppliers through portals such as the EPA FLIGHT.[56]

Recent plans and rules emphasize infrastructure rebuilding and enhanced economic competition. This is the case of the proposed 2022 Inflation Reduction Act,[57] a fiscal reform tackling tax loopholes and increasing tax enforcements, and raising funds for energy security and climate change, potentially abating 40% of CO_2 emissions until 2030, and covering 80% of the Nationally Determined Contribution (NDC) to the 2015 Paris Agreement, under the United States Framework Convention on Climate Change.[58] The NDC pledges to reduce economy-wide net GHG emissions by 50% to 52% below the 2005 level by 2030.[59]

6.2.5 *Subnational Efforts*

A variety of subnational climate policies, measures, and initiatives have been trying to fill in the gap created at the federal level over the last 20 years. There is vast literature on this topic, and new proposals frequently appear.[60] Created after the 2017 withdrawal of the US from the Paris Agreement, the "We Are Still In" movement has gained a lot of support and spotlight, as a beam of hope for the nonfederal leadership in terms of a climate ambition that could be replicated abroad. Also, 24 states joined the US Climate Alliance, pledging to reduce net GHG emissions from their states by at least 50% to 52% below 2005 levels by 2030 and to achieve net-zero GHG emissions no later than 2050. How these governments will achieve these targets without federal action is uncertain, given the limitations of legal authorities and jurisdictions over GHG emissions sources. Mandatory GHG reduction programs have been established since 2009 in 11 states participating in the Regional Greenhouse Gas Initiative (RGGI) and since 2013 in California (together with the Canadian province of Quebec). Vehicle emissions standards were set by California and followed by 14 states (a rule preempted by the Trump Administration). Renewable electricity, low-carbon fuel portfolio standards, and incentives for electric vehicles and/or hybrids reinforce such initiatives.

Actions during the two President Donald Trump administrations (2017–2021, and particularly 2025 to present) have created several regulatory hardships and hence legal precedents for national climate policies. In 2022, these have contributed to set the stage for the Supreme Court's pivotal 2022 ruling in West Virginia v.

[56] EPA Facility Level GHG Emissions Data (n.d.).

[57] US Senate Democrats. Proposed 2022 Inflation Reduction Act. https://www.democrats.senate.gov/imo/media/doc/inflation_reduction_act_of_2022.pdf. Accessed Oct 17, 2025.

[58] Energy Innovation (2022).

[59] UNFCCC NDC Registry (2022).

[60] Congressional Research Service (2021).

EPA,[61] which invoked the "major questions doctrine," holding that agencies must have clear congressional authorization to decide issues of vast "economic and political significance." The Court ruled that the Clean Power Plan's generation-shifting approach represented such a transformative expansion of EPA authority that it required explicit congressional approval, which was lacking.[62] This ruling did not strip the EPA of its authority to regulate GHGs, but it erected a formidable legal barrier against the kind of systemic, flexible mechanisms that many experts argue are necessary for cost-effective decarbonization.

Previously in 2021, a coalition of environmental groups had filed a petition urging the EPA to list GHGs as criteria pollutants and establish NAAQS for CO_2.[63] Following a legal settlement, the EPA was obligated to respond by February 2024; they denied the petition, arguing that the criteria pollutant framework is "ill-suited" for a global pollutant like CO_2 and that its current sector-based approach is more effective.[64] This rationale considered that GHG NAAQS would represent a "major question": CO_2 standards could be interpreted as mandating a fundamental restructuring of the US energy and economic systems, almost certainly triggering a legal challenge that the current Supreme Court would likely resolve against the EPA. Proponents of GHG NAAQS, including members of Congress, argue that it is the most science-driven and comprehensive tool available, compelling nationwide action to achieve a protective atmospheric concentration of CO_2.[65] Yet, the EPA's denial reflects a pragmatic assessment that such a path is currently a legal and political dead end. The debate has shifted from science and policy effectiveness to statutory interpretations and the limits of executive agency power, moving more intensively after year 2025 from a stance of cautious advancement to one of active and systematic dismantlement, pursuing a multi-pronged attack on the foundations of federal climate authority.

Confronting the vast scientific evidence amassed for decades, swift works have been executed in order to roll back previous regulations on vehicle emissions and power plants, replacing them with toothless rules cementing a narrow, ineffectual interpretation of the EPA's Clean Air Act authority.[66] Beyond specific regulations, a profound transformation of the federal bureaucracy explicitly calls for the politicization of the federal workforce, allowing for the firing of thousands of career civil servants and their replacement with political appointees loyal to the

[61] US Supreme Court, 2022. West Virginia v. Environmental Protection Agency, 597 U.S. https://www.supremecourt.gov/opinions/21pdf/20-1530_n758.pdf. Accessed Oct 17, 2025.

[62] US EPA, 2019. Repeal of the Clean Power Plan; Emission Guidelines for Greenhouse Gas Emissions From Existing Electric Utility Generating Units; Revisions to Emission Guidelines Implementing Regulations. 84 FR 32520. June 19, 2019.

[63] Center for Biological Diversity (2023).

[64] US EPA (2024).

[65] Markey and Lee (2023).

[66] Fried (2024).

administration's deregulatory agenda,[67] causing damages that will persist long after the present administration ends.[68]

Faced with a shift in federal policies, many local governments and a substantial part of American society remain committed to climate action, engaging in global climate diplomacy, and representing the US nonfederal perspective at UN climate negotiations. For instance, the "We Are Still In" movement claims to comprise, as of 2025, nearly 4000 leaders representing 159 million people and a collective $9.46 trillion in GDP. Its "We Are Taking Action" campaign encourages members to submit new ambitious climate contributions. Diverse in their scope, these initiatives emphasize renewable energy, efficiency, and better climate policy advocacy.[69]

State legislatures have become the primary architects of present US climate policy. Public corporate disclosure of GHG emissions is being required in several states.[70] At least 10 states have introduced "climate superfund" bills in 2025, charging major fossil fuel emitters for climate damages ("Polluter Pays") and directing the revenues to state-led adaptation and mitigation projects. Proposals also include a "private right of action," empowering residents to sue polluters directly for climate impacts.[71]

Modernizing the electricity grid is considered a priority to many states, focusing on transmission reform to meet rising energy demand and improve reliability. Key policies include promoting grid-enhancing technologies (GETs), reforming siting and permitting processes for new lines, and creating state-level transmission authorities, particularly in Western states without regional grid operators. Also, Just Transition state legislation seeks to establish new environmental justice offices and advisory bodies in Texas, Minnesota, Illinois, Massachusetts, and New York.[72]

Although this patchwork of state regulations represents advances, it also complicates compliance for national businesses, posing challenges in terms of climate policies, harmonization, and robustness. The US climate policy landscape after 2025 is defined by a profound divergence between federal and subnational

---

[67] The Heritage Foundation (2023).

[68] CNote (2024); Compliance and Risks (2025).

[69] We Are Still In (2025).

[70] New York State Senate, 2023. Senate Bill S3456A, Climate Corporate Accountability Act. https://www.nysenate.gov/legislation/bills/2023/S3456. Accessed Oct 17, 2025; Colorado General Assembly, 2025. House Bill 25-1119, Greenhouse Gas Emissions. https://leg.colorado.gov/bills/hb25-1119. Accessed Oct 17, 2025; New Jersey Legislature, 2024. Senate Bill no. 4117, Climate Corporate Data Accountability Act. https://www.njleg.state.nj.us/bill-search/2024/S4117. Accessed Oct 17, 2025; Illinois General Assembly, 2023. House Bill 3673, Climate Corporate Accountability Act. https://www.ilga.gov/legislation/BillStatus.asp?DocNum=3673&GAID=17&DocTypeID=HB&SessionID=112&GA=103. Accessed Oct 17, 2025.

[71] California Legislature, 2023. Senate Bill 260, The Climate Corporate Data Accountability Act. https://leginfo.legislature.ca.gov/faces/billNavClient.xhtml?bill_id=202320240SB260. Accessed Oct 17, 2025; Hawaii State Legislature, 2024. Senate Bill S.B. no. 2505, Relating to Climate Change. https://www.capitol.hawaii.gov/session/orderdocs/sb2505_cd1_.htm. Accessed Oct 17, 2025.

[72] Climate XChange (2025).

ambitions. Future outcomes will likely depend on the ability to maintain momentum, ensure regulatory coherence across states, and withstand potential political and legal challenges from the federal level.

6.3 Brazil: Air Pollution Control

The US 1970 Clean Air Act provided the basis of air pollution control in Brazil, and in practical terms the US EPA is still considered the main reference for enforcement of related sources, despite all the advancements in other jurisdictions such as the European Union.

6.3.1 Early Years: Influences of the Clean Air Act

Since the 1960s, acute episodes of air pollution in the disorderly grown São Paulo Metropolitan Region have raised concerns for controlling black smoke, particulate matter, strong odors, and other emissions released mostly by industries. Discomfort and pressures on emergency medical services led, in the early 1960s, to the creation of a Commission for Control of Water and Air Pollution involving four municipalities around the State Capital (the cities of Santo André, São Bernardo do Campo, São Caetano do Sul, and Mauá). Measurements of pollutants in the atmosphere were restricted to monthly rates of sulfation, settling dust, and corrosivity. In 1972, air quality monitoring data from 14 stations began to be reported daily to the population through press bulletins. In the early 1970s these duties were incorporated into the State Health Department and, in 1975, transferred to São Paulo State Environment Agency (CETESB).

CETESB had been created in 1973, benchmarking the US EPA regulations. Continuous monitoring of air quality and enforcement of pollution control by sources started in 1975 with a program called "Operation White," with intense monitoring activity of industrial atmospheric pollution sources that allowed for a consolidation of emission data. One year later the enactment of Law no. 997/1976 and its regulation approved by Decree no. 8.468/1976 allowed CETESB to implement a program to reduce industrial emissions of particulate matter and sulfur dioxide emissions,[73] heavily based on the AP-42.[74]

The Brazilian federal legislation that regulates the quality of the environment, relating to air pollution, began with 1975 Decree-Law 1413,[75] controlling industrial

[73] CETESB (2022).

[74] US EPA (2025c).

[75] Brazil. Decreto-Lei no 1.413 de 14 de agosto de 1975 (Decree-Law #1413, On Pollution Control Caused by Industrial Sources). https://legislacao.presidencia.gov.br/atos/?tipo=DEL&numero=1413&ano=1975&ato=fc8kXTU5UMnRVT6ff Accessed Aug 9, 2025.

activities. Later, 1980 Law 6803 provided for basic guidelines for industrial zoning in critical areas of pollution, setting rules for location but not addressing specifically emission limits.[76]

6.3.2 The New Constitution

Responding to the pressures resulting from the 1972 Stockholm United Nations Conference on Man and the Environment, the 1981 Law 6938 established the Brazilian National Policy for the Environment.[77] Such pressures came mainly from multilateral financing organizations such as the World Bank and the Inter-American Development Bank, requiring environmental components in feasibility studies of infrastructure and production projects.[78]

Law 6938/1981 defines pollution as the degradation of quality environment resulting from activities that directly or indirectly: (1) harm the health, safety, and well-being of the population; (2) create adverse social and economic conditions; (3) adversely affect the biota; (4) affect the aesthetic or sanitary conditions of the environment; (5) release materials or energy that do not comply with established environmental standards. A polluter is defined as a natural or legal person, in public or private law, responsible, directly or indirectly, for activity causing environmental degradation. Also, Law 6938 gave the National Environmental Council Environment (CONAMA), among others, the competence to establish, privately, norms and national standards for the control of pollution by motor vehicles, aircraft, and vessels, upon hearing the competent ministries, and to establish norms, criteria, and standards related to the control and maintenance of the quality of the environment with a view to the rational use of environmental resources. Based on the powers assigned to it by Law 6938, CONAMA has been establishing, through resolutions, the norms to control the emission of air pollutants from stationary and mobile sources, including the consideration of motor vehicles.

The 1988 Brazilian Federal Constitution incorporated the content of Law 6938 and carried out the division of legislative and administrative powers of the entities of the Federation.[79] It thus establishes, as a common competence of the Union, the States, the Federal District and Municipalities, to protect the environment and combat pollution in any of its forms and determines that it is incumbent upon the Union,

---

[76] Brazil. Lei n 6803 de 2 de julho de 1980 (Law #6803, On basic guidelines for industrial zoning in critically polluted areas). http://www.planalto.gov.br/ccivil_03/leis/l6803.htm. Accessed Aug 9, 2025.

[77] Brazil, 1981. Lei 6938 (Law 6938 On the National Environmental Policy). http://www.planalto.gov.br/ccivil_03/leis/l6938.htm. Accessed Aug 9, 2025.

[78] Pereira (2007).

[79] Constitution of the Federal Republic of Brazil, 1988. Conselho Administrativo de Defesa Econômica. https://www.gov.br/cade/en/content-hubs/legislation/brazilian-constitution/constitution-of-the-federal-republic-of-brazil-1988. Accessed Aug 10, 2022.

the States and the Federal District to legislate concurrently on environmental protection and pollution control, with general rules from the Union. The Constitution treats the environment as a collective right, whose preservation is the duty of the public power and the collective. Right and duty apply to pollution control, and apply to all from present and future generations. Conducts and activities considered harmful to the environment will subject any offenders, whether individuals or legal entities, to criminal and administrative sanctions, irrespective of the obligation to repair the damage caused.

Enforcement is ensured by the 1998 Federal Law 9605.[80] The so-called Environmental Crimes Law provides for criminal and administrative sanctions derived from conduct and activities harmful to the environment, including actions to cause pollution of any nature at such levels as to result in or that could result in harm to human health, or that cause the death of animals or significant destruction of flora. It also includes anyone who fails to adopt, when required by the competent authority, precautionary measures in the event of risk of serious or irreversible environmental damage. The proper definition of pollution, however, does not explicitly cover greenhouse gases. Fearing liabilities under this law is a strong reason for the fierce opposition of many sectors toward enforcing climate law in Brazil.

6.3.3 *GHG as Pollutants in Brazil*

Despite the progress in legislation and enforcement, anthropogenic GHG emissions still represent a form of pollution not yet regulated in Brazil. A legal interpretation derives from the 1988 Federal Constitution, article 225, which considers the environment as a collective good, whose preservation for present and future generations is the duty of public authorities and the community.[81]

The 2006 CONAMA Resolution 382 established maximum limits for the emission of atmospheric pollutants by certain stationary sources,[82] and the 1986 Resolution 18 initiated the Vehicle Air Pollution Control Program,[83] named PROCONVE.[84] In both cases, GHGs were not covered.

---

[80] Brazil, 1998. Lei 9605 (On Penal and Administrative Sanctions Derived from Conducts and Activities Harmful to the Environment). http://www.planalto.gov.br/ccivil_03/leis/l9605.htm. Accessed Aug 9, 2025.

[81] Brazil. Constitution of the Federal Republic of Brazil - 1988, Conselho Administrativo de Defesa Econômica. https://www.gov.br/cade/en/content-hubs/legislation/brazilian-constitution/constitution-of-the-federal-republic-of-brazil-1988. Accessed Aug 10, 2022.

[82] CONAMA. Resolução 382, de 26 de dezembro de 2006. https://www.ibama.gov.br/component/legislacao/?view=legislacao&legislacao=113047. Accessed Aug 10, 2022.

[83] CONAMA. Resolução CONAMA no 18, de 6 de maio de 1986. Dispõe sobre a criação do Programa de Controle de Poluição do Ar por Veículos Automotores—PROCONVE. http://conama.mma.gov.br/?option=com_sisconama&task=arquivo.download&id=41. Accessed Dec 18, 2025.

[84] CONAMA, 2018. Resolução 490. Estabelece a Fase PROCONVE P8 para veículos automotores pesados novos de uso rodoviário. http://conama.mma.gov.br/?option=com_

Circumstances have changed since then. The latest Nationally Determined Contribution submitted by Brazil to the Secretariat of the Climate Convention provides for concrete mitigation and adaptation measures, particularly those of limiting emissions of the six main greenhouse gases. The target for 2035 is a reduction in the range of 59% to 67% compared to 2005 emissions and to a long-term objective to achieve climate neutrality by 2050.[85] Nevertheless, without considering greenhouse gases as pollutants it will be practically impossible to establish the legal restrictions necessary to comply with such commitments, since GHGs in fact still do not exist in the regulatory framework, accentuating the risks of vulnerability of the national economy in the face of threats caused by global warming.

A movement to classify GHGs as air pollutants gained significant momentum from a landmark 2022 ruling by the Federal Supreme Court, which mandated the federal government to reactivate the National Fund on Climate Change and, critically, recognized the "constitutional dimension" of the climate crisis, implicitly reinforcing the legal basis for stringent regulation of GHGs.[86] Building on this judicial momentum, the most significant post-2022 action occurred in March 2023. CONAMA, under the reinstated President Luis Inácio da Silva administration, passed Resolution no. 557. This resolution officially amended the definition of "air pollutants" in the national registry to include "greenhouse gases, substances, and aerosols that contribute to the alteration of the climate system."[87] This administrative act represents a decisive step toward treating GHGs as conventional air pollutants, laying the groundwork for their future regulation under Brazil's air quality standards.

The strategic push for this reclassification has been led by civil society organizations, which argue that this move unlocks more robust regulatory tools. By framing GHGs as air pollutants, they can be integrated directly into the licensing and operation permits for high-emission facilities, such as steel plants and refineries, imposing legally enforceable limits.[88] This approach embeds climate objectives directly

---

sisconama&task=arquivo.download&id=767. Accessed Dec 18, 2025; CONAMA, 2018. Resolução 492. Estabelece as Fases PROCONVE L7 e PROCONVE L8 para veículos automotores leves novos de uso rodoviário. http://conama.mma.gov.br/?option=com_sisconama&task=arquivo.download&id=765. Accessed Dec 18, 2025.

[85] UNFCCC NDC Registry (2025).

[86] Supremo Tribunal Federal (STF), 2022. Arguição de Descumprimento de Preceito Fundamental (ADPF) 760. Relator: Min. Luís Roberto Barroso. Julgamento: 30 de junho de 2022.

[87] CONAMA. Resolução no. 557, de 23 de março de 2023. Diário Oficial da União. https://www.in.gov.br/en/web/dou/-/resolucao-n-557-de-23-de-marco-de-2023-470700055. Accessed Aug 9, 2025.

[88] Brazil Ministry of Science, Technology, Innovations and Communications. Opções transversais para mitigação de emissões de gases de efeito estufa: captura, transporte e armazenamento de carbono, 2017. https://www.gov.br/mcti/pt-br/acompanhe-omcti/cgcl/arquivos/opcoes-de-mitigacao-de-emissoes-de-gee-em-setores-chave/opcoes-transversais-para-mitigacao-de-emissoes-degases-de-efeito-estufa-captura-transporte-e-armazenamento-de-carbono.pdf. Accessed Apr 6, 2026.

into the core of environmental permitting and enforcement, a more direct and potentially more aggressive tool than standalone climate policies.

The present critical phase is the conclusion of the Climate Plan (Plano Clima), with sectoral targets for GHGs measured as CO_2 equivalent, economy wide, and aligned with the NDC by the year 2035 and envisaging net-zero by 2050.[89] It will at a certain phase involve CONAMA for establishing specific National Air Quality Standards for GHGs. The political volatility of Brazilian environmental policy means that the implementation of these standards could be hindered by changes in government or a lack of enforcement capacity. Historically Brazil recognizes the heavy share of land use change in GHG emissions, which in turn drives climate policies and prospects toward the necessary but not sufficient deforestation control, mainly after the landmark carbon neutral year 2050. In all cases, there are no plans for 2060 and beyond. This is a strong reason to acknowledge that presently a very critical phase in policymaking involves CONAMA establishing specific National Air Quality Standards for GHGs, a process that will involve intense negotiation among government agencies, industry, and civil society.

6.3.4 *Circumventing Strategies*

Without legal provisions, no one is compelled to curb emissions of such gases, unless potentially through fragmented judicial decisions. Needless to say, fulfilling the provisions of the NDC depends intrinsically on such regulations. Hence, it is still necessary to have a proposal for a Federal Bill of Law regulating greenhouse gases as pollutants that would cover at least carbon dioxide (CO_2), methane (CH_4), nitrous oxide (N_2O), hydrofluorocarbons (HFCs), perfluorocarbons (PFCs), and sulfur hexafluoride (SF_6).

Setting parameters for the emission of gaseous pollutants and particulate matter from stationary sources began to be carried out through the 1989 CONAMA Resolution 5, which provides for the National Control Program of Air Pollution (PRONAR).[90] Following international standards, PRONAR establishes quality standards according to the uses of the areas considered. Considered a pioneering program in the country, it establishes targets and instruments of action, including the preparation of a national inventory of sources of air pollution and critical areas of pollution.

Two 1990 CONAMA Resolutions, no. 3 and no. 8, complement PRONAR by establishing limits for the concentration of certain air pollutants, based on the World Health Organization guidelines, which take into account concentration limits

[89] MMA (2025).

[90] CONAMA. Resolução no 5, de 15 de junho de 1989. Dispõe sobre o Programa Nacional de Controle da Poluição do Ar—PRONAR. http://conama.mma.gov.br/?option=com_sisconama&task=arquivo.download&id=81. Accessed Dec 18, 2025.

compatible with health and human well-being.[91] Resolution 3 defines standards of air quality based on concentrations of atmospheric pollutants that, if exceeded, could affect the health, safety, and well-being of the population, as well as causing damage to flora and fauna, materials, and the environment in general. It also defines as an atmospheric pollutant any form of matter or energy with intensity and in quantity, concentration, time, or characteristics at odds with the levels established, and that make or may make the air: (1) inappropriate, harmful, or offensive to health; (2) inconvenient to public welfare; (3) harmful to materials, fauna, and flora; (4) harmful to safety, to the use and enjoyment of property, and normal community activities. Pollutants regulated by these resolutions are particulate matter, sulfur dioxide, carbon monoxide, nitrogen dioxide, and tropospheric ozone. From 1986, a series of Resolutions established limits for stationary sources of pollution, covering particulate matter, nitrogen and sulfur oxides, carbon monoxide, lead, fluoride, and ammonia.[92]

Mobile sources such as heavy-duty vehicles (buses and trucks), and commercial and passenger light-duty vehicles (including motorcycles), were first regulated in 1986 by Resolution 18,[93] followed by the 1993 Law 8723,[94] limiting emissions of criteria pollutants (carbon monoxide, hydrocarbons, nitrogen oxides, aldehydes, and particulate matter). Further resolutions updated these limits for more advanced technologies and fuels until recently,[95] still covering conventional, local criteria pollutants.

[91] CONAMA. Resolução no. 3, de 28 de junho de 1990. Diário Oficial da União. https://www.legisweb.com.br/legislacao/?id=100544. Accessed Oct 17, 2025; CONAMA. Resolução no. 8, de 6 de dezembro de 1990. Diário Oficial da União. https://www.legisweb.com.br/legislacao/?id=100549. Accessed Oct 17, 2025.

[92] CONAMA. Resolução 382 de 26 de dezembro de 1986. Estabelece os limites máximos de emissão de poluentes atmosféricos para fontes fixas. http://conama.mma.gov.br/?option=com_sisconama&task=arquivo.download&id=510. Accessed Dec 18, 2025; CONAMA. Resolução 436 de 22 de dezembro de 2011. Estabelece os limites máximos de emissão de poluentes atmosféricos para fontes fixas instaladas ou com pedido de licença de instalação anteriores a 02 de janeiro de 2007. http://conama.mma.gov.br/?option=com_sisconama&task=arquivo.download&id=640. Accessed Dec 18, 2025; CONAMA. Resolução 501 de 21 de outubro de 2021. Altera a Resolução no 382/2006, que estabelece os limites máximos de emissão de poluentes atmosféricos para fontes fixas. http://conama.mma.gov.br/?option=com_sisconama&task=arquivo.download&id=811. Accessed Dec 18, 2025.

[93] CONAMA. Resolução 1. Resolução CONAMA no. 018/1986 - Dispõe sobre a criação do Programa de Controle de Poluição do Ar por Veículos Automotores - PROCONVE. http://conama.mma.gov.br/?option=com_sisconama&task=arquivo.download&id=41. Accessed Dec 18, 2025.

[94] Brazil, 1993. Lei 8723. Dispõe sobre a redução de emissão de poluentes por veículos automotores e dá outras providências. http://www.planalto.gov.br/ccivil_03/leis/l8723.htm. Accessed Aug 11, 2022.

[95] CONAMA, 2018. Resolução 490. Estabelece a Fase PROCONVE P8 para veículos automotores pesados novos de uso rodoviário. http://conama.mma.gov.br/?option=com_sisconama&task=arquivo.download&id=767. Accessed Dec 18, 2025; CONAMA, 2018. Resolução 492. Estabelece as Fases PROCONVE L7 e PROCONVE L8 para veículos automotores leves novos de uso rodoviário. http://conama.mma.gov.br/?option=com_sisconama&task=arquivo.download&id=765. Accessed Dec 18, 2025.

In 2018, a proposal by the State of São Paulo to the Federal Government, based on international regulations,[96] addressed CO_2 in vehicles, measured at the tailpipe. This proposal was opened for public consultation, without being converted into legislation.[97] It was replaced by a program called Rota 2030,[98] established by law and supported by the local industry taking as a basis, instead of tailpipe CO_2 emissions, the cycle covering from well to wheel.[99] With support from the private sector and government, the underlying assumption is loss of competitiveness in Otto cycle bioethanol related to electric vehicles.[100]

Life cycle approaches are deemed by these stakeholders as a good strategy, but they overlook problems related to international alignment and competitiveness with unclear metrics.[101] While the world is converting vehicles to electric, Brazil insists on conventional technologies, which are more inefficient and pollutant. The lifecycle of electricity based on coal is not likely to last, and cleaner power electric vehicles will help in curbing GHGs. Biofuels also perform this task, if flexible fuel vehicles run on these options and not with gasoline—as tends to happen in the real world. Moreover, lifecycle boundaries can be extended, reaching the highly controversial discussions about Indirect Land Use Change (ILUC), by which biofuel production indirectly induces deforestation. The approval section of the IPCC Special Report on Renewable Energy got stuck for 28 hours on the ILUC topic,[102] and the final Summary for Policymakers (SPM) featured sentences such as "the GHG balance may be affected by land use changes and corresponding emissions and removals," "GHG implications related to land management and land use changes in carbon stocks have considerable uncertainties," and stated the following:

> the sustainability of bioenergy, in particular in terms of lifecycle GHG emissions, is influenced by land and biomass resource management practices. Changes in land and forest use or management that, according to a considerable number of studies, could be brought about directly or indirectly by biomass production for use as fuels, power or heat, can decrease or increase terrestrial carbon stocks. The same studies also show that indirect changes in terrestrial carbon stocks have considerable uncertainties, are not directly observable, are complex to model and are difficult to attribute to a single cause. Proper governance of land use, zoning, and choice of biomass production systems are key considerations for policy makers.[103]

Many trade barriers, including future border tax adjustments, consider these aspects.

---

[96] EC (2017).

[97] IBAMA (2018).

[98] Brazil, 2018. Lei 13755. Estabelece requisitos obrigatórios para a comercialização de veículos no Brasil; institui o Programa Rota 2030 - Mobilidade e Logística; dispõe sobre o regime tributário de autopeças não produzidas. http://www.planalto.gov.br/ccivil_03/_Ato2015-2018/2018/Lei/L13755.htm. Accessed Aug 11, 2022.

[99] ANFAVEA (2020).

[100] Abreu (2017); AutoIndústria (2020); Brazilian Ministry of Mines and Energy (2021).

[101] Elgowainy et al. (2016); Moreira et al. (2022).

[102] Edenhofer et al. (2011).

[103] Edenhofer et al. (2011), pp. 18–19, 19, 19–20.

Legislation covering biofuels indirectly acts on GHGs. The most important in this respect are the RenovaBio Program, 2017 Law 13576[104] and the 2019 Decree 9888.[105] The latter explicitly refers to compulsory annual targets for reducing GHG emissions from fuel sales. In practice this is a quota-based Renewable Portfolio Standard, as legislation that rules over the minimum content of ethanol in gasoline, covered by law since 1938,[106] accelerated by the 1975 Proálcool Program,[107] and incorporated in 1993 environmental legislation to control local pollutants,[108] with many other provisions for minimum content in fuel blends, covering not only bioethanol but also biodiesel.

6.3.5 *Subnational Efforts*

Subnational governments, including states and regions, have an active voice in the UNFCCC process, and positive benchmarks can be identified. Notwithstanding, replicating US initiatives to other jurisdictions is not straightforward and several legal restrictions apply, particularly those represented by constitutions, and this is exactly the case of Brazil.

The Brazilian "We Are Still In" motto was adopted by states, more as a political platform than as a proper form of advancing ambition. It was, above all, a protest against setbacks in environmental governance at federal level, particularly those related to soaring deforestation rates in the Amazon region and to limiting participation of civil society in the decision-making processes. An assessment of subnational policies in Brazil shows that limiting GHG emissions at state level practically did not occur, despite attempts to establish targets and time frames in major economies such as São Paulo and Rio de Janeiro.[109] Even considering the limits imposed by the 1988 Constitution for States—such as privative federal ruling in the energy sector,

---

[104] Brazil, 2017. Lei 13576. Dispõe sobre a Política Nacional de Biocombustíveis (RenovaBio). http://www.planalto.gov.br/ccivil_03/_Ato2015-2018/2017/Lei/L13576.htm#art6. Accessed Aug 11, 2022.

[105] Brazil, 2019. Decreto 9888 Dispõe sobre a definição das metas compulsórias anuais de redução de emissões de gases causadores do efeito estufa para a comercialização de combustíveis. http://www.planalto.gov.br/ccivil_03/_Ato2019-2022/2019/Decreto/D9888.htm. Accessed Aug 11, 2022.

[106] Brazil, 1938. Decreto Lei 737. Torna obrigatória a adição de alcool anidro à gasolina produzida no país. https://www2.camara.leg.br/legin/fed/declei/1930-1939/decreto-lei-737-23-setembro-1938-350748-publicacaooriginal-1-pe.html. Accessed Aug 11, 2022.

[107] Brazil, 1975. Decreto 76593. Institui o Programa Nacional do Álcool. https://www2.camara.leg.br/legin/fed/decret/1970-1979/decreto-76593-14-novembro-1975-425253-publicacaooriginal-1-pe.html. Accessed Aug 11, 2022.

[108] Brazil, 1993. Lei 8723. Dispõe sobre a redução de emissão de poluentes por veículos automotores e dá outras providências. https://www.planalto.gov.br/ccivil_03/leis/l8723.htm. Accessed Aug 11, 2022.

[109] Lucon (2021).

finances, production and consumption—activism was mostly restricted to narratives presented at climate change conferences. Countless indirect actions on land use, traffic, economic incentives, voluntary agreements, and others, also intend somehow to circumvent the lack of GHG emission limits in the country.

One of the principles of the National Climate Policy, Law 12187, is to encourage and support the participation of states and municipalities in actions to combat climate change.[110] Some of these federative entities have adopted specific legislation, in general with a strong programmatic content. This has a pedagogical value—characteristic of Brazilian environmental legislation—but lacks objectivity. The following survey analyzes these laws focusing on one of their most important elements: metrics, defined through goals and deadlines. This is probably the most critical point for approval, as it implies responsibilities and demands on the part of society, something well beyond the typical festivity of launch events.

Few federation entities have established these guidelines; Brazil itself took 17 years between the Climate Convention and the Copenhagen COP21 to establish the first legal targets for mitigating emissions, through the 2009 Climate Policy. The limited assumption of subnational goals (as well as implementation of climate neutral pledges) is a good indicator for governors and mayors, who are publicly in favor of national goals but are reluctant to commit within their own jurisdictions. In order to avoid controversy, most legislation mentions attracting business and incentives, without however detailing where these incentives would come from.

An overall assessment of subnational policies in the country starts with the experience of the State of São Paulo, which benchmarked California and the EU to adopt in 2009—six years before the national government—an absolute target to mitigate CO_2.[111] The State also committed in 2021 to a net-zero target by 2050. Enthusiasm in announcements were followed by several barriers to implementation, including non-alignment with federal policies (which subsidized fossil fuels and inefficient vehicles), backlashes from pressure groups, bureaucracy by excess of representatives, effects of the post-2012 economic crisis, and gaps in overall awareness affecting, in the end, political will.[112]

A similar experience comes from the abandoned efforts of the State of Rio de Janeiro, which pledged "real, measurable and verifiable measures to reduce anthropogenic greenhouse gas emissions in its territory, including among other instruments the goals of stabilization or reduction of emissions, sectoral efficiency targets and additional mechanisms for exchanging rights obtained."[113] The Rio de Janeiro law was regulated by a decree, defining a general goal of reducing the intensity of emissions per economic product by 2030 in relation to 2005. Sectoral goals were also established for the 2030 horizon, and these might be reviewed every five years

[110] Brazil, 2009. Lei 12187. Institui a Política Nacional sobre Mudança do Clima - PNMC. http://www.planalto.gov.br/ccivil_03/_ato2007-2010/2009/lei/l12187.htm. Accessed Aug 11, 2022.

[111] Lucon (2021).

[112] Lucon et al. (2022).

[113] Rio de Janeiro (2011). Decree 43.216/2011. Rio de Janeiro State (in Portuguese). Available at https://www.legisweb.com.br/legislacao/?id=159527. Accessed Dec 20, 2025.

through a state climate change plan, which was not established. Sectoral targets are well defined, but for a very distant date (2030 in relation to 2005) without plans or other documents having been presented that demonstrate intermediate steps that justify the real, measurable, and verifiable measures.[114]

The State of Paraíba is, in turn, a case study for copy-and-paste legislation. It has adopted a contrafactual target, reproducing the Brazilian 2009 commitments (Nationally Appropriate Mitigation Measures, or NAMAs) and is based on an undisclosed business-as-usual emissions benchmark. Postponing details is another measure, as in the case of Rio Grande do Sul State, attributing to a future and still not found strategic environmental assessment a promised establishment of GHG emission reductions. The Paraná State is a case of watering down legislation, in which GHG emission reduction targets were initially mentioned, but were later replaced by a voluntary label granted to companies that reduce their emissions by more than 0.5% per year. Minas Gerais State opted for voluntarism, through decrees granting benefits in the environmental license to companies that adhere to a voluntary emission registry. Postponement was also the case of Espírito Santo State, which committed to establishing targets to reduce its emissions by 2025, in a percentage to be defined when the second emissions inventory is consolidated, to be designed in 2012, with a base year in 2010. The inventory was published without setting any target. Finally, in a programmatic way, Mato Grosso and Mato Grosso do Sul States legislations foresaw GHG emission reduction targets, but these have still not been set.[115]

Overall, subnational legislation in Brazil has emphasized credits from the Kyoto Protocol's Clean Development Mechanism, and narratives are now being directed toward climate neutral pledges, with high expectations around the market-driven mechanisms of the Paris Agreement Article 6. Although it remains uncertain how these targets will be attained, there is a very positive factor in the alignment of all these policies around the Brazilian NDC and the Climate Change Convention as a whole.

6.4 Conclusion

The post-2022 developments in the United States and Brazil reveal a shared need for more potent regulatory instruments to combat climate change, despite divergent pathways shaped by distinct political and institutional contexts. In the United States, the path is predominantly judicial and adversarial. Progress is driven by litigation and petitions against a reluctant federal agency, all under the shadow of a skeptical Supreme Court. The EPA's denial of the NAAQS petition reflects a pragmatic

[114] Rio de Janeiro (2011). Decree 43.216/2011. Rio de Janeiro State (in Portuguese). Available at https://www.legisweb.com.br/legislacao/?id=159527. Accessed Dec 20, 2025. See Lucon (2021).

[115] Lucon (2021).

caution, fearing legal reversal and administrative unworkability.[116] The American approach remains incremental, favoring existing Clean Air Act tools over the systemic transformation a CO_2 NAAQS could trigger. Conversely, Brazil has taken a more administrative and proactive route. The 2023 CONAMA resolution, buoyed by a supportive judiciary in the Supreme Federal Court and a reinvigorated federal executive, is trying to move from legal theory to regulatory action, embedding GHGs into its air pollution control lexicon.

Future climate policies depend on the pivotal concept of regulating GHGs as criteria pollutants. Brazil has seized the initiative with a definitive administrative change, while the United States remains locked in a high-stakes legal and policy debate. Both nations demonstrate that existing air quality laws offer a powerful, if contested, vehicle for climate action. The ongoing struggles in both countries will not only determine their own decarbonization trajectories but will also serve as critical case studies for other nations considering how to leverage legacy environmental laws to confront the defining global challenges of human-caused climate change and science-based GHG mitigation levels.

Climate emergency exposes the limitations of "no regrets" programs, which provide gains in efficiency and reputation but are insufficient to meet the necessary, science-based GHG mitigation levels.[117] Despite all the efforts by other countries—particularly those from the European Union— there are great expectations about the outcomes of GHG enforcement and control in the United States.

A breath of hope lies in the Executive Order on protecting public health and the environment and restoring science to tackle the climate crisis,[118] by which all executive departments and agencies must address federal regulations and other past actions in order to confront the climate crisis. It is not clear if the former EPA regulations will be put in place again.

The United States is a mature society, where all the litigation around the Clean Air Act created solid foundations for transformational policies, which can be replicated by other countries. Certainly, reenacting direct GHG reduction rules in the United States can give a necessary impulse to such a movement, as shown in the history of environmental enforcement in Brazil.

References

Abreu RS (2017) Rota 2030 e a importância do Bioetanol. http://pages.cnpem.br/wectbe/wp-content/uploads/sites/83/2017/08/Ricardo_Sim%C3%B5es_de_Abreu_MAHLE.pdf. Accessed 18 Dec 2025

[116] US EPA (2003)

[117] Morgenstern and Pizer (2007).

[118] The White House (2021).

Agencia Brasil (2018) Bolsonaro says Brazil may “quit” Paris Agreement. https://agenciabrasil.ebc.com.br/en/politica/noticia/2018-12/bolsonaro-says-brazil-may-quit-paris-agreement. Accessed 29 Aug 2022

America Is All In (2025) We Are Still In: Home. https://www.wearestillin.com/. Accessed 17 Oct 2025

ANFAVEA (2020) Mobilidade Sustentável de Baixo Carbono. http://www.anfavea.com.br/docs/Release%20MSBC.pdf. Accessed 20 Dec 2025

Angelo C (2022) Brazil continues to violate Paris Agreement with new climate target. OC | Observatório do Clima, 7 April. https://www.oc.eco.br/brasil-segue-violando-acordo-de-paris-com-nova-meta-do-clima/. Accessed 29 Aug 2022

AutoIndústria (2020) Eficiência energética e emissões: Benefícios do Rota 2030 e riscos do Proconve. AutoIndústria, February 6. https://www.autoindustria.com.br/2020/02/06/eficiencia-energetica-e-emissoes-beneficios-do-rota-2030-e-riscos-do-proconve/. Accessed 11 Aug 2022

Bang G, Hovi J, Sprinz DF (2012) US presidents and the failure to ratify multilateral environmental agreements. Climate Policy 12(6):755–763. https://doi.org/10.1080/14693062.2012.699788

Birkmann J et al (2022) Poverty, livelihoods and sustainable development. In: Pörtner H-O et al (eds) Climate Change 2022: Impacts, Adaptation and Vulnerability. Contribution of Working Group II to the Sixth Assessment Report of the Intergovernmental Panel on Climate Change. Cambridge University Press, Cambridge

Brazilian Ministry of Mines and Energy (2021) Combustivel do Futuro. September 3. https://www.epe.gov.br/pt/publicacoes-dados-abertos/publicacoes/combustivel-do-futuro. Accessed 20 Dec 2025

CAT (2022a) Brazil. Climate Action Tracker. https://climateactiontracker.org/countries/brazil/. Accessed 29 Aug 2022

CAT (2022b) USA Climate Action Tracker. https://climateactiontracker.org/countries/usa/. Accessed 29 Aug 2022

Center for Biological Diversity (2023) Lawsuit Seeks List of Polluters Asking Trump for Clean Air Act Exemptions. https://biologicaldiversity.org/w/news/press-releases/lawsuit-seeks-list-of-polluters-asking-trump-for-clean-air-act-exemptions-2025-06-25/. Accessed 9 Aug 2025

Centro Brasil no Clima (2022) Governadores pelo clima. 7 March. https://centrobrasilnoclima.org/governadores-pelo-clima/. Accessed 29 Aug 2022

CETESB (2009) Inventário de Emissões das Fontes Estacionárias do Estado de São Paulo. Manual de Preenchimento. Companhia Ambiental do Estado de São Paulo. https://sistemasinter.cetesb.sp.gov.br/inventariofontes/Manual_de_Preenchimento.pdf. Accessed 29 Aug 2022

CETESB (2022) Qualidade do Ar. https://cetesb.sp.gov.br/ar/. Accessed 2 Aug 2022

Cissé G et al (2022) Health, wellbeing and the changing structure of communities. In: Pörtner H-O et al (eds) Climate Change 2022: Impacts, Adaptation and Vulnerability. Contribution of Working Group II to the Sixth Assessment Report of the Intergovernmental Panel on Climate Change. Cambridge University Press, Cambridge

Climate XChange (2025) Webinar recap: 2025 State climate policy trends and opportunities. https://climate-xchange.org/2025/03/webinar-recap-2025-state-climate-policy-trends-and-opportunities/. Accessed 17 Oct 2025

CNote (2024) Climate Action: The shifting landscape of U.S. climate action: Insights for 2025. https://www.mycnote.com/blog/the-shifting-landscape-of-us-climate-action-insights-for-2025/. Accessed 17 Oct 2025

Compliance & Risks (2025) US state specific climate disclosure regulatory activities in 2025. https://www.complianceandrisks.com/blog/us-state-specific-climate-disclosure-regulatory-activities-in-2025/. Accessed 17 Oct 2025

Congressional Research Service (2021) R46947 U.S. climate change policy. https://crsreports.congress.gov/product/pdf/R/R46947. Accessed 18 Dec 2025

EC (2017) European Commission. Proposal for a Regulation of the European Parliament and of the Council setting emission performance standards for new passenger cars and for new light commercial vehicles as part of the Union's integrated approach to reduce CO2 emissions from light-duty vehicles and amending Regulation (EC) No 715/2007 (recast). https://eur-lex.europa.eu/legal-content/EN/TXT/HTML/?uri=CELEX:52017SC0650&rid=6. Accessed 29 Aug 2022

Edenhofer O, Pichs-Madruga R, Sokona Y et al (2011) Renewable energy sources and climate change mitigation: special report of the intergovernmental panel on climate change. Cambridge University Press, Cambridge

EEA (2019) EMEP/EEA air pollutant emission inventory guidebook—European Environment Agency. https://www.eea.europa.eu/themes/air/air-pollution-sources-1/emep-eea-air-pollutant-emission-inventory-guidebook/emep. Accessed 29 Aug 2022

Elgowainy A et al (2016) Cradle-to-Grave Lifecycle Analysis of U.S. Light Duty Vehicle-Fuel Pathways: A Greenhouse Gas Emissions and Economic Assessment of Current (2015) and Future (2025–2030) Technologies. ANL/ESD-16/7. Argonne National Laboratory. https://doi.org/10.2172/1254857

Energy Innovation (2022) Closing the Emissions Gap Between the IRA and 2030 NDC: Policies to Meet The Moment. https://energyinnovation.org/report/closing-the-emissions-gap-between-the-ira-and-ndc-policies-to-meet-the-moment/. Accessed 17 Oct 2025

EPA Facility Level GHG Emissions Data (n.d.). https://ghgdata.epa.gov/ghgp/main.do. Accessed 9 Aug 2025

Eskander S, Fankhauser S, Setzer J (2021) Global lessons from climate change legislation and litigation. Environ Energy Policy Econ 2:44–82. https://doi.org/10.1086/711306

Franta B (2022) Weaponizing economics: Big oil, economic consultants, and climate policy delay. Environ Polit 31(4):555–575. https://doi.org/10.1080/09644016.2021.1947636

Fried J (2024) What Trump 2.0 could mean for the environment. E&E News, January 16. https://www.eenews.net/articles/what-trump-2-0-could-mean-for-the-environment/. Accessed 9 Aug 2025

Gardiner and Theobald (2011) International construction cost survey. http://www.gardiner.com/assets/files/files/973bd8f7bd7c6f4038153dc47a3705fc26138616/ICCS%202011%20%C2%A3%20Version.pdf. Accessed 29 Aug 2022

Hovi J, Sprinz DF, Bang G (2012) Why the United States did not become a party to the Kyoto Protocol: German, Norwegian, and US perspectives. Eur J Int Relat 18(1):129–150. https://doi.org/10.1177/1354066110380964

IBAMA (2018) Consulta Pública sobre controle de emissões de gases de efeito estufa por veículos automotores novos. IBAMA. https://www.gov.br/ibama/pt-br/assuntos/notas/copy_of_notas/consulta-publica-sobre-controle-de-emissoes-de-gases-de-efeito-estufa-por-veiculos-automotores. Accessed 11 Aug 2022

Kosnik LR (2018) Cap-and-trade versus carbon taxes: which market mechanism gets the most attention? Climatic Change 151(3):605–618. https://doi.org/10.1007/s10584-018-2330-z

Lucon O (2021) Governança multinível climática no Brasil: o papel dos governos subnacionais. In: Rolim MJCP (ed) Pimentel C. Caminhos Jurídicos e Regulatórios para a Descarbonização no Brasil, Forum, pp 191–216

Lucon O, Buchianeri V, Morello S (2022) PEMC 10 anos Política Estadual de Mudanças Climáticas. SIMA. https://smastr16.blob.core.windows.net/home/2022/04/relatorio-pemc-3.pdf. Accessed 18 Dec 2025.

Mangino J (2010) Prevention of Significant Deterioration and Title V Greenhouse Gas Tailoring Rule. US EPA Operating Permits Group Office of Air and Radiation. Presentation, Office of Air Quality Planning and Standards. June. https://archive.epa.gov/apti/video/web/pdf/tailoring.pdf. Accessed 18 Dec 2025

Marengo JA, Jimenez JC, Espinoza J-C et al (2022) Increased climate pressure on the agricultural frontier in the Eastern Amazonia–Cerrado transition zone. Sci Rep 12(1):457. https://doi.org/10.1038/s41598-021-04241-4

Markey EJ, Lee B (2023) Letter to Administrator Michael S. Regan. December 13, 2023. https://www.markey.senate.gov/imo/media/doc/231213_letter_to_epa_re_carbon_naaqs1.pdf. Accessed 9 Aug 2025

Masson-Delmotte V, Zhai P, Pirani A et al. (eds) (2021) Climate Change 2021: The Physical Science Basis. In: Contribution of Working Group I to the Sixth Assessment Report of the Intergovernmental Panel on Climate Change. Cambridge University Press, Cambridge. https://doi.org/10.1017/9781009157896

MMA (2022) Floresta+ Program. REDD+ Brasil. http://redd.mma.gov.br/en/floresta-program. Accessed 29 Aug 2022

MMA (2025) Plano Nacional de Mudança do Clima: Plano de Mitigação. Ministério do Meio Ambiente. https://www.gov.br/mma/pt-br/composicao/smc/plano-clima/plano-clima-mitigacao/plano-clima-mitigacao. Accessed 17 Oct 2025

Mooney C, Eilperin J (2017) EPA website removes climate science site from public view after two decades. Washington Post, 29 April. https://www.washingtonpost.com/news/energy-environment/wp/2017/04/28/epa-website-removes-climate-science-site-from-public-view-after-two-decades/. Accessed 29 Aug 2022

Moreira JR, Pacca SA, Goldemberg J (2022) The reduction of CO2e emissions in the transportation sector: plug-in electric vehicles and biofuels. Renew Sustain Energy Transit 2:100032. https://doi.org/10.1016/j.rset.2022.100032

Morgenstern RD, Pizer WA (eds) (2007) Reality check: the nature and performance of voluntary environmental programs in the United States, Europe, and Japan. Resources for the Future, Washington, DC

O'Neill B, Aalst MV, Ibrahim ZZ et al (2022) Key risks across sectors and regions. In: Pörtner H-O et al (eds) Climate Change 2022: Impacts, Adaptation and Vulnerability. Contribution of Working Group II to the Sixth Assessment Report of the Intergovernmental Panel on Climate Change. Cambridge University Press, Cambridge

Office of the Federal Register (2007) Presidential Documents. Executive Order 13432—Cooperation among agencies in protecting the environment with respect to greenhouse gas emissions from motor vehicles, nonroad vehicles, and nonroad engines. FR Vol. 72, No. 94. https://www.govinfo.gov/content/pkg/FR-2007-05-16/pdf/07-2462.pdf. Accessed 29 Jan 2026

Pereira JDS Jr (2007) Legislação Brasileira sobre Poluição do Ar. Brasília: Câmara dos Deputados. https://bd.camara.leg.br/bd/bitstream/handle/bdcamara/1542/legislacao_poluicao_ar_jose_pereira.pdf. Accessed 2 Aug 2022

Philodemos AB, Scopel CASR (2022) An important step for the Brazilian carbon market – Environmental. Machado Meyer. https://www.machadomeyer.com.br/en/recent-publications/publications/environmental/an-important-step-for-the-brazilian-carbon-market. Accessed 29 Aug 2022

Politica por Inteiro (2022) Carbon: a Decree by the Brazilian government is out, but not the market. May 20. https://www.politicaporinteiro.org/2022/05/20/carbon-the-decree-is-out-but-not-the-market/. Accessed 29 Aug 2022

Pompeo MR (2019) On the U.S. Withdrawal from the Paris Agreement. United States Department of State, November 4. https://2017-2021.state.gov/on-the-u-s-withdrawal-from-the-paris-agreement/. Accessed 29 Aug 2022

Pörtner H-O et al (eds) (2022) Climate change 2022: Impacts, adaptation and vulnerability. In: Contribution of Working Group II to the Sixth Assessment Report of the Intergovernmental Panel on Climate Change. Cambridge University Press, Cambridge.

Rajão R, Rochedo P, Davis J et al. (2021) Brazil's new climate target backtracks and allows an increase in deforestation. CSR. https://csr.ufmg.br/csr/wp-content/uploads/2021/04/Rajao_21_Brazil_NDC_Backtracking_FINAL.pdf. Accessed 29 Aug 2022

Reis A, Lugao F, Pimentel L (2022) Brazil's government establishes parameters for a regulated carbon market. Mattos Filho. https://www.mattosfilho.com.br/en/unico/brazils-parameters-carbon-market/. Accessed 29 Aug 2022

Setzer J, Vanhala LC (2019) Climate change litigation: A review of research on courts and litigants in climate governance. WIREs Climate Change 10(3):e580. https://doi.org/10.1002/wcc.580

Shukla P, Skea J, Reisinger A (2022a) Climate Change 2022. Mitigation of Climate Change. Working Group III Contribution to the Sixth Assessment Report of the Intergovernmental

Panel on Climate Change. Summary for Policymakers. Intergovernmental Panel on Climate Change. https://www.ipcc.ch/report/ar6/wg3/downloads/report/IPCC_AR6_WGIII_SPM.pdf. Accessed 23 Feb 2026

Shukla P, Skea J, Slade R et al. (2022b) Climate Change 2022: Mitigation of Climate Change. Contribution of Working Group III to the Sixth Assessment Report of the Intergovernmental Panel on Climate Change. IPCC. https://www.ipcc.ch/report/ar6/wg3/. Accessed 29 Aug 2022

Stavins RN (2019) Carbon Taxes vs. Cap and Trade: Theory and Practice. Discussion Paper ES 2019-9. https://www.enelfoundation.org/content/dam/enel-foundation/topics/2019/11/heep/Stavins%20HPCA-Enel%20Found%202019%20paper%20191104.pdf. Accessed 29 Aug 2022

The Climate Group (2025) Under2 Coalition, Climate Group. https://www.theclimategroup.org/under2-coalition. Accessed 17 Oct 2025

The Heritage Foundation (2023) Project 2025: Mandate for Leadership. Washington, DC. https://www.project2025.org/. Accessed 9 Aug 2025

The White House (2013) Remarks by the President in the State of the Union Address. https://obamawhitehouse.archives.gov/the-press-office/2013/02/12/remarks-President-state-union-address. Accessed 11 Aug 2022

The White House (2021) Executive Order on protecting public health and the environment and restoring science to tackle the climate crisis. https://bidenwhitehouse.archives.gov/briefing-room/presidential-actions/2021/01/20/executive-order-protecting-public-health-and-environment-and-restoring-science-to-tackle-climate-crisis/. Accessed 9 Aug 2025

UNEP (2021a) Emissions Gap Report 2021, UNEP - UN Environment Programme. http://www.unep.org/resources/emissions-gap-report-2021. Accessed 29 Aug 2022

UNEP (2021b) Regulating Air Quality: The First Global Assessment of Air Pollution Legislation, UNEP - UN Environment Programme. http://www.unep.org/resources/report/regulating-air-quality-first-global-assessment-air-pollution-legislation. Accessed 29 Aug 2022

UNFCCC (1992) Convention documents. https://unfccc.int/process-and-meetings/the-convention/history-of-the-convention/convention-documents. Accessed 11 Aug 2022

UNFCCC (2022a) Global Stocktake. https://unfccc.int/topics/global-stocktake/global-stocktake. Accessed 29 Aug 2022

UNFCCC (2022b) Nationally Determined Contributions Registry. https://unfccc.int/NDCREG. Accessed 29 Aug 2022

UNFCCC NDC Registry (2022) United States of America Nationally Determined Contribution. https://unfccc.int/NDCREG. Accessed 17 Oct 2025

UNFCCC NDC Registry (2025) Federative Republic of Brazil. Paris Agreement Nationally Determined Contribution (NDC). Brasília, November 13, 2024. https://unfccc.int/sites/default/files/2024-11/Brazil_Second%20Nationally%20Determined%20Contribution%20%28NDC%29_November2024.pdf. Accessed 9 Aug 2025

Unterstell N, Martins N (2022) NDC: Analysis of the 2022 update submitted by the Government of Brazil. Politicaporinteiro. https://www.politicaporinteiro.org/wp-content/uploads/2022/04/Brazils-NDC-2022-analysis_V0.pdf. Accessed 29 Aug 2022

US EPA (2003) EPA Denies Petition to Regulate Greenhouse Gas Emissions from Motor Vehicles. https://www.epa.gov/archive/epapages/newsroom_archive/newsreleases/694c8f3b7c16ff6085256d900065fdad.html/. Accessed 17 Oct 2025

US EPA (2009) Endangerment and cause or contribute findings for greenhouse gases under Section 202(a) of the Clean Air Act: EPA's Response to public comments. Volume 9: The endangerment finding. Washington DC: US Environmental Protection Agency Office of Atmospheric Programs. https://www.epa.gov/sites/default/files/2021-05/documents/rtc_volume_9.pdf. Accessed 29 Jan 2026

US EPA (2013) Summary of the Clean Air Act. https://www.epa.gov/laws-regulations/summary-clean-air-act. Accessed 2 Aug 2022

US EPA (2015a) Clean Air Act Permitting for Greenhouse Gases. https://www.epa.gov/nsr/clean-air-act-permitting-greenhouse-gases. Accessed 29 Aug 2022

US EPA (2015b) Coalbed Methane Outreach Program (CMOP). https://www.epa.gov/cmop. Accessed 29 Aug 2022
US EPA (2015c) Evolution of the Clean Air Act. https://www.epa.gov/clean-air-act-overview/evolution-clean-air-act. Accessed 29 Aug 2022
US EPA (2015d) Next steps and preliminary views on the application of Clean Air Act permitting programs to greenhouse gases following the Supreme Court's decision in Utility Air Regulatory Group v. Environmental Protection Agency. https://www.epa.gov/nsr/next-steps-and-preliminary-views-application-clean-air-act-permitting-programs-greenhouse-gases. Accessed 9 Aug 2025
US EPA (2015e) Progress Cleaning the Air: Voluntary Partnership Program Accomplishments. https://www.epa.gov/clean-air-act-overview/progress-cleaning-air-voluntary-partnership-program-accomplishments. Accessed 29 Aug 2022
US EPA (2016a) EPA's Voluntary Methane Programs for the Oil and Natural Gas Industry. https://www.epa.gov/natural-gas-star-program. Accessed 29 Aug 2022
US EPA (2016b) Landfill Methane Outreach Program (LMOP). Available at: https://www.epa.gov/lmop. Accessed 29 Aug 2022
US EPA (2016c) Voluntary Programs. High GWP Gases. Climate Change. https://www3.epa.gov/climatechange/highgwp/voluntary.html. Accessed 29 Aug 2022
US EPA (2021a) Climate change regulatory actions and initiatives. https://www.epa.gov/climate-change/climate-change-regulatory-actions-and-initiatives. Accessed 9 Aug 2025
US EPA (2021b) EPA proposes new source performance standards updates, emissions guidelines to reduce methane and other harmful pollution from the oil and natural gas industry. https://www.epa.gov/controlling-air-pollution-oil-and-natural-gas-industry/epa-proposes-new-source-performance. Accessed 9 Aug 2025
US EPA (2021c) Final rule - Phasedown of hydrofluorocarbons: Establishing the allowance allocation and trading program under the AIM Act. https://www.epa.gov/climate-hfcs-reduction/final-rule-phasedown-hydrofluorocarbons-establishing-allowance-allocation. Accessed 9 Aug 2025
US EPA (2021d) EPA Reboots Climate Change Website. https://www.epa.gov/newsreleases/epa-reboots-climate-change-website. Accessed 29 Aug 2022
US EPA (2022) White Paper: Available and emerging technologies for reducing greenhouse gas emissions from combustion turbine electric generating units. https://www.epa.gov/stationary-sources-air-pollution/white-paper-available-and-emerging-technologies-reducing. Accessed 9 Aug 2025
US EPA (2024) EPA response to petition for rulemaking to list greenhouse gases as criteria air pollutants and set national ambient air quality standards for greenhouse gases. February 2. https://www.epa.gov/system/files/documents/2024-02/ghg-naaqs-petition-response-2024.pdf. Accessed 9 Aug 2025
US EPA (2025a) The origins of EPA. https://www.epa.gov/history/origins-epa. Accessed 20 Dec 2025
US EPA (2025b) Clean Air Act Overview. https://www.epa.gov/clean-air-act-overview. Accessed 20 Dec 2025
US EPA (2025c) AP-42: Compilation of air emissions factors. https://www.epa.gov/air-emissions-factors-and-quantification/ap-42-compilation-air-emissions-factors-stationary-sources. Accessed 20 Dec 2025
US EPA (2025d) Clean Air Act Requirements and History. US EPA, Washington, DC. https://www.epa.gov/clean-air-act-overview/clean-air-act-requirements-and-history. Accessed 26 Jan 2026
We Are Still In (2025) 'We Are Still In' coalition launches campaign to drive wave of local climate action to deliver on America's pledge. https://www.wearestillin.com/news/we-are-still-coalition-launches-campaign-drive-wave-local-climate-action-deliver-americas. Accessed 17 Oct 2025
Wold C, Hunter D, Powers M (2013) Climate change and the law, 2nd edn. LexisNexis, New Providence, NJ

Wood J (2018) The Pros and Cons of Carbon Taxes and Cap-and-Trade Systems. The School of Public Policy Publications 11(30). Available via SSRN. https://papers.ssrn.com/abstract=3289810. Accessed 29 Aug 2022

WRI (2022) Climate Watch Data. World Resources Institute. https://www.climatewatchdata.org/. Accessed 29 Aug 2022

Chapter 7
BRICS Response to Climate Governance Crisis in Pandemic Times

Douglas de Castro and Danielle Mendes Thame Denny

Abstract This chapter investigates the BRICS (Brazil, Russia, India, China, and South Africa) coalition's response to the dual crises of climate change and the COVID-19 pandemic. Utilizing a constructivist framework and content analysis via Voyant Tools, the study examines joint declarations from 2017 to 2021 to assess the group's institutional governance capacity. The analysis reveals that despite the existential threat posed by climate change, the BRICS' institutional response remains "highly insufficient," primarily due to a developmental model heavily reliant on intensive land use, forestry, and extractivist projects. The COVID-19 pandemic acted as an intervening variable, exacerbating existing vulnerabilities in the Global South and shifting political priorities toward immediate national interests and economic recovery. Through its constitutional integration of "ecological civilization" and the promotion of a green Belt and Road Initiative, China is increasingly acting as an agenda-setter for a new model of sustainable development within the bloc. The chapter concludes that the BRICS platform currently lacks the institutional learning and steering capacity necessary for concerted climate policy. It argues for a transition from non-binding soft law toward more robust, binding cooperation mechanisms that integrate multi-hazard risk assessments and prioritize an ecological transition over traditional, asymmetric economic growth.

D. de Castro
Lanzhou University, Lanzhou, Gansu, China

D. M. T. Denny (✉)
Research Centre for Greenhouse Gas Innovation, University of São Paulo (USP), Luiz de Queiroz College of Agriculture (Esalq), Piracicaba, Brazil

© The Author(s), under exclusive license to Springer Nature Switzerland AG 2026
J. E. Núñez (ed.), *Perspectives on Crises*,
https://doi.org/10.1007/978-3-032-23836-8_7

7.1 Introduction

In the fictional yet based on reality book *The collapse of Western civilization*, Oreskes and Conway provided a clear picture of the nature of things regarding climate change.[1] The authors tell how Western civilization approached the climate crisis that ultimately led to an irreversible and unpleasant state of events for humankind. The book is divided into three parts: "The coming of the Penumbral Age" (the state of denial that climate change is a "real" problem); "The frenzy of fossil fuels" (consumption is not the problem); and "Market failure" (there is no limitation for capitalism, as the end of history[2] has already shown). In the epilogue, the authors present the only country that had the chance to survive the "Great Collapse": China. The logic behind the country's success in resisting climate change is explained by the steps taken to liberalize the economy while retaining the centralization of the government and politics, which enables planning for the long term.

Although a piece of fiction, Oreskes and Conway's text somehow reflects the debates and actions toward the climate change crisis faced by humankind. Despite the robust scientific knowledge and accumulated empirical evidence,[3] the international community has not been able to provide appropriate responses through multilateral institutions. *Au contraire*, there has been a high degree of apathy and back-and-forth stances observed in international law and the Conference of the Parties (COP), thus increasing the inequality between developed and developing countries, with the latter being more exposed to the harmful effects of climate change and distant from the desired goals of sustainable development. Note that the emergence of the pandemic and the election of ultra-nationalist governments around the globe contribute to the lack of results of the international climate regime since they demote the issue to the low-politics realm of the states, and thus, a secondary target. The focus is isolationism (i.e., "make America great again") and not coordinated multilateral global responses to pressing crises.

The pandemic outbreak in 2020 has exacerbated the inequalities among developed and developing countries, thus acting as a catalytic factor to decrease international solidarity on many fronts.[4] It put pressure on the international climate regime, which is already suffering from an unjustifiable apathy considering the existential threat that climate change, pollution, and biodiversity loss[5] represent to humankind.[6] In addition, the social distortions brought by the pandemic, plus the vulnerability and lack of resources for adaptation to climate change, represent a threat to international security. For example, adaptation is one of the major problems for developing countries as it requires pattern changes that demand high sources of

---

[1] Oreskes and Conway (2014).

[2] Fukuyama (2006).

[3] IPCC IP on CC (2022).

[4] Denny et al. (2021).

[5] UNFCCC (2022).

[6] Manzanedo and Manning (2020).

financing and technology, capacity building, and urgency, which in times of pandemic and post-pandemic become harder to obtain.[7]

In an article published in 2005, the now well-known Anthony Fauci argued that infectious diseases like COVID-19 are intrinsically connected to humankind, and therefore destined to emerge and re-emerge from time to time.[8] The primary factors for the emergence of viruses are economic development and land-use change, human demographics and behavior, international travel, and trade. All of these factors are at the core of the struggle that developing countries face in the international system, with the by-products, to name a few, of environmental degradation and the potential for the appearance of new kinds of threats, as we observed in the COVID-19 case. Thus, combining the existing climate change crisis and the COVID-19 outbreak brought the countries to primarily attend to their own national interest.

Is there an option, especially for developing countries, to overcome the limitation of international institutions on addressing climate change, while achieving sustainable development and dealing with the pandemic or recovering from it? This was one question that oriented a series of virtual roundtables in 2020, in the face of the pandemic.

The international order created in the post-war era built a stronghold of resistance in the developing countries vis-à-vis the developed ones. The ghosts of colonialism under new and disguised forms[9] have been detected by developing countries that shared experiences and perceptions about the imposed development model. The Bandung Conference in 1955[10] set the tone for the resistance of the Global South based on ideational factors that create a collective identity and shape alliances beyond the material dimension. It emerged as an alignment movement that recognized the vulnerability of developing countries in confronting their challenges, especially considering those countries demanding collective action to which they have barely contributed, such as in the case of climate change.

The constructivist approach[11] to interstate relations argues that ideas, values, and shared experiences are central variables for understanding how states interact. Unlike materialist perspectives, which prioritize economic or military power, constructivism emphasizes that identity, social norms, and the construction of meaning shape both cooperation and conflict. In the context of the Global South, this perspective is particularly significant.[12] Countries across Asia, Africa, and Latin America, while heterogeneous, share historical legacies of colonialism, experiences of peripheral development, and common aspirations for political and economic autonomy. These symbolic and historical dimensions underpin practices of

[7] Mertz et al. (2009).

[8] Fauci (2005).

[9] Dehm (2016).

[10] Appadorai (1955).

[11] Wendt (1999).

[12] Castro and Denny (2020).

solidarity, discourses of resistance, and the building of alliances in multilateral forums such as the following:

(1) Group of 77 (G77), a coalition of developing countries established in 1964 within the framework of the United Nations. It was created to promote collective economic interests and strengthen negotiating capacity on major international issues. Today, it has expanded to more than 130 member states, making it the largest intergovernmental organization of developing countries in the UN system.
(2) Community of Latin American and Caribbean States (CELAC), founded in 2010, is a regional bloc that unites 33 countries from Latin America and the Caribbean, aiming to promote political dialogue, integration, and cooperation among its members while reducing dependence on extra-regional forums such as the Organization of American States (OAS). It functions as a voice for the region in global affairs, particularly on issues of development, climate, and trade.
(3) The object of this paper, the BRICS (Brazil, Russia, India, China, and South Africa) coalition that brings together five major emerging economies that represent significant shares of global population, GDP, and trade. Established in the mid-2000s, it serves as a platform for cooperation in political, economic, and security matters. The bloc seeks to reform global governance institutions and to enhance South–South cooperation, often presenting itself as a counterbalance to Western-led frameworks. As of January 2025, the BRICS includes 11 countries: Brazil, China, Egypt, Ethiopia, India, Indonesia, Iran, Russia, Saudi Arabia, South Africa, and the United Arab Emirates.[13]

Relations among Global South countries, therefore, cannot be reduced to immediate material interests. They are also structured by shared narratives of justice, self-determination, and recognition, which inform strategies of technical cooperation, regional integration initiatives, and joint positions in international negotiations. The constructivist lens thus provides essential analytical tools to explain why and how Global South states seek to articulate themselves collectively in terms of identity, legitimacy, and shared values, while still confronting structural challenges of inequality and dependence.[14]

This chapter is a product of the abovementioned set of roundtables looking for the best responses to crises and argues that the existing ideational dimension in the relationship between developing countries should play an essential role in the climate change regime, bringing opportunities to increase the regime's effectiveness within the BRICS. Moreover, the countries' shared perceptions, expectations, and experiences about development might be a challenge that at the same time contributes to addressing the evolving bulk of actions and solutions to climate change while dealing with the effects of COVID-19.

[13] Toronto ICB (2025).

[14] Castro and Denny (2020).

This study treats COVID-19 as an intervening variable that exaggerates the lack of international institutional response to collective action problems that leaves developing countries vulnerable[15] due to a lack of appropriate financing and technology transfer, both essential to mitigation and adaptation.[16] In addition to this introduction and the final remarks, the second part will summarize the methodology of building knowledge to instrument this chapter; then there will be some explanations about the use of BRICS as a case study; and a discussion will follow on the many possibilities of its role in tackling climate change.

7.2 Methodological Considerations

This chapter results from a consistent and long process of collaborative research that followed the format of 10 roundtables and was initiated in the year 2020. A group of transdisciplinary experts on climate change from different countries around the world held virtual meetings to explore the particularities that the pandemic brought to the subject. The main conclusion was that there are more similarities than differences between the two global threats (climate change and coronavirus). Long before the COVID-19 outbreak, most of the main problems and challenges were already there, but they were made more blatant with the health crisis. Both require multistakeholder collaboration and global efforts. In contrast, efforts to tackle climate change still lack the urgency it deserves; if correctly designed, public policies to face the sanitary emergency can bring permanent benefits to the climate and inspire better policy designs, more focused on people and the environment, and less on profits.

The pandemic transformed the terms on which discussions on climate change were being held, but questions remain: what is different, what are the new challenges, how can we deal with this new scenario, and what are the pitfalls of the existing regimes? Can we point out examples of new rules, policies, and regulations? Despite the temporary reduction in daily global greenhouse gas emissions (GHGs) during the COVID-19 crisis, lockdowns and isolation-related falls in emissions have not reduced the concentration of GHGs in the atmosphere. Production, distribution, and consumption patterns must change to support climate action and prevent other pandemics. International economics shows, though, that the challenge will be even more significant than it is to overcome the crises with sustainability, because of some new challenges, such as the low price of oil, the digital rights crises, and the human vulnerabilities impacting readiness and resilience to tackle problems. Some policies and practices can respond to such new challenges.

Climate litigation and the transnational enforcement of environmental law are possibilities. Another option is the green new deal policies that are emerging as

[15] Walker et al. (2020).

[16] VijayaVenkataRaman et al. (2012).

fiscal recovery packages conditioned to sustainability; they can entrench or partly displace the current fossil fuel-intensive economic system in the long term. Another possibility is implementing carbon taxes and permits used in "cap and trade" schemes; nowadays, the vast majority of carbon emissions are unpriced. There are also opportunities to foment voluntary sustainability standards, environmental sustainability governance certifications, and corporate responsibility. However, there are some difficulties in implementing such alternatives, like the lack of legally binding commitments internationally, international bureaucracies, the creation of costs and deadlocks, the complex architecture of global governance, and a hard-to-achieve and maintain orchestration of power through local actions, paradiplomacy, and multistakeholder engagement to overcome national government shifts.

Some examples of new rules, policies, regulations, and litigation that have been put in place, such as China's green Belt and Road Initiative and the tendency to pass security emergency laws, put the environment into the realm of security and infrastructure diplomacy. One tendency of the pandemic was to facilitate the deployment of security emergency laws and surveillance practices (biosurveillance, online tracking, censorship, harassment of activists). In any case, both the pandemic and climate change are existential threats to humanity; the difference is the time of impact and, when the effects are not right away, there is a tendency to postpone the measures to deal with the problem to the next administration. So, the immediate response to the pandemic should be used to inspire and coordinate sustainable long-term reactions to the climate crisis. How the pandemic challenges are interpreted and assessed now will determine the future of the civilization in which we live in the next decades and possibly the success of the climate change responses. In any case, only global responses can deal with the impending risk of mass extinction that climate change poses to our generation.

Some policies and practices need to be refocused. For example, action can be taken to accelerate the construction of clean power projects (including distributed energy) and electric vehicle charging infrastructure. Both are areas with a developed supply chain, established know-how, and developers ready to pounce, often with sites already identified. Also, there can be greater incentives for the trade-in of old polluting vehicles for clean new ones, thus fueling demand for high-value, innovative products, and tapping into the renewed desire for better air quality. And when that personal vehicle is preferable over public transport, it helps to avoid exposure to others during a pandemic. A green stimulus program would make it easier for those with the means to buy new vehicles to choose electric. And in this type of challenge, BRICS partnerships can play an important role.

Above all, the pandemic is a systemic human development crisis: the level of poverty, healthcare capacity, access to the internet, and social protection can determine how severe the effects of a crisis might be. Facing the challenges of crises such as climate change, poverty, and biodiversity loss, the world is at a crossroads, demanding a new form of international governance that is constantly focused on tackling multiple crises.

7.3 BRICS as a Case Study

The BRICS platform is the case selected for the purposes of this inquiry because it represents the argued theory as the members share experiences in the development process, as well as the challenges in their encounters with developed countries. The platform adopts ontological and epistemological stances that have the capacity to engender cooperation and mutual assistance among its members.

The present study adopts content analysis as its research technique, with a view to systematizing the case study and its analytical boundaries. The objective of the content analysis is to establish a systematic framework for the various forms of communication present in the corpus. This process involves the identification of qualitative and quantitative indicators for the words employed in the texts. Consequently, this analysis yields hermeneutical units of analysis, which function as theoretical markers within the scope of this investigation.[17]

The content analysis is justified by the research object, which seeks explanations for behaviors associated with the notion of intentionality and awareness in the engagement of the BRICS with the climate change regime. The existence of subjective elements that are in a state of flux between the mind, words, and actions establishes a posture that demonstrates sufficient ideational factors. This, in turn, clarifies perceptions and misperceptions in the interstate relationship,[18] providing a framework for understanding how practices and discourses construct subjectivities, which is helpful in grasping the manner in which states internalize climate norms.[19]

The construction of inferences permeates the logical process. The analyzed and coded messages undergo interpretation to determine the state of mind, data, subjectivities, ideologies, and phenomena hidden behind the use of terms. Therefore, applying content analysis systematizes the knowledge, making qualitative analysis rigorous.[20]

To accomplish the content analysis task, we use the online version of Voyant Tools.[21] The Voyant application facilitates exploratory and content analysis of the corpus to identify the operationalization of hermeneutical units, as well as their correlation and context. Consequently, as the investigation progresses, it was anticipated that the argument would gain traction in terms of the inferences and empirical amplitude.[22]

The primary documents that comprise the corpus are the declarations issued by the BRICS from 2017 to 2021. The corpus also comprises the 14th Five-Year Plan[23] and the Ecological and Environmental Protection Guidelines for Overseas

[17] Bardin (2000); Krippendorff (2012).

[18] Jervis (2017).

[19] Foucault (1987).

[20] Bardin (2000).

[21] Geoffrey and Sinclair (2020).

[22] Gibbs (2008).

[23] CSET (2021).

Investment and Cooperation Construction Projects.[24] These documents are of particular significance in light of China's participation in the climate change regime and its response to the COVID-19 crisis, when compared to the participation and response of other BRICS countries. A separate analysis of China's responses is expected to identify the indicators of these responses, thus highlighting the substantial contributions of the country to environmental governance, with implications for the health dimension.[25]

Beyond the BRICS, experiences from other regions highlight the uneven nature of global responses. The European Union, for instance, launched the European Green Deal[26] and the Fit for 55 package,[27] integrating post-pandemic recovery measures with an accelerated transition toward climate neutrality through carbon pricing instruments and structural funds for green innovation. In the United States, the approval of the Inflation Reduction Act in 2022[28] marked the largest climate investment in the country's history, combining fiscal incentives with job creation in clean energy sectors.

In Africa, the Great Green Wall Initiative[29] has sought to address climate, water, and food security crises simultaneously, although it remains heavily dependent on international cooperation and external financing. Meanwhile, Small Island Developing States (SIDS),[30] such as Fiji and Tuvalu, have advanced localized adaptation strategies—from planned community relocations to embedding climate risk metrics into national policies—yet remain highly vulnerable to sea level rise and pandemic-related economic volatility.

These contrasts reveal that, while developed countries were able to link post-COVID recovery to robust green stimulus packages, Global South countries faced fiscal and institutional constraints that limited their ability to respond and adapt effectively.

7.4 BRICS' Role in Tackling Climate Change

In this part of the chapter, three levels of analysis are made considering the challenges of addressing climate change during the pandemic. First is the positioning of each member of the BRICS (using China as the controlling case), second is the positioning of the BRICS as an international institution, and third is the correlation

[24] CDB (2022).

[25] Spracklen (2016).

[26] European Commission (2019).

[27] EU (2021).

[28] Rep. Yarmuth JA [D-K-3 (2022) H.R.5376 - 117th Congress (2021-2-022): Inflation Reduction Act of 2022. https://www.congress.gov/bill/117th-congress/house-bill/5376. Accessed Oct 1, 2025.

[29] GGW (2021).

[30] UN (1992).

between climate change and COVID-19 responses, considering the developing status of the BRICS countries.

7.4.1 *Countries' Positioning*

The assessment of each country's positioning regarding climate change is a two-fold strategy. First, we look into the Climate Action Tracker (CAT) database[31] to identify how the countries are handling their emissions vis-à-vis the targets related to the Paris Agreement. The Climate Action Tracker is an independent scientific analysis that tracks government climate action and measures it against the globally ratified Paris Agreement aim of "holding warming well below 2°C, and pursuing efforts to limit warming to 1.5°C." A collaboration of two organizations, Climate Analytics and the NewClimate Institute, the CAT has been providing this independent analysis to policymakers since 2009.[32]

Second, a normative layer is added to the analysis by looking into the Environmental Justice Atlas[33] database to find the state of the countries' vulnerability due to climate change in their respective territories. The Environmental Justice Atlas represents a form of citizen science that involves the documentation and cataloging of social conflicts pertaining to environmental issues. This is achieved through the registration and mapping of cases of environmental conflicts by users, who in this capacity transform their personal experiences into data that supports research, advocacy, and policymaking. The objective of including this normative layer is to identify the shared challenges of adapting to climate change and the degree of vulnerability that imposes severe socioeconomic effects, especially in the context of developing countries.

We present the data collected in the Climate Action Tracker in Table 7.1.

As observed from the indicators above, the countries in the BRICS stand very close in their position regarding climate change. As for the indicator "overall rating," the data shows that the countries are in a state of insufficient action toward compliance with the goals set by the Paris Agreement.[34] However, the results in Table 7.1 are not far from the global indicators that also point to a gap between the threat and the efficient responses to address the challenge.[35]

The indicator "sources of emissions" highlights land use and forestry as challenges for the BRICS countries, which can be linked to the priority of the economic

[31] CAT (2020).

[32] CAT (2020).

[33] Ej Atlas (2020).

[34] UNFCCC (United National Framework Commission on Climate Change), Paris Agreement to the United Nations Framework Convention on Climate Change, Dec. 12, 2015, T.I.A.S. No. 16-1104. U.N. Doc. FCCC/CP/2015/L.9/Rev/1.

[35] Townend (2023).

Table 7.1 Made by the Authors using the data collected from the Climate Action Tracker (CAT 2020)

	Overall Rating	Net Zero Target	Sources of Emissions	Historical Position	Policies and Action
BRAZIL	Highly Insufficient	2050	Land use and forestry	Source of emissions	Insufficient
RUSSIA	Critically Insufficient	2060	Land use and forestry	Sink	Highly Insufficient
INDIA	Highly Insufficient	2070	Land use and forestry	Information Incomplete	Almost Sufficient
CHINA	Highly Insufficient	2060	Land use and forestry	Information Incomplete	Insufficient
SOUTH AFRICA	Insufficient	2050	Land use and forestry	Information Incomplete	Almost Sufficient

The indicators were selected to demonstrate the positioning of the countries in managing the climate change issue vis-à-vis the international obligations assumed

agenda for developing countries.[36] While developed countries have wealthy economies, advanced technological industries, sophisticated trade policies, and stable political systems, in the Global South, countries have economies based on agricultural activities, especially the production of commodities for exportation, and economic dependence on the developed countries and international institutions.[37]

The indication by the Climate Action Tracker that the source of emissions is concentrated in land use and forestry (although deforestation might be more appropriate in this case) is not surprising within the developing context of the BRICS countries. The impacts of climate change due to higher land use will generate adverse effects that will hit the most vulnerable people and will damage, even more, the economy that seeks to create development.[38]

Dealing with vulnerability to the effects of climate change requires adaptation and mitigation, which involves a significant financial and technological commitment from developed countries to support developing countries. However, despite the existential threat hanging over everyone's heads, this is not what we observe in the climate change regime. Instead, the observation is the failure of the developed countries to comply with their commitments.[39]

Achieving an equilibrium between environmental protection and social and economic development is contingent on two primary variables related to large-scale cooperation: firstly, the endorsement of multilateral institutions and platforms, given the inherently interconnected nature of environmental challenges; and secondly, the involvement of non-state actors. For instance, at a time when national policy was completely in denial about climate change, the Brazilian Corporate

[36] Townend (2023).

[37] Odeh (2010).

[38] Smith et al. (2022).

[39] Roberts et al. (2021).

Council for Sustainable Development issued a formal communication to the Brazilian government.[40]

The open letter presented the urgent concerns raised by Brazil's environmental policies at the time, and the language employed was unambiguous: "the Brazilian business sector, through institutions and companies in the industrial, agricultural, and service sectors, today reaffirm their public commitment to the agenda of sustainable development." The private sector expressed particular concern about the negative perception of Brazil's handling of environmental issues in the Amazon, which could impact the country's international reputation.

The negative international perception has the potential to cause significant harm to Brazil, both in terms of its reputation and the effective development of fundamental business and projects for the country, which highly depend on commodity exports and international trade. Several of the signatory companies are involved in developing business solutions based on the bioeconomy, with a focus on added value and product traceability, including in the Amazon region, thereby making the Amazon a key source of development and a climate solution.

On the one hand, it was acknowledged that scaling up beneficial practices is possible, predicated on the implementation of coherent policies that promote the environmental, social, and governance agenda. Conversely, the letter highlighted the importance of implementing rigorous monitoring procedures to address environmental irregularities and criminal activities in the Amazon and other biomes within Brazil.[41] The mapping of environmental conflicts within the BRICS countries reveals the development pressures that simultaneously generate ecological and social tensions among the most vulnerable and marginalized people.[42]

It has been well established by the available scientific knowledge that developing countries are the most vulnerable to climate change. Table 7.2 presents representative cases in which the development model based on competition over natural resources generates social and economic conflicts. As stated by the International Organization for Migration,[43] the most vulnerable groups of countries in the world are the least developed countries (LDCs), landlocked developing countries (LLDCs), and Small Island Developing States (SIDS). They are disproportionately affected by the negative impacts of climate change due to their structural constraints and geographical disadvantage.[44]

The population's vulnerability to climate change is directly linked to the lack of adaptation by developing countries, which face the adverse effects of severe climate conditions. The vulnerability with no conditions to mitigate the impact of climate

---

[40] CEBDS (2020).

[41] CEBDS (2020).

[42] Ej Atlas (2020).

[43] UN (1951).

[44] IOM (2019).

Table 7.2 Made by the Authors using the data collected from the Environmental Justice Atlas (Ej Atlas 2020)

	Number of Conflicts	Main Cause(s)	Representative Case	Example of a Case
BRAZIL	174	Oil projects and mining	Conexão Abrolhos	In October 2019, the National Petroleum Agency of Brazil, without an exploitation license, auctioned four oil and gas blocks close to the Abrolhos region. The mitigation areas established for these blocks are insufficient to protect the Marine Park, and Brazil lacks a structured system to take action in the event of any disaster. High risk to the local traditional communities of fishermen.
RUSSIA	71	Oil projects and mining	Vostok mega oil project, Taymyr, Arctic Russia	An oil development is underway in the Arctic region of Russia. The project is located near Dudinka town in the Taymyr region. The project brings threats to Indigenous livelihoods and traditional ways of life.
INDIA	346	Development projects	Sterlite copper smelter unit, Tamil Nadu	Vedanta Group's Sterlite copper smelter unit began operating in Tuticorin, Tamil Nadu, in 1996. Protests began almost immediately, with hundreds of fishermen blockading the port with their boats to prevent ships carrying copper ore from unloading in March and October 1996. However, this did not prevent operations from continuing. In July 1997, 165 women in a neighboring factory, Ramesh Flowers, fainted because of a toxic gas leak from Sterlite. Some of these women later had miscarriages.

(continued)

Table 7.2 (continued)

	Number of Conflicts	Main Cause(s)	Representative Case	Example of a Case
CHINA	156	Water and gas projects	Friends of Nature sued State Grid for refusing to purchase clean energy in Gansu	In August 2016, Friends of Nature (FON) sued State Grid Gansu Electric Power Co, the provincial grid enterprise in Gansu, China, since the company refused to purchase all of the electricity produced from wind and solar generators (also known as wind and solar curtailment, which means the reduction of output of a renewable source below what it could have otherwise produced) within its geographic boundary. Furthermore, as the amount not produced with renewable energy sources was substituted with coal-fired power, FON indicated that the company's behavior led to an increase in air pollution and GHG emissions, which have direct implications for climate change.
SOUTH AFRICA	60	Energy and mining projects	Ezulwini gold and uranium mining	The Witwatersrand is a region containing a mountain ridge of gold-bearing rock, which is mostly located in the Gauteng province of South Africa. The gold is located in reef beds, which were first discovered in 1886. The beginning of gold mining in the Witwatersrand region resulted in it becoming the most densely populated region of South Africa, with settlements initially constructed for the miners, the mining area grew and developed due to supporting industries moving in.

change leads to implications for social and economic development, forced migration, loss of livelihood, and other disruptive scenarios.[45]

Therefore, we observe the interplay between the lack of adequate responses by the countries due to developmental pressures and their reduced capacity for adaptation. In the next section of the chapter, we examine the potential intervention of the BRICS in addressing this conundrum.

[45] Thornton et al. (2014).

7.4.2 BRICS: Influences on the Countries' Responses

Although the BRICS constitutes an informal group of emerging economies, the meetings and declarations issued by the group can be considered morally binding among the countries, thus possessing some strength in governing behaviors. BRICS is an international regime. Regime theory is an approach within international relations theory, a subdiscipline of political science, which seeks to explain the occurrence of cooperation among states by focusing on the role that regimes play in mitigating international anarchy and overcoming various collective action problems among states.[46] Like many social institutions, international regimes may or may not be formally articulated or organized.

The traditional notion of regimes posits that they constitute a series of norms, resolutions, and principles within the international system,[47] providing a more substantial framework for establishing order. This encompasses not only the sources of international law but also the political and diplomatic actions of state actors and the activities of non-state actors (soft law).[48] The majority of BRICS countries are reliant on their economies to ensure their independence (without significant military power), as evidenced by India, Brazil, and South Africa.

Because of that reliance, BRICS adopted a dual approach: firstly, at the multilateral level, it has promoted the principle within the UN that economic and social progress in developing countries is a collective international responsibility; and secondly, at the South–South level, it has encouraged developing countries to pool their resources and capabilities, thereby reducing their dependence on the Global North. This vision consolidated South–South cooperation as a practice of solidarity and partnership, thus departing from the donor-recipient model that characterizes traditional aid.[49]

While the BRICS constitute an informal association under international law, their summits and collective decisions generate institutional authority that exerts a binding influence on member states. This dynamic highlights how even loosely structured forums may produce forms of governance and normative expectations that shape state behavior in global climate politics. The declarations issued by the BRICS are considered soft law, which are normative stipulations in non-binding texts.[50] The extent to which commitment and compliance are manifested within the international legal system is contingent upon the role of non-binding norms, such as declarations, guidelines, and resolutions, that influence state behavior in the absence of legally binding obligations.[51]

---

[46] Bradford (2007).

[47] Krasner (1983).

[48] Nye (2005).

[49] Chaturvedi (2015).

[50] Nye (2005).

[51] Shelton (2000).

These norms play a significant role in shaping expectations, building consensus, and complementing formal treaties, particularly in areas where political or legal constraints make binding agreements difficult, such as "super wicked problems" like climate change.[52] States frequently opt for soft law due to its capacity to engender flexibility, mitigate the hazards associated with non-compliance, and foster collaboration among a diverse array of actors. The degree of compliance with such norms is contingent on several factors, including the clarity and precision of the obligations, the existence of monitoring and review mechanisms, and the broader political and institutional context. The concept of law, in its hard and soft forms, exists on a continuum where non-binding norms have the capacity to engender genuine commitment and behavioral change, particularly in the domains of human rights, environmental law, arms control, and trade. In the absence of legal enforceability, soft law can serve as a mechanism for fostering solidarity, providing normative guidance, and promoting governance in international relations.[53]

A first exploratory analysis of the BRICS' declarations from 2017 to 2021, respectively, the Xiamen Declaration, Johannesburg Declaration, Brasilia Declaration, Moscow Declaration, and New Delhi Declaration, reveals the high incidence of "cooperation" (455) and "development" (247). To work with the terms as hermeneutical units and to measure the covariation between them, we refer to them as variables. Stop words and expected words, such as BRICS, are excluded due to the lack of context or correlation with the object of this study.

The higher incidence of the terms "cooperation" and "development" in the documents was expected, as both are at the center of the BRICS' objectives. However, considering that this study aims to explain and understand institutional responses to climate change, the correlation between cooperation and development and the sustainability concept should be investigated. Additionally, the variable "security" appears 189 times, and its ontology may be correlated with the sustainability concept related to environmental security. Moreover, the complexity and development of global issues require a broader and encompassing concept of national security that includes matters related to natural resources and the environment.[54] As such, environmental security refers to "[how] environmental change puts national security at risk, how it may be a factor in violent conflicts, and the ways in which environmental change puts human security at risk."[55]

Therefore, the content analysis in the corpus should follow the correlation between cooperation, development, and security with sustainability. Finally, strong or weak correlations should indicate evidence of institutional responses to climate change. In Fig. 7.1, we observe the trends of the variables in the last five joint declarations issued by the BRICS. As the countries alternate the place where the summits happen each year, the host country can push certain aspects of the agenda,

52 Shelton (2000).

53 Chaturvedi (2015).

54 Mathews (1989).

55 Barnett (2009).

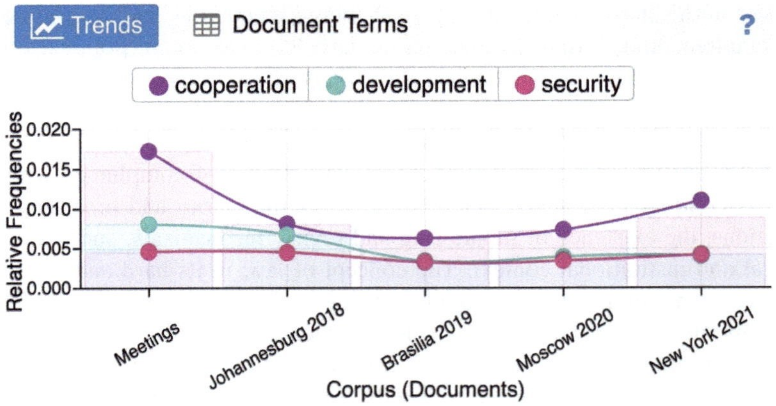

Fig. 7.1 Occurrence of terms in the BRICS' declarations using Voyant Tools (Geoffrey and Sinclair 2020)

becoming an agenda-setter, which suggests that the scope is determined by the practices and access points in the host countries in a two-level game of politics.[56]

As we look at the variables' frequency, oscillation, and the distance between them, we observe a pattern of stability from Johannesburg (2018)[57] to New Delhi (2021)[58] that reflects the data provided in the first part of this chapter. The development model is based heavily on the intensive extractivist approach that relies heavily on land use and forestry, as evidenced in Table 7.1. Therefore, the pressures over land and natural resources by development projects based on oil and gas and mining exploration generate environmental and social tensions among the countries' most vulnerable and marginalized people (see Table 7.2).

A closer look at the frequency of the variables in each of the declarations (Fig. 7.1) shows a relatively stable frequency in the declarations of Johannesburg,[59] Brasília,[60] Moscow,[61] and New Delhi,[62] even considering the potential interference of the COVID-19 pandemic that hit the world at the end of 2019, which makes it even worse to account for their response considering the shift of priorities in developing countries

The deviant case is the Declaration of Xian[63] which presents a higher incidence of the variable "cooperation," which is related to the increasing participation of China in the international system since the inauguration of President Xi Jinping

[56] Putnam (1988).
[57] BRICS (2018).
[58] BRICS (2021).
[59] BRICS (2018).
[60] BRICS (2019).
[61] BRICS (2020).
[62] BRICS (2021).
[63] BRICS (2017).

2013, but maintains stability in the other two variables at the same level as the other declarations.[64] Looking back to the beginning of the 2010s, pressures on the environment and its adverse effects on the population were the cause of severe concern for the authorities. The BRICS nations' huge populations, remarkable growth rates, and increasingly influential positions in global politics, means that the future of the global environment will depend largely on the decisions these politicians make today.[65]

Although China is a country with issues to be tackled in land use and forestry, along with the socio-environmental implications that these bring, the Chinese central government has shifted its focus on investments from infrastructure to technology, including green technologies, thus becoming central to the debates involving environmental protection and development within a new development model.[66]

According to the Net Zero Readiness Index 2021,[67] China is among the top five countries in the index for decarbonization readiness in land use, forestry, and agriculture, losing ground to New Zealand and in front of the United States, Sweden, and Singapore. This assessment provides initial evidence that technology is essential for the other countries of the BRICS to address decarbonization when assessing the changes or adjustments in their development model under the environmental sustainability umbrella.[68]

President Xi Jinping has made it clear that one of his agendas is the promotion of the governance of the environment. He declared: "We must raise awareness of the need to respect, protect, and accommodate ourselves to nature, follow the basic state policy of resource conservation and environmental protection, and give high priority to conserving, protecting the environment, and promoting its natural restoration."[69]

In March 2018, the Chinese Constitution was amended for the fifth time since 1954 to incorporate the "ecological civilization development" concept,[70] which marks a high degree of concern for ecological issues at the constitutional level. Ecological civilization means that humans can benefit from nature and create wealth for nature; in other words, humans must protect nature while transforming nature into a harmonious interaction between man and nature.[71] The amendment of the Constitution of 2018 includes the Five-Sphere Integrated Plan,[72] featuring the development of socialism with Chinese characteristics encompassing economic,

---

[64] Kent (2013).

[65] Wu (2011).

[66] Kroeber (2016); Naughton (2018).

[67] KPMG (2021).

[68] Economy (2019).

[69] Xi (2018).

[70] Hansen et al. (2018).

[71] Hansen et al. (2018).

[72] CPC (2023).

political, cultural, social, and ecological development, thus elevating the plan to constitutional status.[73]

Commitments made by China internally to deal with environmental issues reflect the country's push for the building of ecological civilization as a new model of development, which sees nature not as an object dominated by humankind but as a world in which humans are a part, and thus are responsible for the processes of adaptation and transformation.[74] In addition, the construction of the concept of ecological civilization points to a new type of international relations, which seeks to share development results at the economic level, safeguard the shared values of humankind at the cultural level, pursue universal security at the social level, and pursue global security at the ecological level.[75]

The 14th Five-Year Plan is the policy guide for central and local governments, which heavily relies on development.[76] The priority of the term "development" (mentioned 565 times in the document), and its high correlation to the terms "research," "economic," and "people's," reflect the efforts of China in switching the development model, as stated earlier. Furthermore, including people brings a whole range of social aspects embedded in climate change effects.

At the international level, the ecological dimension develops strong language. This emphasis is related to the severe criticism that the Belt and Road Initiative received due to the absence of governance structures to oversee environmental and labor standards in the recipient countries of the investments.[77] For that reason, and reflecting a new approach toward realizing ecological civilization at home and abroad, the Chinese government issued the Ecological and Environmental Protection Guidelines for Overseas Investment and Cooperation Construction Projects.[78]

The environmental dimension is highly associated with companies and protection in the Guidelines, again reflecting the ecological civilization concept in the international business conducted by China and its SOEs (state-owned enterprises) in Belt and Road Initiative countries, thus exporting these values (which generally seems not to be the case in the BRICS).[79] Thus, China is becoming an agenda-setting country in the international system. Although this fact brings some discomfort to other nations, especially the United States and its allies, China is making significant contributions to the global governance of the environment, which is very important in understanding the process of agenda-setting in the BRICS meetings but at the same time it is necessary to confirm the focus on national interests even in the multilateral forum.

[73] Wang et al. (2022).

[74] Kunh (2019).

[75] Coenen et al. (2021).

[76] Creemers et al. (2022).

[77] Cai (2017); Anwar (2019).

[78] MEE and MOFCOM (2022).

[79] Li et al. (2021).

Considering the content analysis of the Guidelines vis-à-vis the individual analysis conducted on the positioning of each country, it is highly probable that countries are transferring their national interest to the institutional level. The declarations, as a result of the agenda-setting capability of the country host and the common challenges faced by the countries, are deemed to reflect the national interest, moving the member countries away from the original intention of forming the multilateral forum as stated by the BRICS Center of the University of Toronto: "Since 2008, the leaders of Brazil, Russia, India, and China—the BRIC countries—have met annually to discuss issues of global significance."[80] South Africa was not mentioned here because it was not part of the original group.

Within such high-level meetings, in terms of the agenda and the shared challenges as Global South countries, it would be expected that some institutional learning and steering capacity would be generated, which are elements of governance capacity.[81] The lack of institutional learning and steering capacity leads to an inevitable lack of concerted policy implementation that would benefit the countries in addressing the developmental problems that contribute to climate change.

An empirical stance of the argument is reflected in the utterance of Sergey Lavrov, the Russian foreign minister, in the article "BRICS strategic partnership for global stability, shared security and innovative growth." The tone regarding multilateralism is somehow confrontational, reflecting more on the domestic perceptions than the group:

> Structural imbalances in the world economy are yet to be overcome. A serious threat to global economic growth is posed by such unfair competition practices as unilateral economic sanctions, trade wars and flagrant abuse of the US dollar status as the world reserve currency. The international community is yet to find effective responses to a whole number of critical challenges of our time—from terrorism to climate change. Moreover, there are attempts to replace the international legal system, established after the Second World War with the UN Charter as its main source, with the so-called "rules-based order," where "rules" being invented in secret, in "small groups," and then, depending upon a political situation, impose[d] on the whole world.[82]

Furthermore, in broader terms, the analysis of the governance of climate change or the lack thereof within the BRICS requires an understanding of the correlation between the variables and a variable that presents the governance indicators. To that end, the closest term to climate change is sustainable development, and the correlations are shown in Table 7.3.

The correlations and contexts between the variables and sustainable development in Appendix show no direct association to climate change governance that might be expressed in terms such as greenhouse effect, emissions, national target, carbon emission, fossil fuels, sea level, or climate disasters.[83] The proper institutional response to an existential threat would be language that reflects that

[80] Toronto ICB (2025).

[81] van Popering-Verkerk et al. (2022).

[82] Lavrov (2019).

[83] McCarthy et al. (2012)

Table 7.3 Correlations and contexts between the variables and sustainable development made with Voyant Tools (Geoffrey and Sinclair 2020)

	Sustainable Development
Cooperation	4
Development	60
Security	7
Total	71

preoccupation and concerted lines of action that surpass the economic development portion of the national interest to a holistic concern and encompass an appeal for all interests, including the national.

While much of the discussion on climate governance during the pandemic has centered on governments and multilateral regimes, civil society played a critical role in shaping agendas and pushing for accountability. In Brazil, for example, a data blackout occurred during the most critical moments of the pandemic. Crucial public health information that had been publicly disclosed for decades was suddenly classified as top secret, contrary to national laws that require transparency and accountability. In this case, it was the organization of society that was fundamental in quickly coordinating and providing data estimates based on informal sources.[84] At the local level, communities mobilized to resist what threatened their livelihoods and ecosystems—reinforcing the evidence already highlighted in environmental conflict datasets. These examples show that policymaking and societal mobilization are deeply intertwined: in moments when governments deprioritized climate action due to pandemic pressures, civil society actors helped sustain momentum, shape legal norms, and anchor climate justice in public debates.

7.4.3 Correlation Between Climate Change Responses and COVID-19

As we observed in Sects. 7.4.1 and 7.4.2, the responses to the climate change crisis under a country and institutional approach are far from being enough vis-à-vis the existential threat humankind faces. To that end, the adverse effects and the challenge of adapting or mitigating the effects are more severe in developing countries. The outbreak of COVID-19 has placed an extra burden on Global South countries, with implications that will be felt in full in the following decades. A direct response to the pandemic was the shutdown of the countries looking after their national interest while facing the common global problem posed by the virus. To that end, developing countries have to deal with associated economic effects that hit the core of their economies, namely commodities exportation and tourism.[85]

[84] Denny et al. (2020).

[85] Frankel et al. (2020).

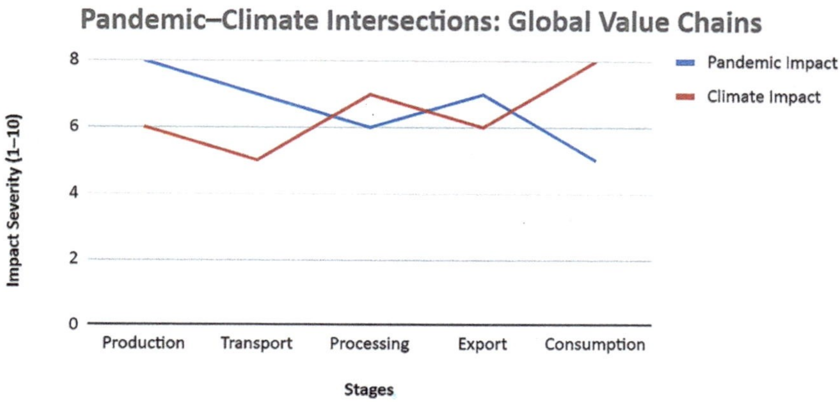

Fig. 7.2 Pandemic–climate intersections in global value chains

Figure 7.2 compares the relative severity of disruptions caused by the COVID-19 pandemic and climate-related shocks across five stages of global value chains: production, transport, processing, export, and consumption. The values reflect composite indicators synthesized from international reports by the Food and Agriculture Organization,[86] the World Trade Organization,[87] and the International Monetary Fund.[88] The assigned values (scale 1–10) do not represent official statistical series but were derived from the qualitative synthesis of the international reports. The figure is therefore intended as an analytical illustration, highlighting patterns and intersections identified by the authors, rather than as a mere reproduction of primary quantitative datasets of the reports.

The pandemic exerted its strongest pressure on production and transport due to restrictions on mobility, labor shortages, and border closures. By contrast, climate-related impacts were particularly evident at the consumption and processing stages, where extreme weather events (droughts, floods, wildfires) and ecosystem degradation disrupted agricultural output, energy supply, and food systems. Export activities were affected by both crises, as lockdowns delayed shipping and climate shocks reduced commodity availability. Overall, the graph demonstrates that while the pandemic created acute short-term disruptions, climate change continues to generate chronic systemic risks that cascade across value chains, amplifying vulnerabilities in both developed and developing economies.

The disruption of the countries and the global economy was felt immediately as projects and strategies had to be modified because of the "war" against the virus. Therefore, addressing climate change for some became a secondary issue to the political agenda as, after all, the lockdowns and other restrictive measures to contain

[86] FAO of the UN (2022).

[87] WTO (2022).

[88] IMF (2023).

the virus could decrease air pollution.[89] Global South countries were already dealing with several economic and social issues before the pandemic, some of them connected to the pathways for development, and thus with direct linkage with climate change. An online survey in the United Kingdom (necessary to say that it is one of the few at that point) measured the psychological implications of the dual challenge of climate change and COVID for young people, and concluded that the

> COVID-19 pandemic and climate change are affecting the well-being of UK young people in distinct ways, with implications for health service, policy, and research responses. There is a need for mental health practitioners, policymakers, and other societal actors to account for the complex relationship between climate agency, distress, and mental well-being in young people.[90]

It is reasonable to infer that the toll on young people in the Global South is exponentially higher considering their exposure to a whole array of economic and social problems caused by the development process.[91] The World Economic Forum, during the pandemic years, has been discussing the impacts and solutions to the exacerbating effects of the virus in the most vulnerable economies, identifying that in comparison to "what we thought six months ago, the economic outlook has worsened significantly in some emerging market and low-income economies where infections are rising rapidly."[92]

Suzanne Nossel (PEN America) and Leslie Vinjamuri (Chatham House) argue that the increase in food insecurity around the world, with more than 345 million people experiencing limited or uncertain access, is the result of complex interlinkages related especially to the pandemic, climate change, and the conflict in Ukraine. The inequalities among peoples and nations that were already acute before the pandemic became "several-fold worst, and the prospects are very dark if no global commitment emerges soon."[93]

The economic repercussions of overlapping crises have been particularly severe for developing economies. The collapse of global supply chains during the pandemic exposed the vulnerabilities of major commodity exporters such as Brazil and South Africa, which faced disruptions in agricultural and mineral exports that underpin their fiscal stability. At the same time, the combined effects of COVID-19, the war in Ukraine, and climate-related shocks generated unprecedented levels of inflation in food and energy markets. Rising input costs amplified social tensions, while currency depreciation and debt pressures constrained governments' abilities to implement countercyclical measures.

More recent assessments, such as the 2025 IMF World Economic Outlook Update,[94] emphasize the uneven recovery trajectory: advanced economies benefited

---

[89] Venter et al. (2021).

[90] Lawrance et al. (2022).

[91] Egger et al. (2021).

[92] Chun et al. (2022).

[93] Nossel and Vinjamuri (2022).

[94] IMF (2025).

from strong stimulus packages and financial buffers, whereas many emerging markets and low-income countries experienced mounting fiscal risks, deteriorating debt sustainability, and limited fiscal space to invest in climate resilience. These dynamics underscore the structural asymmetries in the global economy, where the Global South bears disproportionate costs while lacking the financial instruments to stabilize growth during systemic shocks.

The exception is China,[95] the control case in this study, which has shown that some steps have been taken to tackle climate change even during the pandemic by committing to peak carbon emissions by 2030 and carbon neutrality by 2060.[96] As pointed out by Cory Combs, the country is on a path of transformation and transition from a model dependent on heavy industry and construction to one that relies on technology, especially the strand that helps the country to achieve sustainable goals.[97] The country remained firmly committed to the energy transition process during the pandemic, which will have significant implications for global environmental (and trade) governance and spillover effects across the Global South.

7.5 Final Remarks

The main takeaway from the roundtables on responses to crises that inspired this chapter was that temporary reductions in daily global GHG emissions resulting from lockdowns and isolation had little effect on permanently reducing the concentration of GHGs in the atmosphere. Production, distribution, and consumption patterns must change in order to support climate action and prevent other pandemics. However, international economics shows that the challenge of overcoming the crises with sustainability will be even greater than expected because of multiple global crises. The short-term prospects for renewables are rocky amid economic upheaval, war, and fluctuating oil prices. However, in the long term, if governments integrate support for clean energy into economic recovery programs, renewables could emerge stronger than ever and good results can be achieved even without extreme measures.

The institutional response of the BRICS to climate change has been very weak and has become even weaker during the COVID-19 pandemic. Despite climate change posing an existential threat to these countries and increasing their vulnerability, the cooperation platform seems to focus more on the economic development dimension when guiding their actions. However, each country's need to increase its own level of development based on national interests is inconsistent with the platform's objectives. This highlights the urgent demand for alternative models of cooperation to facilitate an ecological transition. These models must be based on experience of dealing with the asymmetrical interests of developed countries and neoliberal international institutions.

---

[95] IMF Conference (2020).

[96] UN (2021).

[97] Combs (2022).

In addition, the institutional response does not consider countries' international commitments to sustainable development that were already made, particularly in relation to the climate change regime. Developing countries face mounting challenges in terms of mitigation, adaptation, and resilience, which have been exacerbated by the COVID-19 pandemic, placing additional strain on an international economy that was already in a fragile state prior to the pandemic and, at the same time, the crisis has intensified existing fault lines within countries, deprived society of public data, and strengthened nationalist and climate change denial movements.

In light of the findings discussed here, future risk assessment and management strategies should explicitly incorporate the lessons from overlapping crises. It is crucial to recognize that systemic shocks rarely occur in isolation: pandemics, climate change, biodiversity loss, transboundary pollution, and geopolitical disruptions often reinforce one another, amplifying vulnerabilities. Therefore, assessment frameworks need to move away from single-risk models toward multi-hazard and cascading risk approaches, capable of capturing how disruptions propagate across global value chains, food systems, and social norms.

Institutional responses have revealed significant gaps in coordination and implementation capacity, which points to the necessity of strengthening multilateral platforms with more binding mechanisms for cooperation beyond soft law. At the same time, risk management should implement adaptation and resilience indicators into mainstream development planning, particularly in Global South economies that remain heavily dependent on commodities and are disproportionately exposed to climate extremes. Civil society and local knowledge must be integrated into monitoring and accountability processes, as these actors have often sustained continuity when governments have deprioritized long-term risks.

The use of fiscal and financial instruments to stabilize the economies of developing countries while they invest in climate resilient infrastructure must be expanded. Risk governance must also become anticipatory rather than reactive, linking early warning systems, climate modeling, and health surveillance to create cross-sectoral risk dashboards. This would enable governments and institutions to detect compound threats in real time and coordinate prompt responses. Without such anticipatory capacity, countries in the Global South will continue to bear the brunt of asymmetric costs, as was evident during the COVID-19 pandemic and many climate-related disasters. Incorporating these principles into future assessments would provide a more robust basis for managing risks to the global commons and safeguarding sustainable development.

In conclusion, institutional change within the BRICS is welcome in order to align the cooperation platform more closely with the countries' expectations and experiences, taking into consideration not just the economic dimension of the development process. The subjective dimension that brings the BRICS together should be strong enough to increase the level of cooperation between them, forming a more robust governance structure and risk assessment and management capabilities based on political and legal multilateral decisions. Furthermore, the binding relationship created would be robust enough to generate positive ripple effects in global governance and address the challenges to the global commons.

Acknowledgments We gratefully acknowledge support of the RCGI – Research Centre for Gas Innovation, hosted by the University of São Paulo (USP) and sponsored by FAPESP – São Paulo Research Foundation (2014/50279-4 and 2020/15230-5) and Shell Brasil, and the strategic importance of the support given by ANP (Brazil's National Oil, Natural Gas and Biofuels Agency) through the R&D levy regulation, as well as the Center for Carbon Research in Tropical Agriculture (CCARBON) at the University of São Paulo, sponsored by the São Paulo Research Foundation (FAPESP) under grant 21/10573-4.

Appendix

Correlation among variables and sustainable development		
Left	Term	Right
Stressing the importance of environmental	cooperation	to sustainable development of our
scientific, technical, innovation and entrepreneurship	cooperation	for sustainable development and to
for creative and sustainable cultural	cooperation	, and we note the various
benefits of sustainable development. International	cooperation	in this field, as in
on economic growth and sustainable	development	. We will strive to coordinate
alleviation and reduction through skills	development	and achieving universal and sustainable
system to sustainable growth and	development	, and agree to better leverage
promote infrastructure construction and sustainable	development	of BRICS countries. 32. We
cultural diversity in promoting sustainable	development	, and encourage BRICS countries to
promoting sustainable economic and social	development	, and to strengthening BRICS partnership
in realizing education-related sustainable	development	goals. 28 63. We believe
Ending Tuberculosis in the Sustainable	development	Era: A 29 Multisectoral Response
the 2030 Agenda for Sustainable	development	and the building of broad
a fairer international order, sustainable	development	and inclusive growth, and to
implementation of the 2030 Sustainable	development	Goals as we foster a
and 3 security, advancing sustainable	development	as well as ensuring the
the 2030 Agenda for Sustainable	development	and the Sustainable Development Goals
Sustainable Development and the Sustainable	development	Goals (SDGs), to provide equitable
round innovation-driven and sustainable	development	, in its three dimensions – economic
Level Political Forum on Sustainable	development	(HLPF), in coordinating and reviewing
supportive of the global sustainable	development	agenda, balanced economic growth and
on the basis of sustainable	development	in an integrated way, addressing
and entrepreneurship cooperation for sustainable	development	and to enhance inclusive growth

Correlation among variables and sustainable development		
Left	Term	Right
be inclusive and support sustainable	development	and prosperity of all countries
and poverty eradication and sustainable	development	in Africa. We therefore reaffirm
our support for sustainable infrastructure	development	in Africa, including addressing the
the bedrock for sustainable economic	development	and growth; boosting productivity and
so as to promote sustainable	development	in BRICS countries. 78. We
to sustainable economic and social	development	, we welcome the initiative to
Ending Tuberculosis in the Sustainable	development	Era: A Multisectoral response, in
peace and security, advance sustainable	development	and ensure the promotion and
express our commitment to sustainable	development	in its three dimensions - economic
enjoy the benefits of sustainable	development	. International cooperation in this field
the 2030 Agenda for Sustainable	development	and call for redoubled efforts
NDB) in infrastructure and sustainable	development	financing. We stress the need
resources for infrastructure and sustainable	development	projects in BRICS and other
including in digital infrastructure, skills	development	, particularly for young people, sustainable
peace and security, advance sustainable	development	, ensure the promotion and protection
the achievement of the Sustainable	development	Goals. We underscore the importance
and providing for Africa's sustainable	development	. We reaffirm our readiness to
sustainable, balanced and inclusive economic	development	and growth in the post
the 2030 Agenda for Sustainable	development	. Policy priorities in our countries
three pillars of the Sustainable	development	Agenda – economic, social and environmental
finance, digital economy and sustainable	development	, to facilitate the speedy economic
promotion of investment for sustainable	development	. We also take note of
may promote international trade, sustainable	development	and inclusive growth. 57. We
resources for infrastructure and sustainable	development	projects in Bank's member states
economies to meet the Sustainable	development	Goals. At the same time
of energy in promoting sustainable	development	. Ensuring access to affordable, reliable
COVID 19 recovery, achieving sustainable	development	and allowing for an inclusive
the 2030 Agenda for Sustainable	development	and recognize that eradicating poverty
an indispensable requirement for sustainable	development	. We recognize that many developing
technological tools to promote sustainable	development	and facilitate affordable and equitable
engagement on these issues. Sustainable	development	and innovative means to achieve
the 2030 Agenda for Sustainable	development	in its three dimensions – economic
the implementation of the Sustainable	development	Goals (SDGs), we believe that

Correlation among variables and sustainable development		
Left	Term	Right
scarcity and sustainable socio-economic	development	. 39. Recognizing the importance of
the 2030 Agenda on Sustainable	development	and its Goals, we reiterate
a vital element of sustainable	development	. We agree to cooperate closely
in the context of sustainable	development	and efforts to eradicate poverty
in the context of sustainable	development	. 47. We emphasize that sustainable
and Financial Cooperation for Sustainable	development	50. We welcome the progress
capacity in meeting our Sustainable	development	Goals, especially in light of
BRICS Academic Dialogue on Sustainable	development	Goals 20–21 May 2021
achieving universal and sustainable social	security	systems. 24. We recognize the
maintaining international peace and	security	, advancing sustainable development as well
skills development, food and nutrition	security	and poverty eradication and sustainable
States to maintain peace and	security	, advance sustainable development and ensure
a sustainable system of social	security	, and labor market data exchanges
cooperate to maintain peace and	security	, advance sustainable development, ensure the
the world agricultural production, food	security	and the implementation of sustainable

References

Anwar A (2019) Belt and Road Initiative: What's in it for China? East-West Center. https://www.eastwestcenter.org/news/east-west-wire/belt-and-road-initiative-what's-in-it-china. Accessed 15 Jan 2026

Appadorai A (1955) The Bandung Conference. India Quart 11(3):207–235. https://doi.org/10.1177/097492845501100301

Bardin L (2000) Análise de conteúdo. Edições 70, Lisboa

Barnett J (2009) Environmental security. In: Kitchin R, Thrift N (eds) International encyclopedia of human geography. Elsevier, Oxford, pp 553–557

Bradford A (2007) Regime theory. Oxford Public International Law. https://opil.ouplaw.com/display/10.1093/law:epil/9780199231690/law-9780199231690-e1462. Accessed 1 Oct 2025

BRICS (2017) 9th BRICS Summit – BRICS Leaders Xiamen Declaration – Xiamen, China, September 4, 2017. Ministério das Relações Exteriores. https://www.gov.br/mre/en/contact-us/press-area/press-releases/9th-brics-summit-brics-leaders-xiamen-declaration-xiamen-china-september-4-2017. Accessed 2 Oct 2025

BRICS (2018) 10th BRICS Summit – Johannesburg Declaration – July 27, 2018. Ministério das Relações Exteriores. https://www.gov.br/mre/en/contact-us/press-area/press-releases/10th-brics-summit-johannesburg-declaration-july-27-2018. Accessed 2 Oct 2025

BRICS (2019) XI BRICS Summit Brasilia Declaration. BRICS 2022 China. https://brics2022.mfa.gov.cn/eng/hywj/ODS/202203/t20220308_10649501.html. Accessed 2 Oct 2025

BRICS (2020) XII BRICS Summit Moscow Declaration. Ministério das Relações Exteriores. https://www.gov.br/mre/en/contact-us/press-area/press-releases/xii-brics-summit-moscow-declaration. Accessed 2 Oct 2025

BRICS (2021) XIII BRICS Summit – New Delhi Declaration. Ministry of External Affairs, Government of India. https://mea.gov.in/bilateral-documents.htm?dtl/34236/XIII_BRICS_Summit_New_Delhi_Declaration=&utm_source=chatgpt.com. Accessed 2 Oct 2025

Cai P (2017) Understanding China's Belt and Road Initiative. Lowy Institute. https://www.lowyinstitute.org/publications/understanding-china-s-belt-road-initiative. Accessed 2 Oct 2025

Castro D, Denny DMT (2020) Economic relationship between Brazil and China: an empirical assessment using sentiment and content analysis. Beijing Law Rev 11(1):227–243. https://doi.org/10.4236/blr.2020.111016

CAT (2020) Climate Action Tracker. https://climateactiontracker.org/. Accessed 1 Oct 2025

CDB (2022) Ecological and environmental protection guidelines for overseas investment and cooperative construction projects. China Development Brief. https://chinadevelopmentbrief.org/publications/ecological-and-environmental-protection-guidelines-for-overseas-investment-and-cooperative-construction-projects/. Accessed 1 Oct 2025

CEBDS (2020) Comunicado do Setor Empresarial Brasileiro. https://cebds.org/publicacoes/comunicado-do-setor-empresarial-brasileiro/. Accessed 1 Oct 2025

Chaturvedi S (2015) The logic of sharing: Indian approach to South–South cooperation. Cambridge University Press, Cambridge

Chun, S, Naidoo, K, Sobrinho N (2022) The impact of the IMF's COVID-19 support to developing and emerging economies. IMF. https://www.imf.org/en/Publications/WP/Issues/2022/12/17/The-Impact-of-the-IMFs-COVID-19-Support-to-Developing-and-Emerging-Economies-527076. Accessed 2 Oct 2025

Coenen J, Bager S, Meyfroidt P et al (2021) Environmental Governance of China's belt and road initiative. Environ Policy Gov 31(1):3–17. https://doi.org/10.1002/eet.1901

Combs C (2022) China's course to carbon neutrality – Introduction. Asia Society. https://asiasociety.org/policy-institute/china-climate-introduction-weaving-chinas-climate-policy-tapestry. Accessed 2 Oct 2025

CPC (2023) The five-sphere integrated plan: Eco-Civilization. China's State Council Information Office. http://english.scio.gov.cn/featured/chinakeywords/2023-03/20/content_85178604.htm. Accessed 2 Oct 2025

Creemers R, Dorwart H, Neville K et al. (2022) Translation: 14th Five-Year Plan for National Informatization – Dec. 2021. DigiChina. https://digichina.stanford.edu/work/translation-14th-five-year-plan-for-national-informatization-dec-2021/. Accessed 2 Oct 2025

CSET (2021) CSET original translation: China's 14th five-year plan. Center for Security and Emerging Technology. https://cset.georgetown.edu/publication/china-14th-five-year-plan/. Accessed 1 Oct 2025

Dehm J (2016) Carbon colonialism or climate justice? Interrogating the international climate regime from a twail perspective. Windsor Yearb Access Just 33:129–161. https://doi.org/10.22329/wyaj.v33i3.4893

Denny DMT, Kazim E, Koshiyama A (2020) Catalogo de datos COVID-19. Revista Brasileira de Direitos Fundamentais & Justiça 14(1):43–68. https://doi.org/10.30899/dfj.v0i0.965

Denny DMT, Duarte CS, de Castro D et al (2021) COVID-19 magnifies the vulnerabilities: the Brazilian case. Int J Discrim Law 21(3):272–287. https://doi.org/10.1177/13582291211031374

Economy (2019) The third revolution: Xi Jinping and the new Chinese state. Oxford University Press, Oxford

Egger D, Miguel E, Warren SS et al (2021) Falling living standards during the COVID-19 crisis: quantitative evidence from nine developing countries. ScienceAdvances 7(6):eabe0997. https://doi.org/10.1126/sciadv.abe0997

Ej Atlas (2020) Environmental justice atlas. https://ejatlas.org/. Accessed 1 Oct 2025

EU (2021) "Fit for 55": delivering the EU's 2030 climate target on the way to climate neutrality. https://www.eesc.europa.eu/en/our-work/opinions-information-reports/opinions/fit-55-delivering-eus-2030-climate-target-way-climate-neutrality. Accessed 16 Feb 2026
European Commission (2019) A European Green Deal. https://commission.europa.eu/strategy-and-policy/priorities-2019-2024/european-green-deal_en. Accessed 16 Feb 2026
FAO of the UN (2022) The state of food and agriculture 2021. FAO Knowledge Repository. https://openknowledge.fao.org/items/437c1215-556b-4161-9af6-6-8163f5a1f84. Accessed 2 Oct 2025
Fauci AS (2005) The global challenge of infectious diseases: the evolving role of the National Institutes of Health in basic and clinical research. Nat Immunol 6:743–747. https://doi.org/10.1038/ni0805-743
Foucault M (1987) Vigiar e Punir - Nascimento Das Prisões. Petrópolis, Vozes.
Frankel J, Carranza E, Guerrero I et al. (2020) COVID-19: Effects in developing countries. Harvard Kennedy School. https://www.hks.harvard.edu/more/about/leadership-administration/deans-office/deans-discussions/covid-19-effects-developing. Accessed 2 Oct 2025
Fukuyama F (2006) The end of history and the last man. Free Press, New York
Geoffrey R, Sinclair S (2020) Voyant Tools. https://voyant-tools.org/. Accessed 1 Oct 2025
GGW (2021) The Great Green Wall. Great Green Wall. https://thegreatgreenwall.org/about-great-green-wall. Accessed 1 Oct 2025
Gibbs GR (2008) Analysing qualitative data, 1st edn. SAGE Publications Ltd, Los Angeles
Hansen MH, Li H, Svarverud R (2018) Ecological civilization: interpreting the Chinese past, projecting the global future. Glob Environ Change 53:195–203. https://doi.org/10.1016/j.gloenvcha.2018.09.014
IMF (2023) World economic outlook, October 2023: Navigating global divergences. IMF. https://www.imf.org/en/Publications/WEO/Issues/2023/10/10/world-economic-outlook-october-2023. Accessed 2 Oct 2025
IMF (2025) World economic outlook update, July 2025. Global economy: Tenuous resilience amid persistent uncertainty. IMF. https://www.imf.org/en/Publications/WEO/Issues/2025/07/29/world-economic-outlook-update-july-2025. Accessed 2 Oct 2025
IMF Conference (2020) COVID-19 pandemic in developing countries. IMF. https://www.imf.org/en/News/Seminars/Conferences/2020/11/30/covid19-pandemic-in-developing-countries. Accessed 2 Oct 2025
IOM (2019) Climate change and migration in vulnerable countries. https://publications.iom.int/books/climate-change-and-migration-vulnerable-countries. Accessed 16 Feb 2026
IPCC (2022) AR6 Climate Change 2022: Mitigation of Climate Change. Working Group III. IPCC Sixth Assessment Report. https://www.ipcc.ch/report/ar6/wg3/. Accessed 13 Jan 2026
Jervis R (2017) Perception and misperception in international politics. Princeton University Press, Princeton
Kent ML (2013) Using social media dialogically: public relations role in reviving democracy. Public Relat Rev 39(4):337–345. https://doi.org/10.1016/j.pubrev.2013.07.024
KPMG (2021) Net Zero Readiness Index 2021. https://assets.kpmg.com/content/dam/kpmg/xx/pdf/2021/10/net-zero-readiness-index.pdf. Accessed 16 Feb 2026
Krasner SD (1983) International regimes. Cornell University Press, Ithaca
Krippendorff K (2012) Content analysis: an introduction to its methodology, 3rd edn. Sage Publications, Inc, Los Angeles and London
Kroeber AR (2016) China's economy. Oxford University Press, Oxford
Kunh B (2019) Ecological civilisation in China. Dialogue of Civilizations Research Institute. Available via Researchgate. https://www.researchgate.net/publication/335661761_Ecological_civilisation_in_China. Accessed 2 Oct 2025
Lavrov S (2019) BRICS Strategic Partnership for Global Stability, Shared Security and Innovative Growth. XinhuaNet. https://www.xinhuanet.com/english/2019-11/13/c_138551550.htm. Accessed 13 Jan 2026

Lawrance EL, Jennings N, Kioupi V et al (2022) Psychological responses, mental health, and sense of agency for the dual challenges of climate change and the COVID-19 pandemic in young people in the UK: an online survey study. Lancet Planetary Health 6(9):e726–e738. https://doi.org/10.1016/S2542-5196(22)00172-3
Li C, Sampene AK, Agyeman FO et al (2021) Analysis of the BRICS countries' pathways towards a low-carbon environment. BRICS J Econ 2(4):77–102. https://doi.org/10.38050/2712-7508-2021-4-4
Manzanedo RD, Manning P (2020) COVID-19: lessons for the climate change emergency. Sci Total Environ 742:140563. https://doi.org/10.1016/j.scitotenv.2020.140563
Mathews D (1989) The politics of community. Natl Civic Rev 78(4):271–278. https://doi.org/10.1002/ncr.4100780407
McCarthy DP, Butchart SHM, Wiedenfeld DA et al. (2012) Financial costs of meeting global biodiversity conservation targets: current spending and unmet needs. Science 338(6109):946–949. https://www.science.org/doi/10.1126/science.1229803. Accessed 2 Oct 2025
MEE, MOFCOM (2022) New environmental guidelines released. BRI International Green Development Coalition. http://en.brigc.net/Media_Center/Updates/Green_Belt_and_Road/202204/t20220408_130597.html. Accessed 2 Oct 2025
Mertz O, Halsnæs K, Olesen JE et al (2009) Adaptation to climate change in developing countries. Environ Management 43:743–752. https://doi.org/10.1007/s00267-008-9259-3
Naughton BJ (2018) The Chinese economy: adaptation and growth, 2nd edn. MIT Press, Cambridge
Nossel S, Vinjamuri L (2022) Some assembly required: why the UN's broadest forum matters more than ever. Foreign Affairs. https://www.foreignaffairs.com/world/some-assembly-required. Accessed 13 Jan 2026
Nye JS (2005) Soft power: The means to success in world politics. PublicAffairs Books, Mishwaka
Odeh LE (2010) A comparative analysis of global north and global south economies. J Sustain Dev Afr 12(3)
Oreskes N, Conway E (2014) The collapse of Western civilization: a view from the future. Columbia University Press, New York
Putnam RD (1988) Diplomacy and domestic politics: the logic of two-level games. Int Org 42(3):427–460. https://doi.org/10.1017/S0020818300027697
Roberts JT, Weikmans R, Robinson S et al (2021) Rebooting a failed promise of climate finance. Nat Clim Change 11:180–182. https://doi.org/10.1038/s41558-021-00990-2
Shelton D (2000) Commitment and compliance: the role of non-binding norms in the international legal system. Oxford University Press, Oxford
Smith P, Bustamante M, Ahammad H et al. (2022) 11 Agriculture, forestry and other land use (AFOLU). IPCC Intergovernmental Panel on Climate Change. https://www.ipcc.ch/site/assets/uploads/2018/02/ipcc_wg3_ar5_chapter11.pdf. Accessed 13 Jan 2026
Spracklen DV (2016) China's contribution to climate change. Nature 531:310–311. https://doi.org/10.1038/531310a
Thornton PK, Ericksen PJ, Herrero M et al (2014) Climate variability and vulnerability to climate change: a review. Glob Change Biol 20(11):3313–3328. https://doi.org/10.1111/gcb.12581
Toronto ICB (2025) About the BRICS and BRICS information centre. University of Toronto. http://www.brics.utoronto.ca/about.html. Accessed 2 Oct 2025
Townend R (2023) Governments face losing the battle against climate change. Chatham House. https://www.chathamhouse.org/2022/02/governments-face-losing-battle-against-climate-change. Accessed 1 Oct 2025
UN (1951) International Organization for Migration. IOM UN Migration. https://www.iom.int/homepage. Accessed 1 Oct 2025
UN (1992) About Small Island Developing States (SIDS). Department of Economic and Social Affairs. https://sdgs.un.org/smallislands/about-small-island-developing-states. Accessed 1 Oct 2025

UN (2021) China headed towards carbon neutrality by 2060; President Xi Jinping vows to halt new coal plants abroad. UN News. https://news.un.org/en/story/2021/09/1100642. Accessed 2 Oct 2025

UNFCCC (2022) What is the triple planetary crisis? United Nations Climate Change. https://unfccc.int/news/what-is-the-triple-planetary-crisis. Accessed 9 Aug 2024

van Popering-Verkerk J, Molenveld A, van Buuren A, Leeuwen C (2022) A framework for governance capacity: a broad perspective on steering efforts in society. Adm Soc 54(9): 1767–1794. https://journals.sagepub.com/doi/10.1177/00953997211069932. Accessed 2 Oct 2025

Venter ZS, Aunan K, Chowdhury S et al (2021) Air pollution declines during COVID-19 lockdowns mitigate the global health burden. Environ Res 192:110403. https://doi.org/10.1016/j.envres.2020.110403

VijayaVenkataRaman S, Iniyan S, Goic R (2012) A review of climate change, mitigation and adaptation. Renew Sustain Energy Rev 16(1):878–897. https://doi.org/10.1016/j.rser.2011.09.009

Walker PGT, Whittaker C, Watson OJ et al (2020) The impact of COVID-19 and strategies for mitigation and suppression in low- and middle-income countries. Science 369(6502):413–422. https://doi.org/10.1126/science.abc0035

Wang ZL, Huang WJ, Liu-Lastres B (2022) Impact of user-generated travel posts on travel decisions: a comparative study on Weibo and Xiaohongshu. Ann Tourism Res Emp Insights 3(2):100064. https://doi.org/10.1016/j.annale.2022.100064

Wendt A (1999) Social theory of international politics. Cambridge Core. https://www.cambridge.org/core/books/social-theory-of-international-politics/0346E6FDC74FECEF6D2CDD7EFB003CF2. Accessed 26 Dec 2019

WTO (2022) World Trade Report 2022 Climate change and international trade. World Trade Organization. https://www.wto.org/english/res_e/publications_e/wtr22_e.htm. Accessed 2 Oct 2025

Wu T (2011) China, BRICs & the environment. The Diplomat. https://thediplomat.com/2011/11/china-brics-and-the-environment/. Accessed 2 Oct 2025

Xi J (2018) Xi Jinping: The Governance of China I (trans). 2nd edn. Cypress Book Co. UK Ltd, Beijing

Chapter 8
Repairing Water in the Face of Climate Change: A Tale of Two Communities

Gabriela Cuadrado-Quesada

Abstract Water has come under increasing pressure in recent years, resulting in significant declines in both quantity and quality. Concurrently, the Earth has experienced a marked rise in the frequency and intensity of extreme weather events, particularly floods and droughts. The COVID-19 pandemic further underscored the significance of water for human well-being, especially for drinking and sanitary conditions. This chapter examines the hydrological cycle and its deep entanglement with social contexts, introducing the hydrosocial cycle to better understand human–nature relations and potential responses to water-related challenges. Climate change is examined as a socio-natural phenomenon, which threatens people's homes and livelihoods through its effects on drinking water supplies, energy production, agricultural output, sea level rise, wildfires, and extreme weather. The chapter also reflects on how communities in the Global South are addressing climate-driven changes in water quantity and quality. Specifically, it tells two stories, one from India and one from Costa Rica, based on an empirical analysis of semi-structured interviews, open-ended discussions, and participant observations. Drawing on work around civic innovations and Haraway's plea for "staying with the trouble," these community actions both affirm and subtly transform existing ways of life, offering pragmatic insights into responding to climate impacts on water.

8.1 Introduction

Today Kati Thanda-Lake Eyre is a dry lake, located in the deserts of central Australia, in the state of South Australia. The lake occupies Australia's lowest natural point, which is 15 meters below sea level; however, 100,000 years ago, the lake was completely filled with water and was 10 times larger than today. The lake was

G. Cuadrado-Quesada (✉)
Water Governance Department, IHE Delft, Institute for Water Education, Delft, The Netherlands
e-mail: g.quesada@un-ihe.org

© The Author(s), under exclusive license to Springer Nature Switzerland AG 2026
J. E. Núñez (ed.), *Perspectives on Crises*,
https://doi.org/10.1007/978-3-032-23836-8_8

fed by numerous rivers, and it was surrounded by a lush, green landscape that hosted exotic fauna such as wombats, kangaroos, and marsupial lions.[1] Unfortunately, most of these creatures as well as most of the lake have disappeared due to climate change.

The story of Kati Thanda-Lake Eyre exemplifies how planet Earth is changing, and how it has always been changing. However, the problem we face nowadays is the frequency, speed, and degree of such changes. Planet Earth has been suffering a staggering rise in the number of extreme weather events over the past 20 years, driven mostly by rising global temperatures and other climatic changes. To illustrate, from 2000 to 2019, there were 7348 major droughts and floods around the world, killing 1.23 million people and causing 2.97 USD trillion in economic losses; however, in the two previous decades, i.e., from 1980 to 1999, the planet had 4212 major droughts and floods, 1.19 million deaths, and suffered 1.63 USD trillion in financial losses.[2]

The preceding statement illustrates how climate change affects every aspect of our daily lives—including our own survival as a species. One of the biggest problems with current change in climate is that, even though it is global, it affects some countries and people more than others. It is known that the least-emitting countries combined generate only a minimal fraction of total emissions. However, a few countries with the largest emissions contribute approximately 68% of the total. It also happens to be the case that these countries, including the United States of America, China, Russia, Germany, the United Kingdom, and Japan, are among those which are better positioned to implement alleviation measures for climate change effects, something that is typically not the case among the least-emitting countries in the world.

This situation shows how climate change also poses questions about injustice between countries in the Global North and the Global South. Floods and droughts are better dealt with when strong institutions are in place (e.g., insurances) and these are accompanied by economic support (e.g., agricultural incentives) from governments, as normally seen when such events happen in countries in the Global North. However, when these phenomena occur in the Global South the reality is very different and these events result in entire communities losing the little that they have, and countless people getting sick and/or suffering famine. This is also causing a huge number of climate refugees, which continues to be a global problem without a clear path of action. There is also injustice within countries in the Global North. Many people in countries like the United States of America and the United Kingdom are also very vulnerable to climate change impacts, such as poor people who have the least economic resources to cope with the problems caused by severe climate events.

It is important to note that in order to address global climate change problems there are significant climate policy strategies in place which seek to tackle emissions and protect the environment. We also have global frameworks and agreements

---

[1] See Bureau of Meteorology (2019).

[2] See UNDRR (2020).

to guide governments and societies to a more sustainable path, such as the Sustainable Development Goals (SDGs), the UN Framework Convention on Climate Change, and the Paris Agreement. However, these frameworks are not enough, and a lot more needs to be done.

In particular, this chapter addresses the question: How are different communities tackling the effects of climate change on their water? To answer this question, the chapter uses an empirical analysis of 20 semi-structured interviews; participation in a number of communities' meetings; open-ended discussions; and direct observations of climate change effects on water, local water practices, and community initiatives to deal with climate change effects. Following the evolving scholarship around civic innovations[3] and Donna Haraway's approach of "staying with the trouble,"[4] the chapter frames these communities' responses as creative forms of "living with" climate change and its impacts on water.

8.2 Theoretical Considerations

This section addresses the main concepts mobilized in the analysis, namely: climate change as a socio-environmental justice phenomenon; the hydrological cycle as a sociological cycle; and civic innovations as a way to address the problems caused by climate change. It also discusses the connections among these different concepts.

8.2.1 Climate Change

Almost 40 years ago, atmospheric scientists alerted the world of a large-scale ozone loss over Antarctica.[5] This phenomenon came to be known as the "ozone hole," which the international community managed by adopting binding controls of ozone-depleting substances. All emitters of pollutants agreed to a binding treaty that successfully established global targets and timetables. However, when this same idea of an agreed binding treaty was suggested to address climate change, the results were completely different.[6] The problem of climate change exemplifies that the planet faces a new and more complex problem than the ozone hole, which requires a new paradigm to be addressed but also to frame it, analyze it, and understand it.

Climate change is increasingly causing deadly and destructive consequences around the world. The increased frequency and intensity of extreme weather events like hurricanes, wildfires, and droughts threaten the lives of millions of people.

[3] See Biekart et al. (2016).

[4] See Haraway (2016).

[5] See Stolarski (1986).

[6] See Grundmann (2016).

While climate change affects the entire planet, its impact on people is not equally felt. Climate change impacts mostly people who are already burdened by poverty, inequality, and exclusion—people who have the least ability to cope with the situation. Their struggle to keep their livelihoods and secure their homes and communities is made more difficult every day. Therefore, it is important to frame climate change as a socio-environmental justice problem.[7]

This idea is taken from social sciences scholars[8] that seek to problematize the evident links between climate (nature) and social interactions (injustice). Even though climate change is a threat to everyone's health, air, water, food, and shelter, some groups—i.e., socially and economically disadvantaged ones—face the greatest risks. As time goes on, these groups will suffer the worst impact of climate change. Therefore, to tackle climate change it is necessary to acknowledge and address the social and justice issues, as these are inextricably linked.

Some social justice scholars[9] assert that climate change is also a product of racism. It started with conquest, genocides, slavery, and colonialism. To illustrate, extractive industries such as fossil fuel and mining were built on the backs and over the graves of Indigenous people around the globe, as they were expelled from their land and either killed or subjugated. The harmful impact of climate change is linked to historical neglect and racism. This happened around the entire world.

More recently we can also see how climate change ramifications continue to affect disadvantaged people even in the richest countries of the planet. For example, in 2005 in the United States of America, in the city of New Orleans, Hurricane Katrina caused extensive destruction. More than half of the 1200 people who died were African Americans and 80% of the homes that were destroyed belonged to African American residents. Many of these neighborhoods had received less government funding for flood protection than White neighborhoods.

Another prominent example to illustrate this argument is that of Flint, Michigan. In 2014, officials of Flint, which has a population of 56.6% African Americans, decided to draw its drinking water from the polluted Flint River in order to save money. Previously the city had brought in treated drinking water from Detroit. As the river had been used as an illegal waste dump for many years, the water was corrosive. This meant that the water leached lead from the aging pipelines. Thousands of people in Flint, including children, drank lead-laced water, which caused a terrible increase in lead levels in their blood, putting everyone at high risk for neurological damage. In October 2015, the city began importing water from Detroit again.

[7] See Miranda et al. (2011).

[8] See Moss (2009); see also Klinsky and Brankovic (2018).

[9] See Schell et al. (2020).

8.2.2 The Hydrologic Cycle

Hydrology is described as having origins in ancient philosophy but is understood to have emerged as a true science with the quantitative, basin-scale studies in the seventeenth century—when the hydrologic cycle was recognized (Linton 2010). According to the *Handbook of Hydrology* the hydrologic cycle is:

> the most fundamental principle of hydrology. Water evaporates from the oceans and the land surface, is carried over the earth in atmospheric circulation as water vapor, precipitates again as rain or snow, is intercepted by trees and vegetation, provides runoff on the land surface, infiltrates into soils, recharges groundwater, discharges into streams, and ultimately, flows out into the oceans from which it will eventually evaporate once again.[10]

Jamie Linton in his book, *What is water? The history of a modern abstraction*, introduces a fascinating critique to what he calls the "Hortonian hydrologic cycle" (after the American hydrologist Robert E. Horton). He explicates the hydrologic cycle as "a historical reconstruction of its representation rather than by reciting past investigations into the nature of water itself."[11] This means that since the term was coined, in the United States of America by Horton in 1931, the concept has been based on the mathematical foundation of the water balance equation and as a veritable natural fact, representing water as a constant (cyclical) flow, which intended to make water visible with the objective of accounting for and controlling it. However, this does not include a consideration of different geographical places such as deserts or tropical forests, which can alter how we understand the hydrologic cycle.[12]

It is interesting to note that this critique seeks to highlight that even a concept such as the hydrologic cycle, which in principle is scientific and neutral, is being heavily influenced by its contours, which include landscape, context, climatic conditions, and people and their activities. The way people use water, manage water, recharge water, and pollute water will directly affect the hydrologic cycle.

8.2.3 The Hydrosocial Cycle

Political ecology offers a different paradigm to understand water and the hydrologic cycle—along with what was discussed in the previous section and exemplified by Linton's critique to the hydrologic cycle. Political ecology has studied the many different ways in which the understanding and knowledge about water is constructed and practiced.[13] This implies that it has analyzed the way scientific claims regarding water are formulated and produced, highlighting the different ways in which

[10] See Maidment (1993).

[11] See Linton (2010), p. 126.

[12] Linton (2010), p. 127.

[13] Forsyth (2002).

science and people are interrelated.[14] These authors bring to the discussion the need to acknowledge that social, natural, and also political issues are intertwined into what is considered a "scientific truth" regarding water—and more broadly environmental problems and the possible ways to address them.

The plea of these authors is to highlight how social and political discourses are imposed into neutral scientific explanations or understandings of the world. Scientific paradigms or explanations about water issues such as pollution or scarcity often fail to acknowledge the different responsibilities and risks of different groups of people in society.[15] Therefore, it is important to acknowledge that water issues and problems are often embedded in broader social and political debates.

Therefore, many political ecologists started using the term "hydrosocial cycle," emphasizing the fact that water connects individuals not only materially but also politically and socially. For example, Karen Bakker[16] uses the hydrosocial cycle to illustrate the nuances of scarcity. Acknowledging that water is scarce, according to the hydrologic cycle, tells little about the human use of water, soils, and forests, which can only be defined in relation to human needs, practices, institutions, and technologies. Whether or not water is scarce depends on factors such as population density and distribution, power relations, and socioeconomic-cultural uses. Scarcity, then, is dependent on the hydrosocial, in addition to the hydrologic, cycle. This means that the assessment that intended to be neutral and technical is often neither neutral nor completely technical. If an assessment excluded an understanding of sociopolitical processes, then those issues mostly responsible for the situation, e.g., scarcity and pollution, would not be identified, and moreover, it would reproduce the existing unequal pattern of resource use that had given rise to the situation the assessment was designed to address.

8.3 Civic Innovations

In situations where climate change is rapidly and abruptly affecting the livelihoods of people and where there is an increase in inequity, injustice, and environmental degradation, people are pushed to make changes. Notably, people struggling with climate change problems are not necessarily pushed unidirectionally to water justice or more broadly to environmental justice, as it can also lead to complete despair. However, often it leads a community to push for positive transformations through, for example, civic innovations.

Taking inspiration from an emerging body of work on the concept of civic innovations, put forward by development researchers, this chapter frames communities' responses to climate change as civic innovations. This work emphasizes the

[14] See Acevedo Guerrero (2020); Whatmore (2009); Jasanoff (2004); Gyawali and Dixit (2001).

[15] Acevedo Guerrero (2020); Whatmore (2009); Jasanoff (2004); Gyawali and Dixit (2001).

[16] See Bakker (2003).

positive, creative, and imaginative aspects of the world as opposed to the common approach of focusing on the negative, on problems, and on what is wrong. Using the term "civic innovations" helps to give a useful alternative to such a crises' approach. This term seeks to "build a mosaic of responses by looking at what is happening on the ground where people are living the contradictions of development."[17]

These scholars emphasize that there is a need to question some predetermined ideas such as "development = good" or one universal policy solution, in order to look with openness at the actions on the ground. This means going beyond the structures of development and its logic. With the concept of civic innovation, these scholars acknowledge the contradictions and failures of our current system but also look at what is possible in how people live their everyday lives under current neoliberal capitalism. Civic innovation also seeks to explore the shifts and possibilities in politics, local economics, and in gender and sexual emancipatory movements.

Civic innovation proposes an alternative discourse that connects in interesting ways the private and public, the domestic and international, the local and the global, as well as the emotional with the technical. At the same time, its aim is to contribute to progressive and creative thinking and to offer a possibility to understand better alternatives to oppressive and daunting situations. Despite acknowledging the fears, doubts, and uncertainties of current times, the overarching purpose is to build connections and openings for social change—focusing on hope in people, cultures, societies, and institutions. Moreover, civic innovation acknowledges that social change happens in all levels of society including at the global, national, local, and—more importantly—at the individual level.[18]

The civic component of the term was established using as inspiration the civic-driven change work done at the International Institute of Social Sciences (ISS), in the Netherlands, whose work focuses on the role of citizens in changing/modifying/reinventing their political-social-cultural-economic contexts. On the other hand, the component of innovations was taken from social and technological sciences that use it to refer to new and creative methods, understandings, mechanisms, and policies. Mainly the proponents of the term refer to innovation as "creative forms of cultural, political and economic resistance and pathways to social change."[19]

The main reasoning behind using the term "civic innovations" is that it allows researchers to explore the current practices of communities in different parts of the world to tackle water problems and create/reinvent a new manner of understanding problems and situations caused by climate change. It offers the possibility of exploring, studying, and analyzing what is happening on the ground where people face water pollution and scarcity, and need to continue with their lives on a day-to-day basis.

Along with the idea of civic innovations the chapter is inspired by Donna Haraway's plea for "staying with the trouble," in which community actions can be

---

[17] See Biekart et al. (2016), p. 3.

[18] See Biekart et al. (2016).

[19] Biekart et al. (2016), p. 5.

seen as creative forms of "living with" climate change that both confirm and subtly change the terms of existence of communities and climate change effects in water. The staying with the trouble approach is a material semiotic approach,[20] which helps to analyze how social and material relations unfold in different practices that will allow discussion in great detail of the transformations of natural resources, in particular water, in landscapes that have been affected by climate change.[21] It can be used to look in particular at changes in water quantity (scarcity) and quality (pollution) and how these translate in water and more broadly in environmental risks. This approach also facilitates a broader understanding of the knowledge and practices around water and other natural resources and facilitates an approach to transform such landscapes into more sustainable, just, and inclusive ones.[22]

Using these frameworks, the chapter discusses two different stories, where communities affected by climate change have managed to address some of the problems, and yields new inspiration for pragmatic ways to deal with climate change effects in water.

8.4 A Tale of Two Communities: Coastal Communities of Santa Cruz, Guanacaste, Costa Rica and Hivre Bazar, Maharashtra, India

Even though Costa Rica is a tropical country, and many areas have significant rainfall, other areas, such as the coastal communities in Santa Cruz, Guanacaste, have not. The average rainfall during the rainy season in the North Pacific is between 1500 and 2000 mm; nevertheless, during the dry season it decreases considerably and can drop to 417 mm.[23] Especially during the past two years, due to the COVID-19 pandemic, these communities have realized the necessity of having water not only for human consumption but also for handwashing, cleaning, and to prevent diseases.

Water quantity (e.g., scarcity) and quality (e.g., saline intrusion) problems in this area are caused by many different factors such as limited development of water infrastructure, accelerated growth in tourism and real estate, and poor control mechanisms of the government to avoid overexploitation and pollution by certain users.[24] Moreover, recently these communities have been affected by severe changes in climate, for example by having less rainfall. As explained before, climate change is not only a natural phenomenon, but rather it is a socio-environmental problem that affects some people more than others. Many people in and around the coastal

---

[20] See Haraway (1991).

[21] See Haraway (2016).

[22] Haraway (2016), p. 11.

[23] See Mora-Alvarado et al. (2012).

[24] See Cuadrado-Quesada (2022).

communities of Santa Cruz have been severely affected by droughts in the last decade, some of them losing most of their crops and cattle.[25]

These coastal communities are a paradise with stunning white sand beaches and dry tropical forest. This area is a common destination for national and international tourism. In the last three decades the area has seen a rapid and widespread growth in tourism and associated real estate development, which for some is a positive achievement.[26] However, for many others, this growth has evidenced the lack of an overarching sustainable plan for the area, as many problems have occurred such as overexploitation of water, destruction of mangroves, deforestation, water pollution, and pollution of the beaches due to a lack of proper sewage.[27]

Since the boom in tourism and real estate started, back in the 1990s, problems of water availability, shortages, and salinity have resulted in the people in the coastal communities of Santa Cruz becoming ever more organized and vigilant in ascertaining who uses water, what for, and how much. Water shortages in these communities are becoming more and more frequent as well as extreme climatic events such as longer dry seasons and shorter rainy seasons.[28] Since then the communities have engaged with the problems and developed different initiatives to try to address them. This chapter frames such initiatives as civic innovations to highlight the role of citizens in these communities in transforming and reinventing their political-social-cultural-economic context, in a creative way that moves toward social change.

The main actors involved in the civic innovations are community-based organizations such as the development associations,[29] environmental associations, and water boards or ASADAs.[30] One factor that these actors have in common is that they are leaders in the communities, work pro-bono, want to improve the well-being in the community in which they live, have a sense of belonging to these communities, and that they care about nature and humans' interactions.[31] It is important to note that these communities are mainly dependent on groundwater.

These community leaders have engaged in addressing certain socio-environmental problems including the effects of climate change on water. Many of these civic innovations have been motivated as a way to repair the damages or consequences faced by the communities. Therefore, these civic responses/efforts have focused on

[25] Cuadrado-Quesada (2022), p. 115.

[26] See Cuadrado-Quesada (2017).

[27] Kuzdas et al. (2016).

[28] Kuzdas et al. (2016).

[29] These are communal organizations that collaboratively pursue the social, economic, and environmental advancement of their community. They work in coordination with governmental institutions and non-governmental organizations to identify community needs, develop strategic plans, and implement initiatives aimed at enhancing the overall quality of life. Their efforts typically span a wide range of areas, including health, education, and environmental sustainability.

[30] These are communal organizations that serve as key actors in the governance of local water systems, particularly through their involvement in the provision of safe drinking water and wastewater treatment processes within their communities.

[31] See Cuadrado-Quesada (2021).

creating awareness on the importance of water protection, climate change impacts, and in repairing environmental degradation in general.

The chapter frames the organization of the coastal communities and their social repair as civic innovations, which include practices of solidarity in alliances with transformative empowerment, which in turn seeks to influence local politics and social movements, and to allow new imaginaries of well-being and opportunities to flourish, even when immersed in a "development plan" that does not address their needs or interests. These civic innovations are as follows:

8.4.1 Environmental Awareness and Aquifer Protection

Many community actors, including the ASADAs, environmental associations, and development associations, have become ever more vigilant in who is using water, how much water is being used, and for what purposes. This involves engaging with many different water users and water experts and having meetings and discussions about water systems with them. These interactions lead to an understanding of how water systems (including groundwater) work, and subsequently the awareness emerges, increasing both the desire to and the likelihood of aquifer protection.

The importance of awareness and its function of expanding local (and national) mindsets, in order to move toward sustainable water use and water protection, is of great significance. Not understanding the manner in which water is being extracted and affected by many different uses and processes—e.g., wastewater discharges—will make it impossible to achieve sustainability and conservation. Along with the organization, discussions, awareness, and better understanding of how water behaves, there is the important task of monitoring of aquifers. Monitoring in this region has been used by the ASADAs, environmental associations, the development associations, and other community leaders to provide important information about the quantity and quality of the aquifers. This has facilitated a great level of engagement in these communities and many now know, for example, which aquifers are healthy, which aquifers are being used beyond their recharge capacity, and which aquifers suffer from saline intrusion and cannot be used anymore.

These civic innovations conducted by the community organizations are clearly motivated by the desire to improve the political-socio-environmental circumstances in which they live, the sense of belonging to these coastal areas—to the beach, the dry forest, and the rurality, and the fact that they care about nature, e.g., the water, soil, sand, sea, trees, and all the little creatures that live there. In particular these civic innovations seek to enhance sustainable use of water. The coastal communities of Santa Cruz have seen their aquifers become dry and saline and therefore the communities felt that a repair needed to be done. They knew they had to do it themselves because no one else would do it for them.

Luckily enough the ASADAs are responsible for authorizing new water connections in these communities. Therefore, the ASADAs can deny new connections if they know that groundwater resources are being used beyond their sustainable limits. Thanks to this legal prerogative the ASADAs have managed to impose some restrictions on groundwater use. For example, in the regions with high scarcity, when new hotels have requested a water connection, the ASADAs have denied the permit. As one interviewee from one of the ASADAs commented: "There are so many hotels being built [...] we cannot provide more permits to hotels and real estate [...] we have experienced water scarcity for many years now [...] particularly in summer [...] there is no more water."[32]

8.4.2 Protection Areas

Many empowered people in the coastal areas of Santa Cruz, including members of the ASADAs, environmental associations, and development associations, have been at the forefront of creating protection areas. The efforts made by these actors have focused on establishing protection areas to protect surface and groundwater sources used by the communities for human consumption. It is important to note that, legally, the ASADAs have many prerogatives to influence the protection of water but also nature more broadly. For example, the ASADAs can purchase the lands around their catchments with the objective of protecting water and guaranteeing their sustainability. Many ASADAs have purchased those lands and implemented reforestation activities, e.g., planting native trees.

Some ASADAs have made important efforts in buying several hectares of land with the only aim of protecting them. They have imposed absolute protection in such areas, where the only activity that is allowed is reforestation and protection. As highlighted by one of the interviewees: "We recently bought 19 hectares [...] these lands have allowed us to protect the water that we use for human consumption [...] our hope is that these lands will be protected forever so we will always have water."[33]

As discussed before, monitoring allows the communities to understand better how groundwater behaves, how much water is in the aquifer, and its quality. In turn, this better understanding of groundwater has enormously facilitated the decision about buying and protecting strategic lands. This civic innovation of buying lands and creating protected areas to guarantee water protection reflects how the ASADAs are working hard on promoting water conservation and overall sustainability in the coastal communities in the North Pacific of Costa Rica. This, was beautifully summarized by one interviewee who said "ASADAs, environmental associations and development associations are doing a great job at using whatever mechanisms we can [e.g., monitoring and buying land] to guarantee water protection for us but more importantly for future generations."[34]

---

[32] Interview Costa Rica, ASADA (July 21, 2022).

[33] Interview Costa Rica, ASADA (July 22, 2022).

[34] Interview Costa Rica, Development Association (*Asociación de Desarrollo*), (July 22, 2022).

Besides being on the other side of the world, there are many similarities between the coastal communities of Santa Cruz and the rural community of Hivre Bazar, Maharashtra, India. This community also mainly relies on groundwater, it has also been severely affected by climate change in the last few decades, and, like in the coastal communities of Santa Cruz, has through different civic innovations managed to flourish despite the adversity.

The community of Hivre Bazar is located in Nagar "Taluka" of Ahmednagar district in the state of Maharashtra, India. The population in Hivre Bazar is 1233 (217 households). Hivre Bazar is fairly homogenous in terms of caste, with the *Maratha* caste (middle caste in caste hierarchy) being the dominant one in terms of both number of households and size of the land they hold. Dalits (Scheduled Caste) account for about 6.5% of the population (81 persons, about 15 households), and they are mostly landless. Also, the size of the operational holdings of farmers vary greatly, from less than a hectare to about 20 ha.[35] Most of the people in the village are dedicated to agriculture, with some of the main crops including sorghum, millets, onions, beans, groundnuts, cucumber, coriander, and spinach. A few people have also taken jobs in the military and as teachers in primary and secondary schools.[36]

The average annual rainfall in the district is 579 mm.[37] The principal form of irrigation in Hivre Bazar is by open wells. Hivre Bazar has, in the past several decades, experienced many problems due to climate change such as droughts. Moreover, the community has suffered socioeconomic deterioration, which has included a lot of problems such as illegal distilleries and alcoholism.[38] The situation has undergone significant transformation over the past two decades.

As in the coastal communities of Santa Cruz, the community of Hivre Bazar has experimented with different civic innovations which have allowed for social repair as these engagements have included practices of solidarity with transformative empowerment within the community. These have managed to influence water protection and overall sustainability, allowing new imaginaries of well-being and the possibility to flourish. These engagements have been valued even more during the past few years, when this community, as with many others around the world, were needing water more than ever to address the COVID-19 pandemic. Below, the most influential civic innovations of the community of Hivre Bazar are discussed.

[35] See Menon et al. (2007).

[36] See Sangameswaran (2006).

[37] See Government of Maharashtra (2014).

[38] See Varghade (2002).

8.4.3 Creating "New" Water

The problematic situation of the community of Hivre Bazar in the 1970s was a key driver to push for civic innovations. Many people, in particular the youth, realized that they needed to do something drastic to overcome the socio-environmental crisis and hence decided to look for a new community leader—a new head of the panchayat.[39] Popatrao Pawar was this new community leader. It is noteworthy to say that with the arrival of Pawar many problems experienced by the community started to be addressed. The local context that includes particularities regarding social, economic, environmental, cultural, and even religious practices related to water and its use are fundamental to understand what and how civic innovations are adopted and implemented in Hivre Bazar. For instance, economic activities such as agriculture significantly influence patterns of water use. In many cases, there has been a deliberate shift from cultivating water-intensive crops (e.g., sugarcane) to more water-efficient alternatives, as part of broader efforts to prevent the overexploitation of water resources—and specifically, to avoid the extraction of water at rates exceeding natural recharge capacities. Such strategies are intended not only to mitigate unsustainable usage but also to promote long-term water availability. Furthermore, by curbing overexploitation, water resources can be distributed more equitably, potentially enabling access for more people.

The creation of "new" water in the community of Hivre Bazar required a need to improve surface storage and expand groundwater recharge. These were both made available through a social and collective effort. The newly created water resource thus warrants being called community water, despite the groundwater component of the water operating primarily under a private property regime. As the water in Hivre Bazar was newly created (producing "new" water), and as its uses and associated rights had not yet been established, people were more willing to craft rules that tilted toward equity and sustainability. This meant that more people were able to access and use this water and that sustainable and equitable components of its use were discussed.

The rules to govern this "new" water emanated at the very local level, as they were drafted in the panchayats in the shape of social norms or customary laws. This means that most people follow them as otherwise they will be sanctioned by the other members of the community. The sanctions might involve social punishment: for example, one participant mentioned that "it is common for some people not to talk to people who are wasting water."[40] The social norms or customary laws are often not written down but internalized and implemented by most people in a certain community.

---

[39] A panchayat is a community governing organization, which functions in rural India. It is a democratic structure at the grassroots level. It is a political organization.

[40] Interview India, local resident (October 3, 2017).

8.4.4 Meteorological Data, Water Knowledge, and Reforestation

Failure to change how water is used and the way in which it is affected by, for example, overuse and pollution will make sustainable use and protection impossible. Information and knowledge about how water behaves, how much is used, and who is using it are also pivotal in addressing existing social inequities, which tend to be exacerbated by climate change. Often water users do not understand how water functions and the threats it faces; however, it is becoming more and more common that people understand the water systems to a certain degree. As the experience of Hivre Bazar shows, raising awareness is not only about information and awareness with regard to how the resource works or functions; it is also about addressing equity concerns such as more adequate (re)allocation and (re)distribution of groundwater.[41]

A civic innovation that is helping to address water concerns in Hivre Bazar is the collection of local meteorological data. The collection, interpretation, and use of meteorological data has facilitated awareness, information, and knowledge regarding water systems in Hivre Bazar. For example, measuring rainfall and monitoring water levels, especially groundwater, has allowed the community to craft groundwater use rules as per availability, taking the form of groundwater budgets and audits.

The Gram Sabha launched such initiatives in 2004, and they have contributed to the community's comprehension of how groundwater levels work, how much groundwater there is, how best to distribute it, and how much groundwater is left for the environment. As a participant commented, "We think the monitoring and an annual groundwater audit has contributed to a more equitable and sustainable use and management of groundwater resources [...]. It has also contributed to greater agricultural productivity."[42]

Knowledge, along with awareness and the generation of information, also translated into the development of other social rules around water management and governance. In average rainfall years, for example, people agreed to certain types of groundwater use in terms of how much area they should have under irrigation in winter and in summer; they further agreed on the application of curbs on irrigation that should be imposed if there is below-average rainfall in summer or winter.[43] Awareness, information, and the overall knowledge regarding water systems were also linked to another relevant civic innovation that is currently going on in Hivre Bazar, that of reforestation.

From the 1990s onwards, reforestation began in the community. Hivre Bazar adopted a holistic focus on a variety of activities, with village groups being responsible for various aspects that included improved water use and overall sustainability. Hivre Bazar focused on reforestation, for which diverse programs and drives have

---

[41] See Cuadrado-Quesada and Joy (2021).

[42] Interview India, local resident (October 7, 2017).

[43] See Menon et al. (2007).

been frequently organized in the village. Currently, they have extensive parts of the community land (common land) dedicated only to reforestation. As highlighted by a participant, "We realized that we needed to reforest those lands [...], and we started to notice the difference thanks to the reforestation programs [...] now we have water all year round, even in summer."[44] As discussed, it was shown that, in Hivre Bazar, the community members' awareness, the knowledge about how water systems work, and reforestation activities have provided the community with a considerable improvement with regard to groundwater availability and access, and the overall sustainability of water resources.

8.5 The Significance of Civic Innovations

The previous examples in Hivre Bazar, Maharashtra, India and the coastal communities of Santa Cruz, Guanacaste, Costa Rica illustrate several engagements and repairs that the communities have done in order to address climate change problems that are affecting surface water and groundwater. These have been efforts outside the boundaries of state institutions, laws, and policies to ground more social, progressive options. All these examples show social repairs done by community organizations, which work separately from the formal, government-led initiatives to deal with climate change.

These prominent examples, where there have been efforts to move toward more social "solutions" than those designed by the government and formal venues, are becoming more and more common in many places around the world. These social repairs are becoming even more commonplace in countries of the Global South where it is more likely to see socio-environmental problems. For example, when situations of inequity, injustice, and environmental degradation become recurrent, like those experienced in Hivre Bazar and in the coastal communities of Santa Cruz, people seem to be willing to make changes, repairs, and innovations.

Of course, these changes, repairs, and innovations do not always necessarily lead to improvements, justice, equitable water access, or sustainable use of water. It is worth noting that, even though the rationale behind social engagements is to improve socio-environmental conditions, often communities face a myriad of problems. Therefore, there is not a straightforward connection between socio-environmental changes, repairs, and innovations and solving socio-environmental problems or crises. It seems that these engagements suggest that we need to complement other efforts, e.g., those made by governments. The role of national institutions, programs, strategies, policies, laws, and regulations is to set certain upper bound norms for addressing climate change effects in water and beyond; however, there is sufficient space and flexibility for local communities to evolve practices, initiatives, changes, innovations and, predominantly, repairs. The overall rationale behind this

[44] Interview India, local resident (October 10, 2017).

would always be to create other practices, rules, and norms to take forward the agenda of water justice, environmental justice, and social justice (in terms of (re) distributive justice, participation, and recognition that respects local contexts).

These two tales show how the concept of civic innovations can be used to understand and explain communities' practices and initiatives such as those in Hivre Bazar and the coastal communities of Santa Cruz that are being used to tackle water problems—due to climate change and beyond. They offer a possible explanation of what is happening on the ground, where people are, on a daily basis, faced with water pollution, salinity, scarcity, and a variety of other related problems. These two stories also illustrate how people and communities are "staying with the trouble," as theorized by Donna Haraway. They show how many community actions are being seen as creative forms of "living with" climate change that both confirm and reinterpret the terms of existence of these communities and the effects of climate change on water. Moreover, they show how transformations of such communities and landscapes to becoming more sustainable, just, and inclusive ones are possible.[45]

8.6 Conclusion

This chapter examined the concept of the hydrologic cycle by exposing its deep entanglement with the social context. It also analyzed the concept of the hydrosocial cycle to explain how the concept is intimately related to human–nature relations. Moreover, it scrutinized the phenomenon of climate change, highlighting that climate change is a socio-natural problem. In particular, the chapter focused on exploring and explaining the different ways in which the coastal communities of Santa Cruz in Guanacaste, Costa Rica and of Hivre Bazar in Maharashtra, India are trying to tackle the effects of climate change on their water. These stories show how the cycle of water is affected by human choices and decisions, thus demonstrating that it is a hydro-socio-logical cycle as opposed to a purely hydrological cycle. Of course, here this only applies to a small part of the hydrological cycle as these are only two communities. However, water is the most basic need for human beings and thus when the water cycle is being affected by human choices all around the world a global hydro-socio-logical cycle is created.

It was found in the research conducted, and in the literature reviewed, that there has been promotion at the rhetoric level of trying to better understand and frame the civic engagements, innovations, and repairs done by communities, especially when it comes to addressing socio-environmental problems and sustainability. Although this study focused specifically on two communities—Hivre Bazar and the coastal communities of Santa Cruz—the findings point to broader patterns that are likely applicable to many other communities, particularly across the Global South. In these contexts, formal institutions, including policies, legal frameworks, and

[45] See Haraway (2016).

regulatory mechanisms, often fall short in effectively addressing the complex challenges posed by climate change, especially in relation to water governance and access. This institutional inadequacy becomes even more pronounced during periods of crisis. For example, during the COVID-19 pandemic, it became starkly evident that existing formal mechanisms were insufficient to ensure equitable and reliable access to water, underscoring the vulnerability of these communities not only to environmental stressors but also to systemic institutional shortcomings in times of emergency.

This chapter makes a three-fold contribution. First, it shows how the concept of civic innovations can be used to make sense and explain efforts done by several communities around the world to deal with climate change, while at the same time using Donna Haraway's plea for "staying with the trouble" to more broadly explain how these community actions can be seen as creative forms of "living with" climate change and providing new inspirations for identifying pragmatic ways to deal with climate change effects on water. Second, it illustrates that, while useful, the concept of innovations might be confusing as the civic practices/initiatives are not always new or innovative but are more like a *repair* that communities need to do to address the many problems they face. Third, it argues for a revisit of the concept of the hydrosocial cycle. Even though this concept was coined to emphasize the fact that water connects individuals not only materially but also politically and socially, it would be useful to also include in the term the "logical" aspect that is currently missing. As water is the most basic need for human beings and the water cycle is being affected by human practices, choices, and decisions all around the world, there is merit in considering, understanding, and explaining the concept as a hydro-socio-logical cycle, highlighting that there is the necessity of it being also logical. The COVID-19 pandemic has evidenced our foremost dependence on water for our health and well-being.

In conclusion, the role of the governments and their institutions, strategies, laws, policies, and regulations at the international, national, and local levels to set ways to address climate change concerns and water-specific problems has proved to be insufficient. Therefore, the way forward to tackle current climate change problems, particularly when it comes to water, is to complement government/formal initiatives with civic repairs. This seems to be a promising manner to handle the problems of climate change, water-related problems and, more broadly, environmental and social justice.

References

Acevedo Guerrero T (2020) Politics of water flows: Water supply, sanitation, and drainage. In: Oxford Research Encyclopedia of environmental science. Oxford University Press, Oxford. https://doi.org/10.1093/acrefore/9780199389414.013.649

Bakker K (2003) An uncooperative commodity: privatizing water in England and Wales. Oxford University Press, Oxford

Biekart K, Hartcourt W, Knorringa P (eds) (2016) Exploring civic innovation for social and economic transformation. Routledge, London
Bureau of Meteorology (2019) Queensland floods: The water journey to Kati Thanda-Lake Eyre. Australian Government. https://media.bom.gov.au/social/blog/2059/queensland-floods-the-water-journey-to-kati-thanda-lake-eyre/ Accessed 25 May 2022
Cuadrado-Quesada G (2017) Gobernanza de las aguas subterráneas, conflictos socio-ambientales y alternativas: Experiencias de Costa Rica. Anuario de Estudios Centroamericanos 43(1):393–418. https://doi.org/10.15517/AECA.V1I1.28852
Cuadrado-Quesada G (2021) Las ASADAS: un análisis jurídico-social de su naturaleza y sus responsabilidades. Revista Jurídica IUS Doctrina 14(1) http://revistas.ucr.ac.cr/index.php/iusdoctrina/issue/view/3115
Cuadrado-Quesada G (2022) Governing groundwater: between law and practice. Springer Nature, Cham
Cuadrado-Quesada G, Joy KJ (2021) The need for co-evolution groundwater law and community practices for groundwater justice and sustainability: insights from Maharashtra India. Water Alternat 14(3):717–733
Forsyth T (2002) Critical political ecology: the politics of environmental science. Routledge, New York
Grundmann R (2016) Climate change as a wicked social problem. Nat Geosci 9:562–563
Gyawali A, Dixit A (2001) Water and science. Hydrological uncertainties, developmental aspirations and uningrained scientific culture. Futures 33(8–9):689–708
Haraway D (1991) Simians, cyborgs, and women: The reinvention of nature. Free Association Books, London
Haraway D (2016) Staying with the trouble: Making kin in the Chthulucene. Duke University Press, Durham, North Carolina
Jasanoff S (2004) Ordering knowledge, ordering society. In: Jasanoff S (ed) States of knowledge: the co-production of science and social order. Routledge, New York, pp 13–45
Klinsky S, Brankovic J (2018) The global climate regime and transitional justice. Routledge, New York
Kuzdas C, Warner B, Wiek A et al (2016) Sustainability assessment of water governance alternatives: the case of Guanacaste Costa Rica. Sustain Sci 11(2):231–247
Linton J (2010) What is water? The history of a modern abstraction. University of British Columbia Press, Vancouver
Maidment D (1993) Handbook of hydrology. McGraw-Hill, New York
Menon A, Singh P, Shah E et al (2007) Community-based natural resource management: Issues and cases from South Asia. SAGE, New Delhi
Miranda ML, Hastings DA, Aldy JE et al (2011) The environmental justice dimensions of climate change. Environ Just 4(1):17–25
Mora-Alvarado D, Mata A, Felipe-Portuguéz C (2012) Agua para Consumo Humano y Saneamiento: Situación de Costa Rica en el Contexto de las Américas 1961–2011. Instituto Costarricense de Acueductos y Alcantarillados, Laboratorio Nacional de Aguas
Moss J (2009) Climate change and social justice. Melbourne University Publishing, Melbourne
Sangameswaran P (2006) Equity in watershed development: a case study in Western Maharashtra. Econ Polit Weekly 41(21):2157–2165
Schell CJ, Dyson K, Fuentes TL et al (2020) The ecological and evolutionary consequences of systemic racism in urban environments. Science 80:3697. https://doi.org/10.1126/science.aay4497
Stolarski RS, Krueger AJ, Schoeberl MR et al (1986) Nimbus 7 satellite measurements of the springtime Antarctic ozone decrease. Nature 322(6082):808–811
UNDRR (2020) Human cost of disaster: An overview of the last 20 years 2000–2019. United Nations Office for Disaster Risk Reduction. https://www.preventionweb.net/files/74124_humancostofdisasters20002019reportu.pdf. Accessed 20 May 2022
Varghade S (2002) Hivrebajarchi yashogatha (The success story of Hivre Bazar). Prafalla Publications, Pune
Whatmore SJ (2009) Mapping knowledge controversies. Science, democracy and the redistribution of expertise. Progr Human Geography 33(5):587–598

Chapter 9
Response to Part II: Global Perspectives from Law and Policy on the Climate Crisis

Carla-Leanne Washbourne

Abstract The chapters in this section provide three geographically and temporally bounded exploratory cases of the evolving shape of legal and policy systems in the climate change context. They look back to some of the earliest modern environmental legislation—the US Clean Air Act (1970)—and forward to speculate upon the nuanced ways in which new knowledge and approaches are emerging from international, national, and local level activities to address climate change. They explore how policy, and specifically legislative, instruments are evolving and might continue to develop in ways that produce more effective, robust, and just social-environmental outcomes.

A key theme unifying the chapters is how we can draw broadly upon precedents that we have set in responding to prior crises in generating responses to the climate crisis. Their authors ask us to consider the lessons we have learned over decades of environmental policy creation and enaction, which policy tools we have at our disposal, and how effective these tools have been to date in enabling climate change action. They also invite us to reflect upon what our responses to fast emerging crises, like the COVID-19 pandemic, can teach us about climate change governance and its diverse temporal and spatial impacts.

9.1 Introduction

As outlined in the introduction to this volume, Part II of the collection provides a set of research-based perspectives on crises through the short-term lens of the COVID-19 pandemic, but with a long-term view fixed on the broader horizons of global challenges, of which climate change is a key facet. The potential impacts of

C.-L. Washbourne (✉)
Centre for Interdisciplinary Methodologies (CIM), University of Warwick, Coventry, UK

Department of Science, Technology, Engineering and Public Policy (STEaPP), University College London, London, UK
e-mail: carla.washbourne@warwick.ac.uk

© The Author(s), under exclusive license to Springer Nature Switzerland AG 2026

J. E. Núñez (ed.), *Perspectives on Crises*,
https://doi.org/10.1007/978-3-032-23836-8_9

climate change loom large over many other global concerns,[1] including the pandemic, like encroaching waves of crisis of increasing magnitude poised to crash down on our day-to-day lives as captured in characteristically light-hearted but hard-hitting fashion in this much shared and edited version of a Graeme MacKay Editorial Cartoon.[2]

The COVID-19 virus and resulting pandemic appeared as a new global threat in 2020 and remains one of the most widespread and impactful global health crises of the last century.[3] The emergence and spread of the virus, with its initially unknown pathologies and wider public health impact, caused swift and wholesale disruption to the global socioeconomic order and triggered the rapid deployment of a range of emergency response systems and emergency powers in local and national governance.[4]

Looking back to the peak of the COVID-19 pandemic, there is still much reflexive work to be done in understanding how effective these responses were. The chapters in this section draw out some of the similarities between framing and response to the pandemic and the climate crisis and ask what one can learn from the other. Through their own areas of research and practical focus, the authors consider whether our current quest to rapidly and equitably tackle and build resilience to climate change could also enable us to work better together to respond to other future shocks and stresses.

9.2 The Chapters

Much of the early discourse on climate change impacts and response was framed through quantitative, physical science insights and technological calls to action. As the scale and scope of the crisis has come into clearer view, and real-world action has started to follow, there is an increasing focus on drawing from broader knowledge bases to understand wider environmental and social effects of policy responses.[5] The chapters all speak in their own way to the (inter)dependence of human and societal outcomes on complex global cycles and intricate connections with more-than-human actors. They bring together theory and practice in this area, drawing upon perspectives from contexts as diverse as innovation studies, political ecology,

[1] While the focus of this section is on climate change, there is a growing recognition that the extinction crisis (biodiversity loss), disruption of global nutrient cycles, pollution, and other global challenges should be considered intimately linked, e.g., Groh et al. (2022); Passarelli et al. (2021); Pörtner et al. (2023).

[2] MacKay (2020) https://i0.wp.com/mackaycartoons.net/wp-content/uploads/2020/03/2020-0311-NATrevised2sm.jpg?w=864&ssl=1.

[3] Naseer et al. (2023).

[4] Béland et al. (2021); Ladi and Wolff (2021).

[5] Hughes (2024); Livingston and Rummukainen (2020); Callaghan et al. (2020); Rashidi and Lyons (2022).

and science and technology studies. Some have specific domains at their core, such as air and water. The governance and use of common pool resources,[6] of which water is a classic case, is becoming increasingly fraught. Effective approaches must seek to better understand these complex, interdependent systems and acknowledge the increasingly visible limits we are approaching in continuing to provide these resources at the quantity and quality needed for human flourishing.[7]

Emulating and echoing the impacts of climate change, and its disregard for borders, the chapters span spatial scales from local community initiatives in India and Costa Rica, to the national policy of Brazil and the US, to climate governance in the BRICS countries.[8] They explore the necessarily multiscalar nature of climate governance and lessons that we can draw from this in our response to future crises. The causes and effects of climate change are not able to be, nor should they be, neatly triaged into the "boxes" that have tended to shape our policy making in the past.[9] Presently a lack of harmonization persists as approaches abruptly stop, change, or disjunct at local, national, or regional boundaries.[10] The chapters explore global governance bodies and processes, frameworks and agreements (e.g., IPCC, SDGs, UNFCCC, Montreal Protocol), regional (EU), cross-national (BRICS), national, federal and state, city, and civic and community innovation and action. They allude to the importance of promoting connectivity and coherence in climate governance and demonstrate that inspiration and action can come from a range of different scales and settings.[11]

Indeed, the chapters are united by concerns of "coherence"[12] and the challenge that emerging and escalating crises can pose to our established and entrenched legal and policy systems. They remind us that the capacity sits with us all—as citizens, as decision-makers and decision-shapers, as scholars—to play a crucial role in bringing highly disparate policies and practices into coherence with our changing global priorities and social norms. In doing so, we can weave a coherent tapestry of policies that enable immediate action while developing a nuanced and ambitious picture of how legal and social systems might continue to transform toward more sustainable futures.

The authors ask, implicitly and explicitly, how we continue to move through a global era of polycrisis, where the environmental and social challenges we face are increasingly interdependent and indivisible. All grapple with what it means to respond to a crisis when already inhabiting a crisis. All articulate the real, imagined,

---

[6] Ostrom (2008).

[7] VanderWeele (2017).

[8] Originally Brazil, Russia, India, China, and South Africa. Since January 2024, BRICS members also include Egypt, Ethiopia, Iran, and the United Arab Emirates.

[9] Birungi (2015).

[10] Fopa Tchinda and Talbot (2024).

[11] Termeer et al. (2013).

[12] "We define policy coherence as an attribute of policy that systematically reduces conflicts and promotes synergies between and within different policy areas to achieve the outcomes associated with jointly agreed policy objectives." Nilsson et al. (2012), p. 396

and self-imposed resource constraints that bound our responses. It is notable that in all of the geographic cases presented there are marked tensions between normative, historical views of economic development, environmental management, and social progress.[13]

The country-level cases explored across the chapters highlight tensions between the need to plot a sustainable trajectory for development and the need to include and value traditional perspectives on resource use and environmental management. They convey important messages about just determination in the face of climate change: a need to recognize the tensions and constructively determine the future role and trajectory of developing and rapidly industrializing economies in the global social-ecological-technological system.[14] In this, many connections can be made to Part I of this volume as climate change impacts speak starkly to issues of justice and human dignity and these impacts play out in the context of colonialism, institutional, and structural racism.

Collectively, the chapters frame the field of climate governance, and climate law in particular, as an area of innovation within legal and policy scholarship and practice.[15] Climate law has needed to rapidly grow into a novel niche with respect to its relationship to global governance, the increasing recognition and need to enshrine the rights of more-than-human entities, and the concomitant need to acknowledge the autonomy and agency of collective voices.[16] It has also needed to take a novel approach to risk and precaution, acting in the face of significant unknowns in the context of polycrisis.[17] At the core, those working within the broad remit of environmental law are united by the capacity it has to take a systems view and increasingly recognize and articulate the nuanced actors that constitute social-ecological-technological systems;[18] enshrine and formalize emerging societal norms around environmental care and protection; and recognize and deliver equity in the distribution of environmental benefits and harms.[19]

[13] Cuadrado-Quesada, Chap. 8, Sect. 8.3, in this volume, articulates that we need to question: "pre-determined ideas such as 'development = good' or one universal policy solution, in order to look with openness at the actions on the ground. This means going beyond the structures of development and its logic."

[14] Markolf et al. (2018).

[15] Turnheim et al. (2018).

[16] Johansson (2023).

[17] "Polycrisis": a series of interconnected and interacting threats. Hoyer et al. (2023). See also Lawrence et al. (2024).

[18] Drumbl and Uhlířová (2021).

[19] Johansson (2023).

9.2.1 *Lucon: Regulating Greenhouse Gases as Criteria Pollutants in the United States and Brazil*

Chapter 6 presents a 50-year comparison of air pollution regulation between the United States and Brazil, two large global emitters "where climate policies are not consolidated."[20] It takes the US as a "global benchmark"[21] based on the groundbreaking work of the Clean Air Act (1970),[22] which set out to "protect public health and public welfare and to regulate emissions of hazardous air pollutants."[23] In the context of growing global enthusiasm for climate change legislation,[24] the chapter explores opportunities for policy innovation in the control of greenhouse gases (GHGs), the current and potential future mechanisms for doing so in the cases of the US and Brazil, and the benefits and vulnerabilities of policy instruments that enable some of the these globally impactful actions at the national and subnational levels.

An introduction to the US case explores the precedent set by the Clean Air Act (1970), which sought to regulate harmful known air pollutants such as sulfur oxides, particulate matter, and carbon monoxide, and remains a notable and influential frontrunner in global environmental legislation.[25] It also explores the enthusiasm (in the early 2020s) for the US Environmental Protection Agency (EPA) to class greenhouse gases as "criteria pollutants"[26] and the accompanying necessity to, therefore, consider such gases as pollutants and control them as close as possible to their sources. The Brazil Case focuses on early attempts to establish provisions for actions akin to the US Clean Air Act, taking this Act as explicit inspiration, such as the establishment of the São Paulo State Environment Agency (CETESB) and developments over the decades following including CONAMA Resolution 5, which provides for the National Control Program of Air Pollution (PRONAR).[27] The author states that:

> without considering greenhouse gases as pollutants it will be practically impossible to establish the legal restrictions necessary to comply with such commitments, since GHGs in fact still do not exist in the regulatory framework.[28]

---

[20] Lucon, Chap. 6, Sect. 6.1, in this volume.

[21] Lucon, Chap. 6 in this volume.

[22] US Congress (1970). Public Law 91-604 An Act to amend the Clean Air Act to provide for a more effective program to improve the quality of the Nation's air (Dec 31, 1970 - H.R. 17255) https://www.govtrack.us/congress/bills/91/hr17255. Accessed Dec 9, 2024.

[23] Lucon, Chap. 6, Sect. 6.2.1, in this volume.

[24] Eskander et al. (2021).

[25] Mosley (2014).

[26] Criteria pollutants "are common in outdoor air, considered harmful to public health and the environment, and [...] come from numerous and diverse sources." US EPA (2026).

[27] CONAMA. Resolução no 5, de 15 de junho de 1989. Dispõe sobre o Programa Nacional de Controle da Poluição do Ar—PRONAR. http://conama.mma.gov.br/?option=com_sisconama&task=arquivo.download&id=81. Accessed Dec 18, 2025.

[28] Lucon, Chap. 6, Sect. 6.3.3, in this volume.

The US–Brazil comparison explores the power and influence of national legislation on the global stage and cites the evolution, translation, and transposition of the US 1970 Clean Air Act to many other democratic jurisdictions worldwide for air pollution command and control.[29] This highlights the potential for significant legislative shifts to occur on the basis of strong consensus and leadership, which can occur based on evidence offered by highly disruptive events such as growing evidence of observable air quality effects on human health and the environment, or the discovery of and rapid response to ozone layer depletion (e.g., the Montreal Protocol[30]).

While enabling significant progress in air pollution reduction and halting ozone layer depletion, the US Clean Air Act (1970) has not yet been formally supplemented to integrate greenhouse gases and the moves to do so have been complex and constrained by current systems and actors. The author highlights the impacts of disconnects in priorities, mechanisms, and practice between legislature, judiciary, and executive in the US, magnified by the increasing polarization of a wide range of policy issues.[31] They go on to explain that:

> several regulatory initiatives have been trying to circumvent direct enforcements of GHG reduction—standards, investments, tax incentives, programs, and support for technology innovation—implemented under various legal authorities.[32]

The chapter includes an extended reflection on the limits of regulatory authority by responsible bodies such as the EPA, also established in 1970, and the "major questions doctrine," the idea that agencies in the US must have clear congressional authorization to decide issues of vast "economic and political significance."[33] Evidence of this significance can be highly disputed and the author notes that recent actions of the EPA have led to a shift in debate around greenhouse gas regulation "from science and policy effectiveness to statutory interpretations and the limits of executive agency power"[34] noting the dominant role of legislative action and litigation in this. In the case of Brazil, the importance of administrative action, activism, and civil society engagement in driving the policy agenda for action on greenhouse gases is highlighted. The use of criminal sanctions for environmental damage is also noted under Federal Law 9605.[35]

---

[29] US EPA (2021).

[30] UNEP (United Nations Environment Programme), 1987 Montreal Protocol on Substances that Deplete the Ozone Layer 1522 UNTS 3, 26 ILM 1541, 1550.

[31] Mccarty (2011).

[32] Lucon, Chap. 6, Sect. 6.2, in this volume.

[33] Lucon, Chap. 6, Sect. 6.2.5, in this volume.

[34] Lucon, Chap. 6, Sect. 6.2.5, in this volume.

[35] Brazil, 1998. Lei 9605 (On Penal and Administrative Sanctions Derived from Conducts and Activities Harmful to the Environment). http://www.planalto.gov.br/ccivil_03/leis/l9605.htm. Accessed Aug 9, 2025.

The chapter reflects on the relationship and relative efficacy of greenhouse gas regulation at state or national levels. While the Paris Agreement[36] focuses on national reporting (via the reporting of nationally determined contributions) and in the US the Clean Air Act (1970) is situated at the national (federal) level, the importance of voluntary initiatives at the state level is also foregrounded, in particular:

> Created after the 2017 withdrawal of the US from the Paris Agreement, the "We Are Still In" movement has gained a lot of support and spotlight, as a beam of hope for the nonfederal leadership in terms of a climate ambition that could be replicated abroad.[37]

This voluntary action ("We Are Still In," a movement by 2025 of "nearly 4,000 leaders representing 159 million people and a collective $9.46 trillion in GDP"[38]), which paralleled actions such as the US Climate Alliance[39] and the Chicago Climate Charter[40] among others, was critical in creating or sustaining subnational (state and city level) action on climate change in the US over this period.[41] It is concluded that the "US climate policy landscape after 2025 is defined by a profound divergence between federal and subnational ambitions."[42] Some emphasis has been given to the opportunity offered by voluntary initiatives, particularly when the national policy environment is unsupportive toward climate action—notably during the first Trump (US) and Bolsonaro (Brazil) administrations.[43] Moves to practically limit greenhouse gas emissions at the state level in Brazil include proposals by several states to set goals or sectoral targets for emissions reduction at a local level. The "We Are Still In" movement, also active in Brazil, is characterized:

> more as a political platform than as a proper form of advancing ambition [...] a protest against setbacks in environmental governance at federal level, particularly those related to soaring deforestation rates in the Amazon region and to limiting participation of civil society in the decision-making processes.[44]

In making its claims for reasons to be hopeful on progress toward considering greenhouse gases as criteria pollutants, the chapter highlights one of the key tensions in climate change governance at all levels—the disconnect between ambition, hope, time, and progress. At the core is a perceived trade-off between a "competitive" and low carbon economy. The chapter highlights the potential within the Brazilian system to leverage strong action in the creation of relevant legislation in moving from "legal theory to regulatory action, embedding GHGs into its air

---

[36] UNFCCC (United National Framework Commission on Climate Change), Paris Agreement to the United Nations Framework Convention on Climate Change, Dec. 12, 2015, T.I.A.S. No. 16-1104. U.N. Doc. FCCC/CP/2015/L.9/Rev/1.

[37] Lucon, Chap. 6, Sect. 6.2.5, in this volume.

[38] We Are Still In (2025); Lucon, Chap. 6, Sect. 6.2.5, in this volume.

[39] US Climate Alliance (2026).

[40] Chicago Climate Charter (2017).

[41] Baumeister (2018).

[42] Lucon, Chap. 6, Sect. 6.2.5, in this volume.

[43] Baumeister (2018); Toni and Feitosa Chaves (2022).

[44] Lucon, Chap. 6, Sect. 6.3.5, in this volume.

pollution control lexicon."[45] Within the US system, the potential is noted for creating significant reform through supplementing or modifying the enactment of established policy instruments like executive orders that can be comparatively responsive,[46] while simultaneously stating that "the widespread use of AP-42 as a regulatory benchmark"[47] had long been expected to evolve to included greenhouse gas emissions. But we are still waiting to see this evolution, which seems increasingly unlikely in the current political climate.

The use of executive orders in the US, and in particular the Executive Order on Protecting Public Health and the Environment and Restoring Science to Tackle the Climate Crisis,[48] was framed as a "breath of hope"[49] in moving forward, bringing a limited justification for action on the basis on impacts on human health and well-being. The order was one of a number signed by President Joe Biden immediately after his inauguration. While it included rejoining the Paris Agreement and other actions to recognize the impact of greenhouse gas emissions and the need to limit them, it did not extend to the inclusion of greenhouse gases as criteria pollutants. While this order was heralded by many as a significant step forward for US environmental policy,[50] it also starkly highlights how climate action—and action on a range of other politically divisive policy issues—can be strongly dependent on the prevailing, and often short-term, political climate. Indeed, in the executive orders emerging in the first days and weeks of the second Trump administration, environmental policy was one of the key targets for "active and systematic" dismantling.[51] In January 2025 an executive order was signed, withdrawing the US from the Paris Agreement for a second time.[52]

9.2.2 Castro and Denny: BRICS Response to Climate Governance Crisis in Pandemic Times

This chapter explores the intimate relationship between climate change and the COVID-19 pandemic, through the lens of climate governance in the BRICS countries.[53] It opens with the claim that:

---

[45] Lucon, Chap. 6, Sect. 6.4, in this volume.

[46] Kennedy (2015).

[47] Lucon, Chap. 6, Sect. 6.2.2, in this volume.

[48] The White House (2021).

[49] Lucon, Chap. 6, Sect. 6.4, in this volume.

[50] Brewer (2022).

[51] Lucon, Chap. 6, Sect. 6.2.5, in this volume.

[52] The White House (2025).

[53] Rinaldi and Martuscelli (2016).

> Despite the robust scientific knowledge and accumulated empirical evidence, the international community has not been able to provide appropriate responses through multilateral institutions.[54]

The authors posit that many countries are already struggling to move forward with their own development, while shaping substantive climate action in the context of an apathetic international climate policy regime.[55]

As others have speculated, the chapter considers whether the peak of the COVID-19 pandemic provided a disruptive reset. It goes on to question whether this could have created space for countries to take ownership of their own development trajectories in which they might have more autonomy to shape ambitious, sustainable, and locally determined climate governance responses:

> This study treats COVID-19 as an intervening variable that exaggerates the lack of international institutional response to collective action problems that leaves developing countries vulnerable due to a lack of appropriate financing and technology transfer, both essential to mitigation and adaptation.[56]

The disruption brought by the pandemic is held up as a possible catalytic factor in further increasing disparities and inequalities between the Global North and South to an untenable level and acting as a prompt for national and international actors to demand new forms of governance that are focused on tackling polycrisis.[57]

The chapter content was initially inspired by a series of virtual roundtables taking place in 2020, bringing together a group of transdisciplinary experts on climate change, which asked: "Is there an option, especially for developing countries, to overcome the limitation of international institutions on addressing climate change, while achieving sustainable development and dealing with the pandemic or recovering from it?"[58] The roundtable participants suggested that they saw more similarities than differences between the two global threats (climate change and COVID-19) and that many of the governance issues being observed in the COVID-19 pandemic response were indeed already present in the response to other global challenges and these were exacerbated, rather than created, by the pandemic.

To explore these ideas further, the authors analyzed the content of climate governance narratives developed by Brazil, Russia, India, China, and South Africa,[59] the founding nations of BRICS (a political and diplomatic coordination forum for emerging economies, established in 2001, currently with 11 members) immediately preceding and following the start of the pandemic, drawing upon declarations issued from 2017 to 2021 as the primary source documents. The importance of the emergence of groups enabling South–South cooperation and capacity building is

---

[54] Castro and Denny, Chap. 7, Sect. 7.1, in this volume.

[55] Castro and Denny, Chap. 7, Sect. 7.1, in this volume; Manzanedo and Manning (2020).

[56] Castro and Denny, Chap. 7, Sect. 7.1, this volume.

[57] Alam et al. (2015); Hoyer et al. (2023).

[58] Castro and Denny, Chap. 7, Sect. 7.1, this volume.

[59] The original BRICS nations were the focus of this work. Since January 2024, BRICS members also include Egypt, Ethiopia, Iran, and the United Arab Emirates.

highlighted, including the G77 (Group of 77, established in 1964, the largest intergovernmental group of developing countries in the UN, promoting their economic interests) and CELAC (Community of Latin American and Caribbean States, established in 2010, a regional political coordinating mechanism representing all 33 countries in Latin America and the Caribbean). The BRICS platform is deemed of particular interest for study due to its membership of emerging economies and its "ontological and epistemological stances that have the capacity to engender cooperation and mutual assistance among its members,"[60] providing a space for experience sharing, learning, and development of novel policies and practice.[61] BRICS countries collaborate on issues related to politics, economy, and trade, and increasingly in developing shared narratives of "justice, self-determination, and recognition," which inform "technical cooperation, regional integration initiatives, and joint positions in international negotiations."[62] BRICS climate governance narratives were analyzed in complement with the Climate Action Tracker[63] and Environmental Justice Atlas,[64] to explore shared challenges in adapting to climate change.

Overall, the chapter attests that the BRICS' institutional response to climate change has been "very weak,"[65] a situation further exacerbated by COVID-19, with significant perceived conflicts and trade-offs between development, climate action, and environmental justice. While there are differences in the level to which different BRICS nations have adopted and enacted climate governance, "countries' shared perceptions, expectations, and experiences about development"[66] remain a common challenge to moving forward on climate action in a substantive way.[67] Analysis of the corpus suggests an ongoing preoccupation with the need to increase levels of "development" established by each country based on the national interest, in a manner inconsistent with the platform's objectives toward sustainability and climate change governance. This extends to a lack of alternative cooperation models to those commonly employed in engaging with developed countries and neoliberal international institutions.[68] Aligned with Chap. 6, the authors note the challenges posed by a lack of legally binding instruments at the international level extending to BRICS in a "complex architecture of global governance, and a hard-to-achieve and

[60] Castro and Denny (2020); Castro and Denny, Chap. 7, Sect. 7.3, in this volume.

[61] Petrone (2019).

[62] Castro and Denny, Chap. 7, Sect. 7.1, in this volume.

[63] CAT (2020).

[64] Ej Atlas (2020).

[65] Castro and Denny, Chap. 7, Sect. 7.5, in this volume; Sampene et al. (2021).

[66] Castro and Denny, Chap. 7, Sect. 7.1, in this volume.

[67] Downie and Williams (2018).

[68] Li and Carey (2014).

maintain orchestration of power,"[69] which is ultimately detrimental to national climate governance commitments and action.[70] The authors posit that:

> Achieving an equilibrium between environmental protection and social and economic development is contingent on two primary variables related to large-scale cooperation: firstly, the endorsement of multilateral institutions and platforms, given the inherently interconnected nature of environmental challenges; and secondly, the involvement of non-state actors.[71]

BRICS is described as having adopted a dual approach on climate change: multilaterally, promoting the acknowledgment of economic and social progress in developing countries as a collective international responsibility, especially within the UN system; and at South–South level, encouraging "developing countries to pool their resources and capabilities, thereby reducing their dependence on the Global North."[72]

The chapter concludes by exploring the importance of voluntary and non-binding agreements in climate governance in BRICS, querying whether these kinds of mechanisms can play an elevated role going forward, in promoting other forms of action and cooperation being "informal" but "morally binding."[73] It highlights BRICS' institutional authority and capacity for "soft law," setting expectations, developing consensus, and supporting the establishment of norms, resolutions, and principles which support formal treaties. Looking forward, the authors suggest that "climate litigation"[74] and the transnational enforcement of environmental law are possibilities for progressing climate governance in BRICS and beyond.[75] Other possibilities explored include the "green new deals"[76] and the hope that some of the post-pandemic fiscal recovery packages are "conditioned to sustainability."[77] This is buoyed by short-term opportunity in the disruption of existing systems, but with the capacity to entrench or partly displace fossil fuel-intensive economic systems at large scale in the longer term. The authors recognize that systemic shocks rarely occur in isolation and that pandemics, climate change, biodiversity loss, transboundary pollution, and geopolitical disruptions often reinforce one another, amplifying vulnerabilities and increasing the need for robust mechanisms for capacity building, resource sharing, and cooperation that BRICS and other platforms seek to offer.

---

[69] Castro and Denny, Chap. 7, Sect. 7.2, in this volume.

[70] Laïdi (2012).

[71] Castro and Denny, Chap. 7, Sect. 7.4.1, in this volume.

[72] Castro and Denny, Chap. 7, Sect. 7.4.2, in this volume.

[73] Castro and Denny, Chap. 7, Sect. 7.4.2, in this volume.

[74] Setzer and Vanhala (2019); Castro and Denny, Chap. 7, Sect. 7.2, in this volume.

[75] Murcott and Tigre (2024).

[76] Boyle et al. (2021).

[77] Castro and Denny, Chap. 7, Sect. 7.2, in this volume.

9.2.3 *Cuadrado-Quesada: Repairing Water in the Face of Climate Change: A Tale of Two Communities*

Turning to climate action at the smallest of governance levels, the scale of local communities and community groups, this chapter explores the use of civic innovations to preempt and tackle the impacts of climate change. It outlines innovations embraced by two communities—Hivre Bazar, Maharashtra, India and Santa Cruz, Guanacaste, Costa Rica—separated by geography but with a shared drive to take action to address current and future climate change impacts on their access to and broader relationship with water. Many of the civic actions documented have emerged in the perceived absence of leadership on the issue by government or other formal institutions and a lack of sufficient strategies, policies, and regulations.[78] The cases are framed by the observation that:

> during the COVID-19 pandemic, it became starkly evident that existing formal mechanisms were insufficient to ensure equitable and reliable access to water, underscoring the vulnerability of these communities not only to environmental stressors but also to systemic institutional shortcomings in times of emergency.[79]

The concept of the hydro-socio-logical cycle is introduced, to acknowledge the way in which the cycle of water is increasingly affected by human choices and decisions, forming the hydrologic system's "deep entanglement with the social context."[80] Human actions have significantly changed the hydrologic system, with the bulk of the responsibility for these changes being with the few countries with the largest emissions. The author explains that while climate change is widely recognized as a threat to health, and to fundamental needs for clean air, water, food, and shelter, the causes and impacts are highly diffracted. They note that the harmful impact of climate change is still, globally, "linked to historical neglect and racism."[81] It is often the most socially and economically disadvantaged groups that face the greatest vulnerabilities and risks.

The chapter draws inspiration from the work of science and technology studies scholar Donna J. Haraway and her call for "staying with the trouble" and embracing the necessity of reimagining human–nature relationships in the current time of polycrisis and destabilization.[82] The two cases illustrate progress through struggle and collaboration, and the role of practices of connection and repair within systems of scarcity and limitation. They illustrate that:

---

[78] Biekart et al. (2016).

[79] Cuadrado-Quesada, Chap. 8, Sect. 8.6, in this volume.

[80] Cuadrado-Quesada, Chap. 8, Sect. 8.6, in this volume.

[81] Cuadrado-Quesada, Chap. 8, Sect. 8.2.1, in this volume.

[82] Haraway (2016).

> community actions can be seen as creative forms of "living with" climate change that both confirm and subtly change the terms of existence of communities and climate change effects in water.[83]

Both cases were developed through "semi-structured interviews; participation in a number of communities' meetings; open-ended discussions; and direct observations of climate change effects on water, local water practices, and community initiatives to deal with climate change effects."[84] They explore the ways in which water system innovations have been developed at the civic or community level. Both cases highlight the centrality and diversity of environmental justice issues in climate change governance. In the case of Hivre Bazar, Maharashtra, India, this includes low-cost approaches to increase water collection and retention and expand groundwater recharge in an otherwise water scarce region. Viewed as "new" resources, these additional reserves have been proactively labeled as a community water resource, separated from the private property regime that otherwise governs many water operations in the region, and enabled the crafting of new rules and approaches for its use, which have "tilted toward equity and sustainability."[85] In the case of Santa Cruz, Guanacaste, Costa Rica, increasing organization of the coastal communities and processes of social repair have led to the empowerment of Rural Aqueduct Associations (ASADAs),[86] environmental associations, development associations, and other community leaders. These actors conduct and instruct monitoring and analyze monitoring data to provide important information about the quantity and quality of the local aquifers, supporting them to take informed decisions and action, including refusal of applications for abstraction and use and direct acquisition of land to protect water sources.

Core to both cases is a reflection on if and how these approaches can be translated or scaled from their local contexts. While much of the discourse on climate action still points toward global agreements for its key frames and narratives, looking to local-scale "civic innovation" can teach us important lessons about creativity, resourcefulness, and processes by which we can create new governance approaches and reciprocate changing social norms.[87] "Civic innovation"[88] acknowledges that social change happens in all levels of society including at the global, national, local, and—more importantly—at the individual level. The cases presented here are, in many ways, a microcosm of the challenges we see and experience at larger governance scales, bringing together multiple actors to take decisions across a complex social-ecological-technological space, in the face of often limited resources and

[83] Cuadrado-Quesada, Chap. 8, Sect. 8.3, in this volume.

[84] Cuadrado-Quesada, Chap. 8, Sect. 8.1, in this volume.

[85] Cuadrado-Quesada, Chap. 8, Sect. 8.4.3, in this volume.

[86] "Un equipo comprometido en promover el desarrollo comunal por medio un servicio sostenible de agua potable y alcantarillado sanitario." AYA (2024).

[87] Sippel and Jenssen (2009); Washbourne et al. (2021).

[88] Biekart et al. (2016).

data. They highlight the importance of policy learning and a need to engage with a wide range of actors to develop meaningful ongoing action.[89]

Reflecting back to the COVID-19 pandemic, this chapter reinforces the centrality of basic resources like water in crisis response and highlights the need to develop robust and resilient systems of resource management to cope with the converging pressures of climate change and inevitable future crises.[90] In short, preparation for nuanced and wide-ranging impacts of climate change goes hand-in-hand with preparation for a range of other disruptive impacts across the social-ecological-technological system, at all scales from local to global.

References

Alam S, Atapattu S, Gonzalez CG et al (eds) (2015) International environmental law and the global South. Cambridge University Press, Cambridge. https://doi.org/10.1017/CBO9781107295414

AYA (2024) Instituto Costarricense de Acueductos y Alcantarillados. https://www.aya.go.cr/ASADAS/Paginas/default.aspx. Accessed 9 Dec 2024

Baumeister S (2018) We Are Still In! Conference report from the 2018 Ceres Conference. J Clean Prod 196:183–184. https://doi.org/10.1016/j.jclepro.2018.06.069

Béland D, Cantillon B, Hick R et al (2021) Social policy in the face of a global pandemic: policy responses to the COVID-19 crisis. Soc Policy Adm 55(2):249–260. https://doi.org/10.1111/spol.12718

Biekart K, Hartcourt W, Knorringa P (eds) (2016) Exploring civic innovation for social and economic transformation. Routledge, London

Birungi P (2015) Breaking "silo" approach key in toppling barriers to merging three pillars of sustainable development, speaker tells high-level political forum. UN Meetings Coverage and Press Releases. https://press.un.org/en/2015/ecosoc6705.doc.htm. Accessed 9 Dec 2024

Boyle AD, Leggat G, Morikawa L et al (2021) Green new deal proposals: comparing emerging transformational climate policies at multiple scales. Energy Res Soc Sci 81:102259. https://doi.org/10.1016/j.erss.2021.102259

Brewer TL (2022) Transforming U.S. climate change policies: 2021 and beyond. Springer Nature, Cham

Callaghan MW, Minx JC, Forster PM (2020) A topography of climate change research. Nat Clim Change 10:118–123. https://doi.org/10.1038/s41558-019-0684-5

Castro D, Denny DMT (2020) Economic relationship between Brazil and China: An empirical assessment using sentiment and content analysis. Beijing Law Rev 11:227–243. https://doi.org/10.4236/blr.2020.111016

CAT (2020) Climate Action Tracker. https://climateactiontracker.org/. Accessed 21 Jan 2026

Chicago Climate Charter (2017) North American Climate Summit. https://northamericanclimate-summit.splashthat.com. Accessed 21 Jan 2026

Downie C, Williams M (2018) After the Paris Agreement: what role for the BRICS in global climate governance? Glob Policy 9(3):398–407. https://doi.org/10.1111/1758-5899.12550

Drumbl MA, Uhlířová K (2021) Actors and law-making in international environmental law. In: Fitzmaurice M, Brus M, Merkouris P et al (eds) Research handbook of international environmental law, 2nd edn. Edward Elgar Publishing, Cheltenham, pp 2–44

Ej Atlas (2020) Environmental justice atlas. https://ejatlas.org/. Accessed 21 Jan 2026

[89] Moyson et al. (2017).

[90] Rockström et al. (2023).

Eskander S, Fankhauser S, Setzer J (2021) Global lessons from climate change legislation and litigation. Environ Energy Policy Econ 2:44–82. https://doi.org/10.1086/711306
Fopa Tchinda A, Talbot D (2024) Barriers and enablers of environmental policy coherence: a systematic review. Environ Policy Gov 34(1):77–92. https://doi.org/10.1002/eet.2057
Groh K, vom Berg C, Schirmer K, Tlili A (2022) Anthropogenic chemicals as underestimated drivers of biodiversity loss: scientific and societal implications. Environ Sci Technol 56(2):707–710. https://doi.org/10.1021/acs.est.1c08399
Haraway D (2016) Staying with the trouble: making kin in the Chthulucene. Duke University Press, Durham
Hoyer D, Bennett JS, Reddish J et al (2023) Navigating polycrisis: long-run socio-cultural factors shape response to changing climate. Philos Transact Royal Soc B Biol Sci 378(1889):20220402. https://doi.org/10.1098/rstb.2022.0402
Hughes H (2024) The IPCC and the politics of writing climate change. Cambridge University Press, Cambridge. https://doi.org/10.1017/9781009341554
Johansson V (2023) Just transition as an evolving concept in international climate law. J Environ Law 35(2):229–249. https://doi.org/10.1093/jel/eqad017
Kennedy JB (2015) "'Do This! Do That!' and Nothing Will Happen": executive orders and bureaucratic responsiveness. Am Polit Res 43(1):59–82. https://doi.org/10.1177/1532673X14534062
Ladi S, Wolff S (2021) The EU institutional architecture in the Covid-19 response: coordinative Europeanization in times of permanent emergency. J Common Mark Stud 59:32–43. https://doi.org/10.1111/jcms.13254
Laïdi Z (2012) BRICS: sovereignty power and weakness. Int Polit 49:614–632. https://doi.org/10.1057/ip.2012.17
Lawrence M, Homer-Dixon T, Janzwood S et al (2024) Global polycrisis: the causal mechanisms of crisis entanglement. Glob Sustain 7:e6. https://doi.org/10.1017/sus.2024.1
Li X, Carey R (2014) The BRICS and the international development system: Challenge and convergence? The Institute of Development Studies and partner organisations. https://hdl.handle.net/20.500.12413/3599
Livingston JE, Rummukainen M (2020) Taking science by surprise: the knowledge politics of the IPCC Special Report on 1.5 degrees. Environ Sci Policy 112:10–16. https://doi.org/10.1016/j.envsci.2020.05.020
MacKay G (2020) Editorial cartoon by Graeme MacKay. The Hamilton Spectator. Wednesday March 11, 2020. Revised May 23, 2020. https://mackaycartoons.net/2020/03/18/wednesday-march-11-2020/
Manzanedo RD, Manning P (2020) COVID-19: lessons for the climate change emergency. Sci Total Environ 742:140563. https://doi.org/10.1016/j.scitotenv.2020.140563
Markolf SA, Chester MV, Eisenberg DA et al (2018) Interdependent infrastructure as linked social, ecological, and technological systems (SETSs) to address lock-in and enhance resilience. Earth's Fut 6(12):1638–1659. https://doi.org/10.1029/2018EF000926
Mccarty N (2011) Chapter 9. The policy effects of political polarization. In: Pierson P, Skocpol T (eds) The transformation of American politics: activist government and the rise of conservatism. Princeton University Press, Princeton, pp 223–255. https://doi.org/10.1515/9781400837502-013
Mosley S (2014) Environmental history of air pollution and protection. In: Agnoletti M, Neri Serneri S (eds) The basic environmental history. Springer International Publishing, Cham, pp 143–169. https://doi.org/10.1007/978-3-319-09180-8_5
Moyson S, Scholten P, Weible CM (2017) Policy learning and policy change: theorizing their relations from different perspectives. Policy Soc 36(2):161–177. https://doi.org/10.1080/14494035.2017.1331879
Murcott MJ, Tigre MA (2024) Developments, opportunities, and complexities in Global South Climate litigation: introduction to the special collection. J Human Rights Pract 16(1):1–24. https://doi.org/10.1093/jhuman/huad070
Naseer S, Khalid S, Parveen S et al (2023) COVID-19 outbreak: impact on global economy. Front Public Health 10. https://doi.org/10.3389/fpubh.2022.1009393

Nilsson M, Zamparutti T, Petersen JE et al (2012) Understanding policy coherence: analytical framework and examples of sector–environment policy interactions in the EU. Environ Policy Gov 22(6):395–423. https://doi.org/10.1002/eet.1589
Ostrom E (2008) The challenge of common-pool resources. Environ Sci Policy Sustain Dev 50(4):8–21. https://doi.org/10.3200/ENVT.50.4.8-21
Passarelli D, Denton F, Day A (2021) Beyond opportunism: the UN development system's response to the triple planetary crisis. United Nations University, New York
Petrone F (2019) BRICS, soft power and climate change: New challenges in global governance? Ethics Glob Polit 12(2):19–30. https://doi.org/10.1080/16544951.2019.1611339
Pörtner H-O, Scholes RJ, Arneth A et al (2023) Overcoming the coupled climate and biodiversity crises and their societal impacts. Science 380:eabl4881. https://doi.org/10.1126/science.abl4881
Rashidi P, Lyons K (2022) Democratizing global climate governance? The case of indigenous representation in the Intergovernmental Panel on Climate Change (IPCC). In: Gills B, Morgan J (eds) Economics and climate emergency. Routledge, London, pp 284–299
Rinaldi AL, Martuscelli PN (2016) The BRICS on climate change global governance. Meridiano 47. J Glob Stud 17:e17020
Rockström J, Norström AV, Matthews N et al (2023) Shaping a resilient future in response to COVID-19. Nat Sustain 6:897–907. https://doi.org/10.1038/s41893-023-01105-9
Sampene AK, Li C, Agyeman FO et al (2021) Analysis of the BRICS countries' pathways towards a low-carbon environment. BRICS J Econ 2(4):77–102. https://doi.org/10.38050/2712-7508-2021-4-4
Setzer J, Vanhala LC (2019) Climate change litigation: A review of research on courts and litigants in climate governance. WIREs Climate Change 10(3):e580. https://doi.org/10.1002/wcc.580
Sippel M, Jenssen T (2009) What about local climate governance? A review of promise and problems. Available at SSRN: https://doi.org/10.2139/ssrn.1514334
Termeer C, Dewulf A, Breeman G (2013) Governance of wicked climate adaptation problems. In: Knieling J, Leal Filho W (eds) Climate change governance. Springer, Berlin, pp 27–39. https://doi.org/10.1007/978-3-642-29831-83
The White House (2021) Executive Order 13990 Protecting public health and the environment and restoring science to tackle the climate crisis. The White House. https://www.whitehouse.gov/briefing-room/presidential-actions/2021/01/20/executive-order-protecting-public-health-and-environment-and-restoring-science-to-tackle-climate-crisis/. Accessed 9 Dec 2024
The White House (2025) Executive Order 14162 Putting America first in international environmental agreements. The White House https://www.whitehouse.gov/presidential-actions/2025/01/putting-america-first-in-international-environmental-agreements/. Accessed 15 Jan 2026
Toni A, Feitosa Chaves C (2022) Bolsonaro's far-right populist environmental and climate diplomacy. Latin Am Policy 13(2):464–483. https://doi.org/10.1111/lamp.12268
Turnheim B, Kivimaa P, Berkhout F (2018) Beyond experiments: innovation in climate governance. In: Turnheim B, Kivimaa P, Berkhout F (eds) Innovating climate governance: moving beyond experiments. Cambridge University Press, Cambridge, pp 1–26. https://doi.org/10.1017/9781108277679.002
US Climate Alliance (2026) States United for Climate Action. https://usclimatealliance.org. Accessed 21 Jan 2026
US EPA (2021) Climate change regulatory actions and initiatives. Available at: https://www.epa.gov/climate-change/climate-change-regulatory-actions-and-initiatives. Accessed 29 Aug 2022
US EPA (2026) US Environmental Protection Agency. https://www.epa.gov/naaqs. Accessed 15 Jan 2026
VanderWeele TJ (2017) On the promotion of human flourishing. Proc Natl Acad Sci 114(31):8148–8156. https://doi.org/10.1073/pnas.1702996114
Washbourne C-L, Bell S, Osborn D (2021) Community responses to climate change. UCL Open Environ 3:e028. https://doi.org/10.14324/111.444/ucloe.000028
We Are Still In (2025) America Is All In. https://www.wearestillin.com. Accessed 15 Jan 2026

Part III
Conclusion

Chapter 10
Conclusion

Natalina Stamile, Rafael González Muñoz, Marlène Sam, and Yarina Amoroso

Abstract This chapter synthesizes the core insights of the volume by showing how the COVID-19 pandemic and the climate crisis are not isolated emergencies but manifestations of deeper structural malfunctions in contemporary legal, political, and ethical systems. Bridging the two pillars of the book—human dignity and climate governance—it argues that global crises act as magnifying lenses, exposing pre-existing inequalities, institutional fragilities, and governance failures that undermine both human dignity and ecological sustainability. Drawing on case studies ranging from Indigenous communities in Brazil to water governance in India and Costa Rica, and from greenhouse gas regulation in the United States and Brazil to the limitations of BRICS climate action, the chapter highlights the need for a polycentric legal architecture that empowers communities, integrates diverse knowledge systems, and recognizes interdependence. Therefore, a multidimensional framework grounded in responsibility, pluralism, and coordinated diversity across legal systems, epistemologies, and levels of governance is required. Finally, human dignity functions as both a mirror that reveals injustice and a compass that guides the ethical and legal reconstruction of a more just and sustainable global order.

N. Stamile (✉)
Department of Law, University of Brescia, Brescia, Italy
e-mail: natalina.stamile@unibs.it

R. G. Muñoz
Faculty of Theatrical Arts at ISA (Universidad de las Artes), La Habana, Cuba

M. Sam
International Cooperation and Partnerships, Ecole Supérieure d'Infotronique d'Haïti (ESIH), Port-au-Prince, Haiti
e-mail: marlene.sam@esih.edu

Y. Amoroso
Centro de Estudios de Gestión de Proyectos y Toma de Decisiones, Universidad de las Ciencias Informáticas, La Habana, Cuba
e-mail: yarina@uci.cu

© The Author(s), under exclusive license to Springer Nature Switzerland AG 2026
J. E. Núñez (ed.), *Perspectives on Crises*,
https://doi.org/10.1007/978-3-032-23836-8_10

10.1 Introduction

This collection was born from a shared preoccupation and growing concern: the urgent need to address two of the most pressing, crucial, and interrelated challenges revealed by recent global crises—the protection of human dignity and the governance of climate change—especially as exposed and exacerbated by the COVID-19 pandemic. The present book, composed of two distinct yet interconnected parts, provides a multidisciplinary, transnational, and ethically grounded reflection on vulnerability, justice, and responsibility in times of global crisis. In his Introduction to *Perspectives on Crises*, Jorge E. Núñez sets the stage for a multidisciplinary and global reflection on how crises—particularly the COVID-19 pandemic but generally all crises—expose and intensify both structural weaknesses and inequalities, as well as systemic malfunctions in legal, political, and socio-environmental systems. These "malfunctions" refer to deeper dysfunctions in the institutional, political, social, and economic frameworks that perpetuate exclusion, hinder resilience, and undermine justice—even before a crisis strikes. It is important to note that the term "malfunction" translates into the French "*dysfonctionnements.*" This expression was notably used in "Haïti et le COVID-19. Des outils pour comprendre et agir," a work that brought together thirty Haitian researchers and field practitioners, who collectively analyzed the phenomenon as early as in April to June 2020.[1] They described the pandemic as a part of a crisis, defining it as a one-off crisis within the general crisis Haiti was already experiencing. In other words, the COVID health crisis revealed and amplified the country's structural difficulties, contributing to an inextricable mix of causes and consequences.[2]

Thus, developed round two main areas—human dignity and climate change—this volume challenges prevailing unidimensional perspectives to global crises and argues instead for a multidimensional, pluralist analysis that respects both sovereignty and individual vulnerability. By this means, it bridges disciplines and geographies, showing that ethical demand for dignity and the ecological imperative for sustainability are inseparable dimensions—or fundamental principles—of global justice. As Núñez states: "In order to develop a better understanding of global issues, a global and interdisciplinary assessment is of central relevance."[3] It is clear, as the Introduction rightly criticizes, that the fragmented, discipline-bound and state-centric responses to crises fail to recognize both the shared global nature of many challenges and their differential local impacts.

For example, while COVID-19 is treated as the reference point, the present volume makes clear that the pandemic is not a standalone crisis; rather, it is a lens through which pre-existing inequalities and/or structural malfunctions become

---

[1] See Lumarque (2020).

[2] For example, see especially: Théodat et al. (2020) who highlight the "failles, ressorts de nos sociétés, dysfonctionnements et défis […] creusement des inégalités, surexposition […] exclusion sociale et plus grande vulnérabilité à la maladie des catégories sociales les plus démunies."

[3] Núñez, Chap. 1, Sect. 1.1, in this volume.

more visible, whether in the form of climate injustice, gender-based violence, institutional fragility and vulnerability, or unequal access to healthcare and resources.[4]

Furthermore, the metaphor of "The Blind Men and the Elephant" is used in the Introduction to highlight the limitations of a single discipline analyses, where each academic field grasps only a part of the larger crisis, thereby missing the (critical) interconnections. This metaphor provides the conceptual foundation for the multidimensional methodology of the present book, which combines empirical insights and normative reasoning across law, political science, international relations, and beyond.

Theoretically, the work adopts what is called a "pluralism of pluralisms," recognizing the coexistence of multiple legal systems, epistemologies, and value frameworks across the world. Rather than proposing uniform solutions, the collection argues for coordinated diversity, where states, communities, peoples, and individuals can cooperate without giving up sovereignty or policy. As Núñez notes: "the global order can progress from a pluralism to a pluralism of pluralisms that is widely sharable."[5] This hypothesis is not utopian. On the contrary, this volume remains grounded in realist legal and political possibilities, recognizing that idealized global justice often fails due to lack of applicability.[6] The objective, then, is to foster practical coordination, rooted in comparative learning across national systems, particularly in law and governance policy. This point is evident when the author states that "accordingly, the conclusions are partial and only aim to give a blueprint of what is possible and realistically achievable in law and policy."[7] Thus, it is useful to stress that the pandemic is not only the object of analysis but also the methodological approach of the book. It provides a common frame of reference that allows all the authors to highlight similarities between seemingly unrelated domains, such as (but not only) gender inequality and environmental degradation.

The section on human dignity unites several contributions under three shared insights: they all focus on the pandemic as a critical challenge; they all return to the foundational principle of human dignity; and they all center their attention on the protection of the most vulnerable. In this regard, it is worth noting: "They amount to a cooperative contribution that enables the shaping of the 'new normality' with respect to human dignity as well as protection of its vulnerability."[8]

---

[4] See also for more details: Pozzolo et al. (2021).

[5] Núñez, Chap. 1, Sect. 1.1, in this volume.

[6] See also Ferrajoli (2021, 2022). Specifically, the author argues for "A Constitution for the Earth." According to Ferrajoli, it is unlike any other constitutional charter, because it must address global challenges unknown in the past, and protect new rights and vital common goods from new and previously unthinkable threats. It is not a utopia. It is the only path to saving the planet, to confronting growing inequalities and the deaths of millions around the world due to hunger and lack of medicine, to addressing the tragedy of forced migration, and to defending against unchecked powers that threaten the safety of entire populations with their nuclear arsenals.

[7] Núñez, Chap. 1, Sect. 1.4, in this volume.

[8] Núñez, Chap. 1, Sect. 1.2, in this volume.

Similarly, the climate change section demonstrates that while the two global threats—COVID-19 and climate change—appear distinct, they reveal and expose overlapping governance failures and the urgent need for multistakeholder collaboration. Finally, the Introduction does not try to provide definitive answers but offers a conceptual and methodological blueprint for more inclusive and pragmatic forms of global justice, a framework that remains sensitive to the plurality of agents (individuals, communities, states) and contexts (local, regional, international). In fact, as Núñez states: "the book proposes to embrace coordination by means of learning from different national legal and political orders and international law."[9] This does not imply homogeneity, but mutual learning and respectful coordination, when sovereignty and human dignity are not considered as mutually exclusive, but rather as interdependent. This is the ethical and political basis of this volume on which all the following chapters develop.

Therefore, the present book is structured in two main parts. Part I examines the concept of human dignity in times of crises and vulnerability (e.g., pandemic and/or post-pandemic), while Part II focuses on governance of climate change and its ethical and legal implications. Both the pandemic and the climate crisis expose similar governance failures and patterns of exclusion, disproportionately affecting vulnerable individuals, populations, peoples, and communities, challenging the very foundations of human dignity.

10.2 Human Dignity in Times of Vulnerability

The first part of this book examines the concept of human dignity, as a legal and ethical foundational (and fundamental) principle, under conditions of vulnerability, exploring how crisis tests and redefines ethics and the frameworks that sustain it. Throughout this section, vulnerability is understood as a structural condition of human existence that exposes individuals, peoples, and communities to harm, while dignity functions as a normative principle that demands protection and respect for that condition. The pandemic has served not only as a public health emergency but also as a powerful magnifier of structural inequalities, institutional fragilities, and social exclusions.[10]

In a nutshell, from theoretical analyses of legal ethics and human fragility, to more context-specific analyses—such as the right to health in emergency settings and the threats faced by Indigenous communities in Brazil—this section reveals a common thread: the urgent necessity to (re)think legal responsibility and institutional obligations in ways that are more inclusive, responsive, and attuned to human vulnerability. Natalina Stamile and Kay Lalor's response chapter (Chap. 5) further

[9] Núñez, Chap. 1, Sect. 1.4, in this volume.

[10] In this regard see also: Ribotta and Lema Añon (2023).

underscores the ethical imperative to engage with dignity not as a static legal concept, but as a dynamic and relational commitment.

Among the key contributions, Chap. 2, "A Legal Ethics of the Vulnerability of Human Beings: Human Dignity and Responsibility to Rethinking the Present Time" by José-Antonio Santos, offers a critical perspective on the role of compassion in the ethical and legal treatment of vulnerable individuals, particularly in end-of-life contexts. While compassion is often invoked as a noble sentiment, the author argues that its role in law should be limited, as it can mask asymmetrical power dynamics and justify morally problematic decisions. As Santos notes "The rhetoric of compassion generates an undesirable situation for the other as unequal, both at the point of departure and that of arrival."[11] Rather than compassion, the text urges us to embrace responsibility as a core value guiding legal and ethical behavior, particularly during the pandemic. Indeed, responsibility is presented not merely as a moral attitude but as a legal principle that involves a commitment to others and to future generations. Drawing from Hans Jonas' ethics of responsibility, Santos states: "responsibility understood as a value and principle serves as a two-sided criterion to offer indications of how to act in the field of ethics and law."[12] In this regard, the legal ethics of vulnerability recognizes the human being as a historical subject—one who must assume responsibility not only for the present but also for the preservation of human dignity and life in the future.

The chapter also challenges both extremes in end-of-life care, therapeutic obstinacy and euthanasia, which, although opposed, can both reflect an unwillingness to accept death as a natural part of life. The need for proportionate palliative care, grounded in the principles of non-maleficence and beneficence, is emphasized as an ethically and legally sound alternative. Thus, as Santos notes, "palliative sedation, administered in proportionate doses, may be convenient to reduce or eliminate pain in a patient who presents a set of differentiated refractory symptoms [as long as] death is not pursued."[13] Moreover, the reflection points against the "slippery slope" argument, that is, where legalizing certain end-of-life practices, such as assisted suicide, may lead to broader and potentially coercive practices. "Supporters of euthanasia are favorable [...] to ideals such as compassion or autonomy, although they promote rules that, despite their good intentions, will only end in coercion and cruelty."[14]

The author concludes that law must not be governed by emotional responses—not even by well-intentioned compassion—but by responsible, measured, and justice-oriented engagement with the needs of the vulnerable. Particularly, "Caring should not be a compassionate act, but an act of responsibility toward vulnerable

[11] Santos, Chap. 2, Sect. 2.4, in this volume.

[12] Santos, Chap. 2, Sect. 2.5, in this volume.

[13] Santos, Chap. 2, Sect. 2.4, in this volume.

[14] Santos, Chap. 2, Sect. 2.4, in this volume.

people."[15] Therefore, the chapter highlights the importance of objectivity, dialogue, and prudence in dealing with pain and suffering.

Finally, the reflection emphasizes that dignity must be understood not as a static legal status, but as a dynamic and relational commitment, particularly in times of global crisis. As such, the legal ethics of vulnerability offers a path forward that integrates realism, ethical coherence, and legal practicality, advocating for inclusive legal structures capable of respecting both individual autonomy and collective responsibility. Therefore, together these insights challenge us to reconsider how legal frameworks can evolve to support human dignity not merely as a formal entitlement, but as a lived experience—especially under the pressures of global crises.

In Chap. 3, "Human Dignity, Right to Health, and Balancing: With Special Focus on Vulnerability in a Public Health Emergency," the authors, Wei Feng and Jingshu Wang, develop a nuanced and theoretically rich account of tensions between human dignity and the right to health in times of public health emergencies, such as the COVID-19 pandemic. In essence, the analysis is based on the assertion that human dignity must be understood in its dual dimensions: both as the dignity of the individual human being and that of the human being as a social entity.

Examining a wide range of philosophical and legal traditions—for example from Mencius and Kant to Radbruch and contemporary constitutional systems—the chapter reveals how dignity has been institutionalized across legal cultures, and yet remains challenged by crises that require the balancing of competing rights and interests. According to Feng and Wang, "the quest is not for a determined hierarchy of rights and values but to acknowledge the significance of rights in concrete circumstance."[16] The traditional assumption that the right to life or health necessarily overrides other rights is problematized. Instead, the authors suggest using Robert Alexy's distinction between principles and rules, which conceptualizes fundamental rights as optimization requirements subject to proportionality.[17]

It is crucial to highlight what the authors call the "hierarchy doubt"—the question of whether life and health always have more significance than fundamental freedoms such as movement, religion, or expression. The chapter critically addresses this point by emphasizing that no right should be considered absolutely (hierarchically) superior but rather should be contextually balanced using structured normative reasoning: "the costs are neither absolute nor permanent—rather they lend themselves to balance."[18]

Furthermore, another important tension is based on the "naturalistic fallacy," the mistaken assumption that mere biological life is synonymous to a life lived in dignity. The chapter strongly argues for distinguishing between life as such and life with dignity, rejecting reductionist approaches that prioritize survival over

[15] Santos, Chap. 2, Sect. 2.6, in this volume.

[16] Feng and Wang, Chap. 3, Sect. 3.3.1, in this volume.

[17] See especially Alexy (2010). For a critical discussion of the theory elaborated by Alexy, see, for instance Stamile et al. (2021); Stamile (2019, 2020, 2023).

[18] Feng and Wang, Chap. 3, Sect. 3.3.1, in this volume.

meaningful existence: "the only way out is precisely to refute the naturalistic strategy of human dignity [...] There should be differentiation between life as such and life with dignity."[19] Here, the concept of personality—combining both the noumenal and phenomenal dimensions of the human being—serves as a bridge between biological existence and moral and legal personhood.

The triage dilemma is also addressed in practical and ethical terms. Feng and Wang criticize simplistic criteria such as age or social utility in allocating life-saving resources. Instead, they place emphasize on proportionality, cautioning against measures that may violate the minimum thresholds of dignity. In this regard, Feng and Wang specifically affirm that "the especially strong requirement of human dignity still has control over the *normative possibilities* to prevent extremely disproportionate treatments of dying patients."[20] Even under extreme conditions, dignity must guide decision-making, ensuring that no life is treated as expendable or instrumentally replaceable.

The chapter also brings to light the social determinants of health, especially in relation to digital technologies and vaccination. Rather than framing these issues as purely technological or administrative, the authors anchor the discussion firmly within the framework of human dignity and social justice. Feng and Wang highlight how inequalities in access to digital technologies, information, and healthcare services exacerbate vulnerabilities during public health emergencies, thus threatening the dignity of marginalized groups. For example, lack of internet access can prevent vulnerable populations from obtaining timely and accurate information about vaccination campaigns or preventive measures, leading to disproportionate health risks.

Furthermore, Feng and Wang stress the importance of transparency, participation, and non-discrimination in public health responses, emphasizing that respect for human dignity requires inclusive policies that address social determinants such as poverty, education, and housing. This approach moves beyond a narrow biomedical perspective to encompass the broader social, economic, and cultural conditions that shape health outcomes.

In relation to vaccination, this chapter addresses debates about mandatory vaccination policies, digital health passports, and privacy concerns. The authors argue that such measures, while potentially justified by public health needs, must be carefully balanced against rights to privacy, bodily integrity, and freedom of movement, always with the normative compass of human dignity guiding proportionality assessments. In light of that, the authors conclude by arguing for a reconceptualization of human dignity in the face of vulnerability—not only recognizing the intrinsic value of every individual but also emphasizing the social dimension of dignity. This dual understanding emphasizes that dignity is both a personal and relational concept, requiring solidarity and collective responsibility in times of crisis. The protection of human dignity thus demands legal and ethical frameworks that can flexibly balance competing rights and interests without sacrificing fundamental

[19] Feng and Wang, Chap. 3, Sect. 3.3.2, in this volume.

[20] Feng and Wang, Chap. 3, Sect. 3.3.3, in this volume.

principles, fostering a "new normality" where dignity remains a core normative value despite the exceptional pressures of public health emergencies.

In conclusion, Chap. 3—through the detailed analysis elaborated by Feng and Wang—significantly enriches the overall argument of the volume by illustrating how human dignity must be (re)thought in times of acute vulnerability, with particular attention to proportionality, social determinants of health, and the relational nature of dignity. This sets the stage for the subsequent chapters, which further explore vulnerability in relation to climate justice and broader institutional responsibilities.

In Chap. 4, titled "Indigenous Dignity Under Threat in the Brazilian COVID-19 Pandemic," by Jairo Lima and Andrei Domingos Fonseca, the focus shifts toward the intersection on human dignity and environmental justice, further expanding the book's central concern with vulnerability in global crisis. Moving forward from the ethical and legal reflections of the previous chapters, this contribution describes how climate change exacerbates existing social inequalities and threatens the dignity of marginalized communities, particularly Indigenous peoples and vulnerable populations in the Global South. Through case studies and normative analysis, the chapter argues for an integrated approach to justice that encompasses both ecological sustainability and social protection. Together, these chapters construct a multidimensional understanding of human dignity that responds to the complex realities of the twenty-first century.

Specifically, Lima and Domingos Fonseca critically analyze the multifaceted crisis faced by Brazilian Indigenous communities during the COVID-19 pandemic. The reflection, elaborated by Lima and Domingos Fonseca, focuses on the idea that Indigenous suffering was not only a consequence of biological risk but largely a result of "the negligence of SESAI health teams and army professionals" and the "significant processes of institutional racism" that led to the underreporting and misclassification of Indigenous COVID-19 cases among "Brown people," thereby obscuring the true extent of the crisis.[21]

This chapter also describes the entanglement of economic interests with public health failures. Beyond institutional negligence, economic interests also played a decisive role in aggravating Indigenous vulnerability. The authors highlight how "agribusiness and large slaughter houses were other means for this contamination process," particularly in Mato Grosso do Sul, where "the first cases of COVID-19 contamination among the Guarani and Kaiowá people occurred through large agribusiness companies," entities directly linked to the destruction of Indigenous lands and the forced labor of Indigenous peoples.[22]

Furthermore, it is useful to note that the authors problematize the controversial authorization of religious missions in Indigenous territories under Brazilian Law no. 14.021/2020, which "enabled the existence of religious missions in territories of

---

[21] Lima and Domingos Fonseca, Chap. 4, Sect. 4.5, this volume.

[22] Lima and Domingos Fonseca, Chap. 4, Sect. 4.5, this volume.

isolated Indigenous peoples and those of recent contact,"[23] a practice that violates the long-established Indigenous strategy of voluntary isolation to protect against diseases introduced by outsiders. This violation is emblematic of the enduring colonial pressures faced by Indigenous peoples, exemplified by incursions of the New Tribes Mission group, which "aimed at changing the policy of noncontact and promoting the Christian conversion of Indigenous peoples,"[24] thus exacerbating their vulnerability during the pandemic.[25]

A key strength of this chapter lies in its detailed account of Indigenous legal resistance. The landmark lawsuit ADPF 709 filed by the Articulation of Indigenous Peoples of Brazil (APIB) and partners before the Brazilian Supreme Court (STF) represents "the first time in history" that Indigenous peoples "went to the STF to demand the protection of Indigenous human dignity."[26] Despite the partial victory granted by Justice Barroso, which included orders to create sanitary barriers and ensure healthcare access, the government's "constant omission" rendered many of these protections ineffective, with "most of the sanitary barriers [...] installed by the Indigenous movements themselves."[27]

In their analysis, Lima and Domingos Fonseca also critically address the broader political context, noting President Bolsonaro's vetoes of critical provisions aimed at safeguarding Indigenous health, which were only partially overturned by Congress. The president's administration prioritized extractive economic policies, pushing forward "Bill no. 191/2020, which aimed [...] to prioritize the opening of the Indigenous lands to mining" even during a global health emergency.[28] This legislative agenda underscores the ongoing "anti-Indigenous" stance of the government, which "has thus fulfilled its campaign promise by not demarcating an inch of Indigenous land."[29]

Importantly, this chapter engages with the legal and ethical complexity of framing these abuses as genocide. It points out that "proving the specific intention to destroy is considerably difficult when faced with government omissions" and highlights how the "cultural aspect corresponds to the extermination of the ethnic difference (ethnocide),"[30] a dimension not fully captured by the Rome Statute. These omissions, however, may still constitute violations of international human rights obligations, revealing the urgent need for domestic reforms and stronger mechanisms of accountability.

Overall, Chap. 4 provides an important critique of the Brazilian state's failure to protect Indigenous dignity during the pandemic, while simultaneously celebrating

[23] Lima and Domingos Fonseca, Chap. 4, Sect. 4.5, this volume.

[24] Lima and Domingos Fonseca, Chap. 4, Sect. 4.5, this volume.

[25] For more details about coloniality see, for example: Quijano (2024) and Mignolo (2005).

[26] Lima and Domingos Fonseca, Chap. 4, Sect. 4.5, this volume.

[27] Lima and Domingos Fonseca, Chap. 4, Sect. 4.6, this volume.

[28] Lima and Domingos Fonseca, Chap. 4, Sect. 4.5, this volume.

[29] Lima and Domingos Fonseca, Chap. 4, Sect. 4.7, this volume.

[30] Lima and Domingos Fonseca, Chap. 4, Sect. 4.6, this volume.

the resilience and the agency of Indigenous peoples through legal activism and communities-led initiatives. This analysis deepens the book's broader argument that safeguarding human dignity in times of crisis demands not only legal recognition but also effective, culturally sensitive, and politically committed action.

Building on this critical examination of state neglect and Indigenous resistance during the pandemic, the concluding chapter of this first section, titled "Human Dignity in Times of Crisis: A Contested Concept," aims to provide a profound reflection on the conceptual and legal complexities of human dignity within the context of crisis, particularly the COVID-19 pandemic. Natalina Stamile and Kay Lalor problematize the almost automatic relation of "crisis" with "emergency" and the related notion of the state of exception, emphasizing how these have normalized exceptional governance modes. In other words, the state of exception has become the rule, and the political sphere is subordinate to economics.[31] This observation constitutes the starting point for the critical interrogation of dignity as both a legal foundation and a contested concept deeply challenged during emergencies.

This chapter, serving as a response to Part I on human dignity, situates human dignity within the broader constitutional and international legal frameworks, citing foundational texts such as Article 1 of the Universal Declaration of Human Rights—"All human beings are born free and equal in dignity and rights"—and regional human rights instruments like the African Charter on Human and People's Rights which enshrine dignity against inhuman treatment. It further highlights the post-World War II constitutional embedding of dignity as an "absolute priority" and "inviolable," linking it indissolubly with fundamental rights in constitutions such as Germany's *Grundgesetz* and the Italian and French Constitutions.[32]

However, Stamile and Lalor caution against uncritical acceptance of dignity's legal status, pointing to its paradoxical, multiplicitous character: described as a "loose cannon" and a "jurisprudential Legoland," dignity is both foundational and slippery, lending itself to divergent interpretations and sometimes to incoherence.[33] In their analysis, the authors reference McCrudden's insight that dignity "appears to become other than impossibly vague only when it is tethered to a coherent community of interpretation,"[34] and allude to how Reva Siegal frames dignity as a judicial tool navigating globalization's tensions.[35]

This complexity foregrounds the normative tensions revealed by the pandemic, which acts as a "magnifying glass" exposing structural inequalities and the intersectional vulnerabilities of marginalized populations.[36] Therefore, it is important to highlight, as this conclusive chapter of the first section emphasizes, how dignity is far from being an abstract or uniform concept, and is profoundly shaped and

---

[31] Stamile and Lalor, Chap. 5, Sect. 5.1, this volume.

[32] Stamile and Lalor, Chap. 5, Sect. 5.1, this volume.

[33] Steinmann (2017), cited in Stamile and Lalor, Chap. 5, Sect. 5.1, in this volume.

[34] McCrudden (2008), p. 723, cited in Stamile and Lalor, Chap. 5, Sect. 5.1, in this volume.

[35] Siegal (2012).

[36] Pozzolo et al. (2021), cited in Stamile and Lalor, Chap. 5, Sect. 5.2, in this volume.

challenged by the social determinants of health, resource allocation dilemmas, and political neglect.

In this context, the authors synthesize the preceding contributions by underscoring two major cross-cutting themes: dignity and responsibility, and dignity, inequality, and vulnerability. Drawing on the work of Feng and Wang in this volume, they highlight the ethical dilemmas arising in healthcare during the crisis—the "hierarchy doubt" between rights, the "triage dilemma," and the negotiation between individual autonomy and social solidarity—illustrating dignity's relational and situational nature. As noted, "dignity is something that is created with and through the other," underlining its inherently social and ethical dimension.[37]

Similarly, Santos frames vulnerability as an unavoidable human condition intensified by the pandemic, reminding us that "the COVID-19 pandemic shows that weakness must be met with responsibility toward the human being in a situation of fragility."[38] This idea echoes Martha Fineman's vulnerability theory, which challenges the traditional legal subject and calls for a collective, relational understanding of rights and responsibility.[39]

Furthermore, it is useful to stress the racialized and colonial dimensions of the denial of dignity for Indigenous peoples in Brazil, who suffered "institutional discrimination, silencing and othering" during the pandemic. Their resistance, the authors suggest, illuminates dignity's dynamic and political nature, as both a form of protection and assertion amid systemic violence.

Finally, Stamile and Lalor close their chapter with the question posed by Judith Butler, who asks: "what consequences this pandemic will have for thinking about equality, global interdependence and our obligations toward one another?"[40] Despite the virus's indiscriminate nature, "social and economic inequality will make sure that the virus discriminates," underscoring how dignity is unequally distributed and contested in crisis—"some human creatures assert their rights to live at the expense of others," perpetuating "the spurious distinction between grievable and ungrievable lives."[41]

Thus, this concluding chapter critically examines how human dignity is not a static legal ideal, but rather a fluid, relational, and contested concept whose meanings and protections are thrown into sharp relief by crisis. It calls for sustained ethical and political engagement with dignity, responsibility, and vulnerability, setting the stage for the broader debates and institutional analyses in the monograph's subsequent chapters.

In light of the analysis on the vulnerabilities explored in Part I, the following section turns to another manifestation of global fragility: the climate crisis, where environmental degradation intersects with social and institutional inequalities.

---

[37] Stamile and Lalor, Chap. 5, Sect. 5.2.1, in this volume.

[38] Santos, Chap. 2, Sect. 2.1, in this volume.

[39] Fineman (2015).

[40] Stamile and Lalor, Chap. 5, Sect. 5.2.2, this volume.

[41] Judith Butler (2020), cited in Stamile and Lalor, Chap. 5, Sect. 5.2.2, this volume.

10.3 Climate Change, Governance, and Justice

Following the discussion on human dignity, Part II extends the lens of vulnerability to the planetary scale revealing how environmental harm reflects and amplifies existing social injustices and inequalities. Specifically, this section unfolds along three complementary dimensions: ethical, legal, and epistemological. Particularly, this second part shifts the focus to the climate crisis, addressing legal responses and governance models under the added pressure of the pandemic. Legal systems are challenged to adapt to ecological disruptions that are transnational in scope and deeply intertwined with economic, political, and health-related vulnerabilities. Contributions explore diverse legal and geopolitical contexts—from the regulation of greenhouse gases in the US and Brazil, to the collective action (or inaction) of BRICS countries, and to community-based responses to climate-driven water crisis. What emerges is a nuanced picture of how climate governance often lags behind scientific and social urgency, and how the most vulnerable populations are often the least protected. The response chapter reflects on the limitations and potential of current legal frameworks to promote climate justice.

In Chap. 6, titled "Regulating Greenhouse Gases as Criteria Pollutants in the United States and Brazil," the author, Oswaldo Lucon, offers a comprehensive and critical analysis of the erosion of regulatory pathways once utilized to control greenhouse gas (GHG) emissions in both the United States and Brazil—two of the world's major emitters. It frames climate change as a systemic, multidimensional threat exacerbating pandemics, conflict, and economic instability, yet notes a conspicuous gap between scientific urgency and the legal-institutional responses required to mitigate its effects. At the core of this discussion lies the observation that environmental governance in both countries has suffered from significant regulatory backsliding, with greenhouse gases still not formally categorized as "pollutants" in many key legal instruments—particularly in Brazil. While Brazil's Federal Constitution (Article 225) enshrines the right to an ecologically balanced environment, and Law 6938/81 establishes the National Environmental Policy, the legal framework remains ambiguous with regard to GHGs, which are not explicitly regulated as pollutants under existing resolutions such as CONAMA 382/2006 or the PROCONVE program.[42] As Lucon notes, "without considering greenhouse gases as pollutants it will be practically impossible to establish the legal restrictions necessary to comply with such commitments,"[43] referring to Brazil's own nationally determined contributions (NDCs) under the Paris Agreement.

[42] CONAMA. Resolução 382, de 26 de dezembro de 2006. https://www.ibama.gov.br/component/legislacao/?view=legislacao&legislacao=113047. Accessed Aug 10, 2022; CONAMA. Resolução CONAMA no 18, de 6 de maio de 1986. Dispõe sobre a criação do Programa de Controle de Poluição do Ar por Veículos Automotores—PROCONVE. http://conama.mma.gov.br/?option=com_sisconama&task=arquivo.download&id=41. Accessed Dec 18, 2025.

[43] Lucon, Chap. 6, Sect. 6.3.3, in this volume.

Furthermore, the author argues that the lack of regulatory clarity allows for circumvention strategies that severely undermine climate mitigation efforts. In Brazil, no legal obligation compels public or private actors to reduce GHG emissions unless imposed through judicial decisions, which tend to be fragmented and reactive rather than systemic.[44] This regulatory vacuum contrasts sharply with the ambition of Brazil's NDC—reducing emissions by 37% below 2005 levels by 2025 and 50% by 2030—yet no federal law currently regulates the six major GHGs: CO_2, CH_4, N_2O, HFCs, PFCs, and SF_6.

Subnational efforts in Brazil, such as those of São Paulo and Rio de Janeiro, have been described as "pedagogical" rather than binding. While São Paulo nearly achieved its self-imposed goal of reducing CO_2 emissions by 20% by 2020, the absence of sectoral targets and clear implementation pathways reveals the symbolic nature of many such initiatives.[45] Therefore, Lucon also highlights the challenge of aligning local policies with federal energy and economic agendas, which have often favored fossil fuel subsidies and inefficient vehicle technologies—an inconsistency that has weakened the efficacy of state-level actions.[46]

The United States, meanwhile, is presented as a cautionary tale of regulatory reversal. After years of litigation-based climate policy under the Clean Air Act, recent Supreme Court decisions—such as West Virginia v. EPA—have narrowed the scope of federal agencies to regulate GHGs. The author focuses on this as part of a broader deregulatory trend, further aggravated by political polarization and the rollback of executive climate orders, especially during the Trump administration. Nonetheless, the chapter also recognizes glimmers of hope in recent initiatives, including President Biden's Executive Order 13990, which mandates that all federal agencies reassess their regulatory frameworks in light of the climate crisis.[47]

The analysis offered by Lucon concludes by underscoring the urgent need for legal-institutional coherence, both in recognizing GHGs as pollutants and in integrating climate commitments into enforceable regulatory mechanisms. The dissonance between climate pledges and legal capacity, in both Brazil and the United States, risks rendering ambitious targets little more than political rhetoric. Without binding, transparent, and enforceable standards, climate governance risks falling into a lost trajectory of ineffectiveness and inaction.

In the following chapter, "BRICS Response to Climate Governance Crisis in Pandemic Times" by Douglas de Castro and Danielle Mendes Thame Denny, several fundamental conclusions can be drawn about the BRICS bloc's response to the climate governance crisis, exacerbated in the context of COVID-19 pandemic. Among the examples presented in the research by Castro and Denny, it is evident that the BRICS' institutional response to climate change has been insufficient and disproportionate to the scale of the existential crisis it represents. Despite sharing

---

[44] Lucon, Chap. 6, Sect. 6.3.3, in this volume.

[45] Lucon et al. (2022).

[46] Lucon, Chap. 6, Sect. 6.3.5, in this volume.

[47] The White House (2021).

socioeconomic vulnerability and a similar position facing climate challenges—characterized by a rating of "Insufficient" or "Highly Insufficient" according to the Climate Action Tracker—the BRICS platform has failed to translate its cooperation and development principles into a concerted and robust climate agenda. The content analysis of joint statements reveals that terms like "cooperation" and "development" are central and recurrent, but their correlation with "sustainable development" and specific climate concepts (emissions, carbon, mitigation) is low. This highlights that the prevailing development model, based on extractivism and dependence on natural resources, remains the priority, creating a fundamental and irreconcilable tension with environmental sustainability goals.

The COVID-19 crisis acted as a catalyst that exacerbated the (existing) structural vulnerabilities of developing countries, deepening the gap with developed nations. The pandemic not only diverted political attention and limited resources from the climate agenda but also imposed additional economic burdens on the pillars of the Global South economies (raw material exports, tourism). This reinforced a retreat toward national interests and further hindered these countries' capacity to implement costly climate adaptation and mitigation measures, creating a vicious cycle where the health and environmental crises feed into each other.

The study seeks to identify the predominance of national interest over multilateral governance within the BRICS forum, where national interests continue to prevail over a solid multilateral vision. The group's agenda seems to reflect the domestic priorities of the host country, lacking the "institutional learning" and "steering capacity" required to enable effective collective action.[48] But, according to the authors, China emerges as an exceptional and potential change agent within the bloc, and a "control case" within the study.[49] Despite sharing many of the structural challenges of its peers, China has undertaken an internal strategic transition toward an "ecological civilization" model,[50] institutionalized at the constitutional level and operationalized in instruments such as the 14th Five-Year Plan and the Ecological and Environmental Protection Guidelines for Overseas Investment. This commitment, along with its technological leadership in decarbonization, positions China as a potential change agent both within and outside of BRICS. However, the analysis suggests that, for now, this momentum has not effectively translated into a transformative climate agenda for the bloc as a whole, but rather manifests primarily as a projection of its national interest and its agenda-setting power.

There is an increasingly urgent need for a paradigm shift. The main conclusion of the chapter is that neither temporary lockdowns nor current weak and fragmented institutional responses are sufficient. A structural change in patterns of production, distribution, and consumption is required. The post-pandemic recovery represents a critical window of opportunity to integrate green stimulus policies that, rather than being a burden, can generate more resilient and sustainable development. For

[48] Castro and Denny, Chap. 7, Sect. 7.4.2, in this volume.

[49] Castro and Denny, Chap. 7, Sect. 7.4.3, in this volume.

[50] Castro and Denny, Chap. 7, Sect. 7.4.2, in this volume.

BRICS to fulfill its potential as a counterbalance in global governance, an internal institutional change is imperative, one that allows it to transcend mere rhetoric of cooperation and build climate governance based on stronger multilateral political and legal decisions that genuinely reflect the shared experiences of the Global South and holistically bring tangible responses to the existential threat of climate change.

In Chap. 8, "Repairing Water in the Face of Climate Change: A Tale of Two Communities," Gabriela Cuadrado-Quesada develops a compelling examination of the impacts of climate change through the lens of water justice, inequality, and community resilience. The chapter opens with the emblematic case of Kati Thanda-Lake Eyre, once a vibrant and water-rich landscape, now a desiccated lakebed symptomatic of broader ecological decline. The use of this example serves not only as an effective narrative device but also as a microcosm of global environmental degradation. The author reflects on the integration of geological and climatological data to substantiate the claim regarding the transformation of the lake over 100,000 years.

The core strength of the chapter lies in its emphasis on the unequal impacts of climate change. The author rightly highlights how extreme weather events have increased in both frequency and severity, as evidenced by United Nations Disaster Risk Reduction (UNDRR) statistics. The comparison of data from 1980 to 1999 and 2000 to 2019 provides an empirical foundation to underscore the urgency of climate crisis. In addition, it is important to stress that the author particularly focuses on climate injustice—both between and within nations. The discussions of Global North–Global South asymmetries, especially in terms of emissions responsibilities and adaptive capacities, is well-articulated and reflects broader discourses in climate ethics and international law. The inclusion of countries like the United States, China, and Germany illustrates the concentration of emissions among a few powerful nations, while less affluent countries—despite contributing minimally to the crisis—face disproportionately severe consequences. This argument aligns with the principles of climate justice, which demand that historical responsibility and differential vulnerability be central to mitigation and adaptation policies. Moreover, this effectively points out the intra-national inequalities within Global North countries. The examples of the Hurricane Katrina disaster and the Flint water crisis offer compelling evidence of how race, class, and environmental governance intersect. These cases demonstrate how marginalized populations—particularly Afro-American communities—continue to bear the brunt of institutional neglect and environmental degradation. The Flint case, in particular, is emblematic of what many scholars describe as "environmental racism."[51] Thus, from a methodological view, the chapter moves forward on its theoretical reflections in empirical research. The use of semi-structured interviews, participatory observation, and community meetings demonstrates a commitment to qualitative depth and community engagement. This participatory approach is in line with contemporary scholarship on civic

[51] In this respect, it is important to emphasize the relevance of this approach, particularly in relation to critical race theory and the environmental justice literature.

innovation and epistemic justice, particularly the idea that local knowledge and community-based responses are essential for adaptive governance in the Anthropocene.

In addition, Cuadrado-Quesada discusses the connection between the hydrological cycle as a sociological cycle and the hydrosocial perspective and its implications for climate adaptation. The chapter's concluding reflections on the limitations of current global frameworks—such as the Paris Agreement and SDGs—are both valid and important. While these agreements set normative aspirations, their lack of enforceability and the persistence of state-centric governance limit their transformative potential. The arguments elaborated by the author point to a more justice-oriented, bottom-up approach to climate governance, echoing arguments made by scholars such as Boaventura de Sousa Santos[52] and Donna Haraway,[53] whose notion of "staying with the trouble" provides a valuable heuristic for navigating complex crisis. In summary, Cuadrado-Quesada provides a multiscalar analysis of climate change, weaving together historical narrative, statistical data, empirical research, and critical theory. The author makes a compelling case for (re)thinking climate governance through the prism of justice, interdependence, and local policy. However, the chapter not only diagnoses the failings of existing institutional responses but also gestures toward more inclusive and resilient forms of climate adaptation.

In the last chapter in Part II, titled "Global Perspectives from Law and Policy on the Climate Crisis," Carla Washbourne examines the evolving landscape of climate governance through a combination of historical, national, and local perspectives. Washbourne centers the discussion within the broader context of polycrisis, highlighting the interconnectedness of environmental, social, and technological systems, and the ways in which legal and policy frameworks have both facilitated and constrained responses to climate change.[54]

The chapter draws on precedents from earlier environmental legislation, notably the US Clean Air Act of 1970,[55] to illustrate how longstanding legal instruments can provide models for contemporary climate governance, while also acknowledging the limitations imposed by political polarization, institutional fragmentation, and resource constraints.[56] As Washbourne indicates, all the authors grapple with what it means to respond to a crisis when already inhabiting a crisis, emphasizing the compounding nature of global challenges and the need for adaptive, multiscalar approaches.

---

[52] Boaventura de Sousa Santos (2014). The author critiques dominant epistemologies and calls for recognition of plural knowledges.

[53] Haraway (2016).

[54] Hoyer et al. (2023); Lawrence et al. (2024).

[55] US Congress (1970). Public Law 91-604 An Act to amend the Clean Air Act to provide for a more effective program to improve the quality of the Nation's air (Dec 31, 1970 - H.R. 17255) https://www.govtrack.us/congress/bills/91/hr17255. Accessed Dec 9, 2024.

[56] Mccarty (2011); Brewer (2022).

Through a series of case studies, the author highlights the diversity of governance responses. At the national level, the author contrasts the United States and Brazil in their regulation of greenhouse gases, noting both the potential for legal innovation and the structural obstacles that can inhibit progress.[57] In the United States, voluntary state-level initiatives, exemplified by the "We Are Still In" movement,[58] have emerged as critical mechanisms for action in the absence of consistent federal leadership, offering "a beam of hope for the nonfederal leadership."[59] Conversely, in Brazil, attempts to implement similar measures have been limited, illustrating how political context shapes the efficacy of climate policies.[60] This comparison underscores the importance of understanding the interplay between federal frameworks, subnational initiatives, and international commitments, particularly in the context of agreements such as the Paris Accord.[61]

At the international level, this final chapter of Part II examines climate governance in the BRICS countries during the COVID-19 pandemic.[62] The author argues that the pandemic functioned as a "disruptive reset," revealing both the fragility of international institutions and the opportunities for emerging economies to exercise greater agency or policy in shaping climate responses.[63] Nevertheless, tensions remain between national development priorities and the collective goals of sustainable climate action, as the "countries' shared perceptions, expectations, and experiences about development"[64] often conflict with cooperative climate objectives. The chapter suggests that non-binding agreements, climate litigation, and post-pandemic recovery measures conditioned on sustainability may provide avenues for strengthening governance in contexts where formal legal mechanisms are weak or inconsistent.[65]

Opening with the shock proposal of a fictional story, Chap. 7 relates how the challenge of climate change has failed to be addressed adequately by multilateral efforts after the COVID-19 pandemic, owing to the election of several ultranationalist and isolationist politicians who place the issue of international climate regime at the low-politic realm, whereas both the pandemic and climate change are existential threats to humanity; the difference is the time of impact, and when the

---

57 Lucon, Chap. 6, this volume.

58 For more details see Baumeister (2018) and We Are Still In (2025).

59 Lucon, Chap. 6, Sect. 6.2.5, this volume.

60 Toni and Feitosa Chaves (2022).

61 UNFCCC (United National Framework Commission on Climate Change), Paris Agreement to the United Nations Framework Convention on Climate Change, Dec. 12, 2015, T.I.A.S. No. 16-1104. U.N. Doc. FCCC/CP/2015/L.9/Rev/1.

62 Castro and Denny, Chap. 7, this volume.

63 Washbourne, Chap. 9, Sect. 9.2.2, this volume. For more details see Manzanedo and Manning (2020) and Passarelli et al. (2021).

64 Castro and Denny, Chap. 7, Sect. 7.1, this volume.

65 Washbourne, Chap. 9, this volume. For more details see Setzer and Vanhala (2019) and Boyle et al. (2021).

effects are not right away. However, the pandemic also transformed the scenario regarding the terms on which the discussions on climate change were to be held.

According to the authors, in contrast to the impact of World War II on the world order, especially for developing countries, the post-pandemic period experienced no majority solidarity event such as the Non-Aligned Movement initiatives. For example the Group of 77 (1964), CELAC (2010), and BRICS (2009–2011) were blocs aimed at serving as platforms for political, economic, and security matters through the promotion of South–South cooperation to counterbalance Western-led frameworks. Their relations are not only based on material interests but also encompass shared narratives, self-determination, and recognition conducive to joint strategies, technical cooperation, regional integration, and common positions in international negotiations and multilateral fora. Thus, the chapter examines the potential intervention of BRICS, a specific regime in international relations theory, in addressing what they define as a "conundrum."[66]

In addition, the chapter highlights how the extremely poor international response to COVID-19 in terms of support funding and technology transfer became "an intervening variable" that deprived vulnerable developing countries of their capacity to mitigate and adapt.[67] The study is based on the long, consistent, and collaborative research effort of a group of transdisciplinary experts on climate change, which started in 2020 within the framework of ten roundtables to address the issue of civilizational decline and downfall in regard to Western civilization, and it uses current data analysis.

The constructivist approach to analyzing interstate relations argues that ideas, values, and shared experiences are central variables for understanding how states interact. In the context of the Global South, this perspective is particularly significant given that the heterogeneous Asian, African, and Latin American nations share historical legacies of colonialism, experiences of peripheral development, and common aspirations for political and economic autonomy.[68]

The pandemic proved to be a systemic human development crisis. Facing the challenges of crises such as climate change, poverty, and biodiversity loss, the world is at a crossroads, demanding a new form of international governance focused on tackling multiple crises, as the population's vulnerability to climate change is directly linked to the lack of adaptation capacity in developing countries. The researchers' main conclusion was that there are more similarities than differences between the two global threats (climate change and coronavirus) and they noted that, if correctly designed, public policies to face the sanitary emergency can bring permanent benefits to the climate as well as inspire better policy designs.

The BRICS platform, whose members share experiences in the development process and challenges in encounters with developed countries, adopts ontological and epistemological stances capable of engendering cooperation and mutual

[66] Castro and Denny, Chap. 7, Sect. 7.4.1, this volume.

[67] Castro and Denny, Chap. 7, Sect. 7.1, this volume.

[68] See especially Quijano (2024) and Mignolo (2005).

assistance, and was selected as a study case. Content analysis was the research technique used to systematize the case study, establish analytical boundaries, and create a systematic framework for the various forms of communication present in the corpus (declarations issued by BRICS between 2017 and 2021, the 14th Five-Year Plan, and the Ecological and Environmental Protection Guidelines for Overseas Investment and Cooperation Construction Projects) using online Voyant Tools. This process identified qualitative and quantitative indicators for the words used in the texts to yield hermeneutical units of analysis, i.e., theoretical markers within the scope of the investigation.

Data analysis was based on the Climate Action Tracker and Environmental Justice Atlas and included feedback and action generated by other players including civil society. A comparative study included experiences from other regions—Europe (European Green Deal), Africa (Great Green Wall Initiative), and Small Island Developing States (SIDS)—highlighting the uneven nature of global responses. While developed countries linked post-COVID recovery to robust green stimulus packages, Global South countries faced fiscal and institutional constraints that limited their ability to respond and adapt effectively.

This analytical framework sets the stage for examining China's role within BRICS as a potential change agent. By combining shared developmental experiences, historical legacies, and policy innovation, the authors highlight how China's strategic emphasis on ecological governance and technological leadership may shape both national outcomes and collective climate responses within the bloc, offering insights into the potential for transformative multilateral action in the Global South.

Finally, Washbourne turns to local and community-level responses, illustrating how civic innovation can address climate impacts on water systems in Hivre Bazar, India, and Santa Cruz, Costa Rica.[69] These cases exemplify the integration of social-ecological systems thinking into practical governance, demonstrating how communities can craft equitable and sustainable management practices even in the absence of formal institutional support.[70] The concept of the hydro-socio-logical cycle captures the deep entanglement between water systems and social contexts, emphasizing the need for governance approaches that are simultaneously adaptive, participatory, and justice-oriented.[71] As Washbourne concludes, "Preparation for nuanced and wide-ranging impacts of climate change goes hand-in-hand with preparation for a range of other disruptive impacts across the social-ecological-technological system," highlighting the broader lessons that local innovations can offer to governance at multiple scales.[72]

Overall, Chap. 9 presents a nuanced and multidimensional analysis of climate governance, emphasizing the importance of coherence, flexibility, and justice in

[69] Cuadrado-Quesada, Chap. 8, this volume.

[70] For more details see Ostrom (2008) and also Haraway (2016).

[71] Cuadrado-Quesada, Chap. 8, this volume.

[72] Washbourne, Chap. 9, Sect. 9.2.3, this volume.

responding to complex global crises. By integrating lessons from historical legislation, national policy frameworks, international governance, and local civic initiatives, Washbourne provides a comprehensive roadmap for understanding the challenges and opportunities inherent in contemporary climate law and policy.

10.4 A Shared Ethical and Legal Horizon

While each part of the book addresses a different thematic field, they converge in some crucial points such as vulnerability, justice, and the future of legal norms. The pandemic and climate crisis, far from being isolated events, reveal deeper systemic failures and call for a (re)imagining and/or (re)defining of legal rules, the question of what the law is, and ethical commitments across borders. At the intersection of human dignity and environmental justice lies a common question: What kind of legal and ethical architecture is required to support human and ecological flourishing in an age of crises? The answers offered in this volume are intentionally diverse, yet they collectively point toward the need for a more integrated, responsive, and ethically grounded legal order.

However, the analysis of the histories of Santa Cruz and Hivre Bazar reveals that conventional institutional responses are not sufficient to address the climate crisis and its impact on essential common goods such as water. A suitable legal and ethical framework for this era must, therefore, transcend traditional paradigms. The challenge is not only about creating new laws but also about designing and establishing a new framework of coexistence that acknowledges the radical interdependence between the human and the ecological. Therefore, from the analysis elaborated in the present volume, some crucial points emerge.

For example, it is important to (re)focus on the ethics of care and co-responsibility, and especially to (re)think in terms of an ethical foundation. In other words, the prevailing ethics, based on individual rights and the exploitation of resources, must evolve toward an ethics of care and co-responsibility. This ethics stance is characterized by the recognition of interdependence. As demonstrated by the concept of the hydrosocial cycle, water (and nature in general) is not an external object, but a fabric of which we are a part. Ethics must shift from a model of domination to one of symbiotic relationship. Another of its characteristics is the primacy of repair, meaning that communities do not act from abundance but from the need to "repair" socio-environmental damage. Ethics must prioritize repairing historical and present damages, recognizing past injustices (such as colonialism, coloniality, and environmental racism) that have led to the current crisis. And finally, there is a need for intergenerational and multi-species responsibility. The comment of an interviewee in Santa Cruz—"guarantee water protection [...] for future generations"[73]—encapsulates this idea. Ethics must extend our moral responsibility beyond current humans, including future generations and ecosystems as a whole.

[73] Cuadrado-Queseda, Chap. 8, Sect. 8.4.2, in this volume.

In light of this, one potential consequence could be to think about a polycentric governance where there is the possibility to recognize the rights of nature. In a nutshell, it is crucial to (re)think and (re)define the legal architecture; that is, the legal framework should be characterized by decentralization and ecologized to accommodate and enhance civic innovations. This implies a polycentric governance structure, namely legal empowerment of local communities. The Rural Aqueduct Associations (ASADAs) in Costa Rica are an example of how legal structures can grant real authority to communities to manage and protect their resources. The legal architecture could recognize the legal personality of commons, following global trends, and the recognition of legal rights for rivers, aquifers, and ecosystems should be explored, allowing communities to represent them in court.[74] The legal framework should also formalize and protect local knowledge systems: the "customary laws" and "social norms" of Hivre Bazar are as crucial as written laws. The legal system must find mechanisms to integrate and protect these local governance systems, ensuring legal security against external interests. Therefore, the last consideration is related to autonomy. Communities need not only the authority to say "no" to destructive projects but also the financial and technical resources to implement solutions, such as purchasing land for protection or implementing monitoring systems.

All of this must be done while considering indivisible human and environmental rights. The crisis in Flint, Michigan, highlighted in the text is a brutal reminder that the right to clean drinking water is a fundamental human right. The legal architecture must treat access to clean water, a healthy environment, and climate justice as indivisible and inalienable rights.

Therefore, it should be useful to build a bridge between ethics and law, based on a hybrid epistemology and/or cognitive justice. In other words, for ethics and law to be effective, we need a change in how we generate and value knowledge. A hybrid epistemology is required that legitimizes multiple knowledges, meaning that the effectiveness of communities can arise from combining scientific monitoring (aquifer data, water levels) with traditional ecological knowledge (reforestation practices, understanding of the local cycle). By this means, the architecture creates

[74] For example, the 2008 Constitution of Ecuador explicitly recognizes the rights of *Pachamama* (Mother Earth), granting nature legal standing to be protected and restored. Constitution of the Republic of Ecuador, 2008, arts. 71–74. See also Perra (2020, pp. 47–70), where the author identifies the phenomenon of the "juridical anthropomorphization of nature and its entities." According to Perra, it is defined as the attribution of legal personality and rights to natural entities such as rivers, forests, or ecosystems. This approach, notes the author, "emerges from the manifestation of the phenomenon of legal anthropomorphization" and that "the environmental protection systems that have opted for a biocentric vision, in addition to maintaining the coherence of the entire system, place themselves on a remarkable plan of effectiveness in solving environmental problems." This approach, grounded in ancestral and Indigenous worldviews, has been constitutionally or judicially recognized in several jurisdictions, not only in Ecuador but also in Bolivia, New Zealand, Colombia, and the Indian State of Uttarakhand, as a means to strengthen environmental protection through a biocentric legal perspective.

spaces where scientific and local knowledge can enter dialogue on equal terms, in what Boaventura de Sousa Santos calls "cognitive justice."[75]

In addition, it is necessary to foster socio-ecological education: both in Costa Rica and in India, awareness was the driving force for change. Educational systems and public policies must promote a deep understanding of hydrosocial cycles and encourage informed citizen participation in the management of commons. For all this, Donna Haraway elaborated an approach of "facing the problem."[76] The law and ethics should not seek universal and abstract solutions but facilitate communities to "live with" the crisis in a creative and adaptive way. This means designing flexible legal frameworks that allow experimentation and continuous learning, as seen with the creation of "new" water and adaptive norms in Hivre Bazar.

If we were to make a synthetic conclusion, we could say that the required legal and ethical architecture is not a single model, but an ecosystem of adaptive governance. It must have, as its compass, an ethics of care that morally obligates us to repair and preserve; as its backbone, it requires a polycentric legal system that empowers communities and recognizes the rights of nature; and as its nervous system, it needs a hybrid epistemology that values all the necessary knowledge for intelligent action.

To conclude, the way forward is not to replace the state, but to complement its actions, often rigid and slow, with the agency, policy, creativity, and resilience of civic action. The fundamental task is to build bridges of legal and ethical nature so that "civic innovations" stop being acts of marginal resistance and instead become the foundation of a new logic for collective human and ecological flourishing.

In other words, through diverse case studies—from the United States to India, from Australia to Brazil—the contributors in this volume show that the climate crisis is not merely ecological but profoundly political, unveiling failures of governance, accountability, and solidarity. For example, the case of Flint, Michigan, demonstrates how the contamination of water supplies represents not only a failure of infrastructure but also a violation of the right to health and equality. Similarly, the chapter on Hivre Bazar in India illustrates the potential of community-based governance in building local resilience and redefining environmental citizenship. Such examples underline the need to embed local knowledge and participation within formal legal frameworks, ensuring that resilience initiatives translate into enforceable rights.

[75] Boaventura de Sousa Santos (2007, 2014).

[76] Haraway (2016).

10.5 Looking Forward

While the preceding analyses map the contours of a shared ethical and legal framework, this section identifies possible directions for future research and policy. All the chapters agree that building resilience requires polycentric cooperation, intergenerational justice, and inclusive governance models that bridge North and South, theory and practice. Therefore, several key reflections emerge from this collective volume. First, the recognition of vulnerability as a legal and ethical category offers a productive framework for guiding institutional responsibilities, particularly in times and in contexts of compounded crises. Second, the call for transnational legal approaches—in both public health and climate governance—highlights the limitations of state-centric models in dealing with global crises and global emergencies. Third, the importance of interdisciplinary dialogue is evident throughout the chapters, suggesting that legal responses must be informed not only by legal doctrine but also by social, environmental, and ethical considerations.

This book is both a reflection and an invitation. It reflects on the lessons (and failures) and limitations of the legal responses to the pandemic, recent crises, and climate change, and invites scholars, policymakers, and legal practitioners to imagine new paths forward. The challenges we face are profound—but so too is the opportunity to build a more just, dignified, and sustainable future in a sustainable world.

Ultimately, beyond institutional reforms or legal innovations, it is our ethical orientation—toward human dignity, justice, and mutual responsibility—that will determine how we navigate the crises of our time. To conclude this volume, we offer a final meditation on crisis and dignity, as both a mirror and a compass in times of rupture.

While the preceding section identifies possible avenues for legal and institutional reform, the following reflections offers a broader philosophical reflection on dignity as an ethical compass in times of rupture. Thus, the first point that we would like to stress is about dignity in times of crisis, that is crisis as threat, revelation, and ethical compass. The word crisis (from the Greek *krisis*) means "decision" or "turning point." It is not merely a collapse, but a moment of judgment in which the established order fractures, revealing the underlying structures of society and—most crucially—the nature of the individuals who compose it. Far from being a purely economic, political, or health-related phenomenon, every profound crisis is, at its core, a stress test for human dignity. This intrinsic and inalienable quality of every human being is challenged, threatened, and—at times—reaffirmed in the crucible of adversity. Understanding the crisis from different perspectives and vantage points allows us to see it not just as a catastrophic event, but as a mirror that reflects a clear image—sometimes terrifying, other times hopeful—of our collective commitment to the value of each life.

Secondly, crisis as threat: the erosion of dignity in the abyss. From a pessimistic perspective, a crisis acts as a dehumanizing force that risks reducing individuals to a state of mere biological survival. In times of economic collapse, dignity—often linked to work and autonomy—begins to erode when people are unable to provide for themselves or their families. Extreme poverty is not only the absence of material resources; it is a condition that denies social participation, limits choices, and turns life into a humiliating struggle. Similarly, during humanitarian or forced displacement crises, the loss of home, community, and cultural identity inflicts a deep wound on human dignity, which depends on the recognition of the other as an equal. Crises often exacerbate existing inequalities, creating a "state of exception" in which fundamental rights are suspended in the name of emergency. Individuals may be reduced to numbers, to cases, or to logistical obstacles—or, in the worse-case scenarios, to collateral damage. The impersonal bureaucracy and depersonalization that often accompany crisis management are damage control mechanisms that, even without malicious intent, corrode the perception of each person's unique worth. In this view, crisis acts as an acid that dissolves the social contract, revealing a Hobbesian landscape where dignity is the first casualty.

The third point focuses on the crisis as revelation, that is dignity as resistance and solidarity. This is a complementary and more hopeful perspective: crisis as a moment of revelation. It is in darkness that light shines brightest, and it is in adversity that human dignity can be manifest with extraordinary force. Crisis may lay bare the injustices and vulnerabilities of a system, but it also exposes the resilience, compassion, and solidarity present within communities. Here, dignity is not a passive concept, but an action. It is found in the quiet resistance of those who maintain moral integrity in the face of corruption or oppression. It becomes visible in the spontaneous solidarity among neighbors, in the tireless work and dedication of health professionals, volunteers, or anonymous citizens who risk their own well-being for others. Through these acts, dignity asserts itself not as an abstract right, but as a concrete practice of mutual recognition. Crisis strips away the superfluous layers of normality and reminds us of our fundamental interdependence. Shared vulnerability becomes the foundation for a renewed solidarity, fraternity, and sisterhood, in which the dignity of one is inextricably tied to the dignity of all.

Finally, it is important also to highlight the point about dignity as compass, that is toward an ethical reconstruction. The most constructive view of any crisis is one that sees it as an opportunity for "re-evolution"—a return to what is essential. Once the emergency phase has passed, a period of reconstruction begins. It is here that human dignity must stand as the ultimate guiding principle. A recovery that merely restores the previous *status quo*—with its same inequities and failures—will be incomplete and fragile. Dignity calls for the redesign of economic systems that prioritize human well-being over abstract growth. It demands political reforms that advance social justice and meaningful participation. It inspires technological progress that empowers and includes, rather than alienates. Crisis forces us to ask: What kind of society do we want to be? The answer must be grounded in the awareness that each person, by virtue of being human, possesses an inviolable value that the state and community are obliged to protect and promote. Dignity becomes the ethical compass that guides us toward a future that is not only more prosperous, but also more just and more human.

In conclusion, crises, in all their rawness and pain, are defining episodes in both personal and collective history. They are not univocal—they can be seen as dehumanizing threats, as revelations of human solidarity, or as opportunities for ethical regeneration. The common thread uniting these perspectives is human dignity. It is both the potential victim of crisis and its most powerful antidote—the foundation upon which any viable future must be built. Ultimately, the true measure of success in the face of a crisis will not lie solely in the recovery of economic indicators or the restoration of order, but in how much we have managed to preserve, honor, and strengthen the inherent dignity of every human being who endured it. In the fault opened by crisis, we do not see only the abyss, but also the possibility of building a bridge—toward a humanity more aware of its own value.

In summary, the contributions to this collection converge on three shared insights: that vulnerability must become a central legal and ethical category; that pluralism—of actors, systems, and epistemologies—is essential for resilient governance; and that global challenges demand coordinated, multi-level responses grounded in human dignity. Together, these insights sketch the contours of a more just and sustainable global order.

This final section of the volume is not merely a conclusion, but the delineation of a new point of departure. By bringing together a wide range of thematic perspectives, the work converges on a powerful realization: vulnerability, justice, and future survival must become the foundational pillars upon which a new global order is reconstructed. The COVID-19 pandemic and the climate crisis, far from being isolated catastrophes, have acted as seismic events that expose the deep structural faults of our legal and ethical systems. They are symptoms of a deeper pathology: the inability of traditional normative architectures—often anchored in the nation-state and in paradigms of infinite growth—to manage systemic risks and protect the most vulnerable.

We thank all the contributors for their generous and thoughtful engagement, which has made this dialogue across themes, disciplines, and geographies not only possible, but intellectually and ethically enriching.

References

Alexy R (2010) A theory of constitutional rights. Oxford University Press, Oxford

Baumeister S (2018) We Are Still In! Conference report from the 2018 Ceres Conference. J Clean Prod 196:183–184. https://doi.org/10.1016/j.jclepro.2018.06.069

Boaventura de Sousa Santos (2007) Beyond Abyssal thinking: from global lines to ecologies of knowledges. Review 30(1):45–89

Boaventura de Sousa Santos (2014). Epistemologies of the South. Justice against Epistemicide. Routledge, New York

Boyle AD, Leggat G, Morikawa L et al (2021) Green new deal proposals: comparing emerging transformational climate policies at multiple scales. Energy Res Soc Sci 81:102259. https://doi.org/10.1016/j.erss.2021.102259

Brewer TL (2022) Transforming U.S. climate change policies: 2021 and beyond. Springer Nature, Cham

Butler J (2020) Capitalism has its limits. https://www.versobooks.com/en-gb/blogs/news/4603-capitalism-has-its-limits. Accessed 17 Dec 2025
Ferrajoli L (2021) Perché una costituzione della Terra? Giappichelli, Torino
Ferrajoli L (2022) Per una costituzione della Terra. L'umanità al bivio. Feltrinelli, Milano
Fineman M. (2015) Fineman on vulnerability and law. In: New legal realism: empirical law and society. http://newlegalrealism.org/2015/11/30/fineman-on-vulnerability-and-law/ Accessed 21 Jan 2026
Haraway D (2016) Staying with the trouble: making kin in the Chthulucene. Duke University Press, Durham, North Carolina
Hoyer D, Bennett JS, Reddish J et al (2023) Navigating polycrisis: long-run socio-cultural factors shape response to changing climate. Philos Transact Royal Soc B Biol Sci 378(1889):20220402. https://doi.org/10.1098/rstb.2022.0402
Lawrence M, Homer-Dixon T, Janzwood S et al (2024) Global polycrisis: the causal mechanisms of crisis entanglement. Glob Sustain 7:e6. https://doi.org/10.1017/sus.2024.1
Lucon O, Buchianeri V, Morello S (2022) PEMC 10 anos Política Estadual de Mudanças Climáticas. SIMA. https://smastr16.blob.core.windows.net/home/2022/04/relatorio-pemc-3.pdf. Accessed 21 Jan 2026
Lumarque J (ed) (2020) Haïti et le COVID-19. Des outils pour comprendre et agir. Presses de l'Université Quisqueya, Port-au-Prince
Manzanedo RD, Manning P (2020) COVID-19: lessons for the climate change emergency. Sci Total Environ 742:140563. https://doi.org/10.1016/j.scitotenv.2020.140563
Mccarty N (2011) Chapter 9. The policy effects of political polarization. In: Pierson P, Skocpol T (eds) The transformation of American politics: activist government and the rise of conservatism. Princeton University Press, Princeton, pp 223–255. https://doi.org/10.1515/9781400837502-013
McCrudden C (2008) Human dignity and judicial interpretation of human rights. Eur J Int Law 19:655–724
Mignolo W (2005) The idea of Latin America. Blackwell Publishing, Oxford
Ostrom E (2008) The challenge of common-pool resources. Environ Sci Policy Sustain Dev 50(4):8–21. https://doi.org/10.3200/ENVT.50.4.8-21
Passarelli D, Denton F, Day A (2021) Beyond opportunism: the UN Development system's response to the triple planetary crisis. United Nations University, New York
Perra L (2020) L'antropomorfizzazione giuridica. Diritto & Questioni Pubbliche 2: 47–70
Pozzolo S, Moreso JJ, Grández PP (eds) (2021) Derecho, derechos y pandemia. Palestra editores, Lima
Quijano A (2024) Foundational essays on the coloniality of power. Duke University Press, Durham, North Carolina
Ribotta S, Lema Añon C (eds) (2023) Mujeres y (des)igualdades de oportunidades: análisis feministas del impacto de las injusticias estructurales y las tensiones coyunturales. Dykinson, Madrid
Setzer J, Vanhala LC (2019) Climate change litigation: a review of research on courts and litigants in climate governance. WIREs Clim Change 10(3):e580. https://doi.org/10.1002/wcc.580
Siegal RB (2012) Dignity and sexuality: claims on dignity in transnational debates over abortion and same-sex marriage. Int J Const Law 10:355–379
Stamile N (2019) Derechos fundamentales ¿Ponderación o subsunción? Algunas reflexiones sobre la polémica entre Robert Alexy y Luigi Ferrajoli. In: Sánchez Brigido R, Longhini C, Villanueva M (eds) Conflictos de derechos fundamentals. Lex Editorial, Córdoba, pp 81–116
Stamile N (2020) La polémica sobre la relación entre derecho y moral: Robert Alexy e Eugenio Bulygin. Derechos y Libertades 42:267–301
Stamile N (2023) El conflicto entre normas en debate: Friedrich Müller y Robert Alexy. In: Villa Rosas G, Toledo C, Nava Tovar A et al (eds) Derecho, argumentación y ponderación. Ensayos en honor a Robert Alexy. Bogotá: Externado de Colombia, Bogotá, pp 385–428

Stamile N, Castilho Gomes N, Almanza Torres D (eds) (2021) Friedrich Müller's Theory of Law/ Zur Rechtstheorie Friedrich Müllers. Archiv für Rechts - und Sozialphilosophie—Beihefte. Franz Steiner Verlag, Stuttgart

Steinmann A (2017) The core meaning of human dignity. Potchef Electr Law J 19:1–32

The White House (2021) Executive Order 13990 on Protecting public health and the environment and restoring science to tackle the climate crisis. The White House. https://www.federalregister.gov/documents/2021/01/25/2021-01765/protecting-public-health-and-the-environment-and-restoring-science-to-tackle-the-climate-crisis. Accessed 17 Oct 2025

Théodat JM, Müller-Poitevien HC, Solages A (2020) Inégalités socio-spatiales en temps de COVID-19. In: Lumarque J (ed) Haïti et le COVID-19. Des outils pour comprendre et agir. Presses de l'Université Quisqueya, Port-au-Prince, pp 105–115

Toni A, Feitosa Chaves C (2022) Bolsonaro's far-right populist environmental and climate diplomacy. LAP Latin Am Policy 13(2):464–483. https://doi.org/10.1111/lamp.12268

We Are Still In (2025) America Is All In. https://www.wearestillin.com. Accessed 15 Jan 2026

MIX
Papier aus verantwortungsvollen Quellen
Paper from responsible sources
FSC® C105338

If you have any concerns about our products,
you can contact us on
ProductSafety@springernature.com

In case Publisher is established outside the EU,
the EU authorized representative is:
Springer Nature Customer Service Center GmbH
Europaplatz 3, 69115 Heidelberg, Germany

Printed by Libri Plureos GmbH
in Hamburg, Germany